Sport, Recreation and Tourism Event Management

Theoretical and Practical Dimensions

Sport, Recreation and Tourism Event Management: Theoretical and Practical Dimensions

Editors

Cheryl Mallen and Lorne J. Adams, Brock University

Photograph by Mike Cheliak

Routledge
Taylor & Francis Group
LONDON AND NEW YORK

First published 2008 by Butterworth-Heinemann

This edition published 2012 by Routledge
2 Park Square, Milton Park, Abingdon, Oxon, OX14 4RN
711 Third Avenue, New York, NY 10017

Routledge is an imprint of the Taylor & Francis Group, an informa business

First Edition 2008

British Library Cataloguing in Publication Data
A catalogue record for this book is available from the British Library

Library of Congress Cataloging-in-Publication Data
A catalog record for this book is available from the Library of Congress

ISBN–13: 978-0-7506-8447-7

Typeset by Charon Tec Ltd (A Macmillan Company), Chennai,
India www.charontec.com

Contents

Contents

Contents

Contents

Acknowledgements

Cheryl Mallen would like to acknowledge a lifetime of support from parents Bob and Betty Brown; friendship and love, which underpin her life, from husband Paddy and children, Bob and Sarah, who have always been the priority in her world.

Lorne Adams would like to acknowledge: his partner, Cyndy, who has been incredibly patient with the time required for this project; Sandie, who accommodated his requests for materials as soon as possible in spite of a busy schedule; Cheryl, the driving force behind this work, whose enthusiasm and excitement for the project made it happen; and his son, Phil, who keeps him grounded.

Preface

**Cheryl Mallen and Lorne J. Adams,
Brock University**

Photograph by Mike Cheliak

Sport, recreation and tourism event management is a vibrant, complex, and growing industry. Growth around the world in this diverse field has stimulated the need for skilled event managers. This peer reviewed, edited text is intended to guide learners to assimilate knowledge for use in the event industry. There are four objectives for this text upon which the chapters are based.

Objectives

The first objective of this text is to provide a foundation of sound theoretical and practical principles in sport, recreation and tourism event management. The second objective is to encourage learners to develop an understanding of the concept of knowledge. This understanding involves the construction of critical interpretations of defining knowledge and determining knowledge requirements for the field. The third objective focuses on presenting an event management planning model, including progressive phases of the model, and the key elements within each phase. The fourth and final objective involves an emphasis on the role of the event manager as a facilitator. The facilitation role involves "thinking through" the requirements for each phase of the event planning model and utilizing a variety of strategies to guide those assigned with planning to stage an event.

Organization of the chapters

The chapters in this text are initially structured around relevant definitions. Chapter 1 defines *traditional* and hybrid or *niche* events that are the focus in this text. Key characteristics for these two foundational types of events are outlined along with an argument for the rise of contemporary diverse niche events within the industry. Chapter 2 focuses on the concept of knowledge and applies the theories of knowledge to develop a unique definition specifically designed for the context of event management. Furthermore, this chapter outlines a knowledge transfer race strategy for the field of event management.

Chapters 3 to 8 are structured to present the phases of an event planning model. Chapters 3 and 4 cover the first phase in the planning model, the event development phase. In this phase, theory on facilitation, governance, networks, policy, volunteer practices, and corporate social responsibility is presented and discussed in the context of event management. Chapter 5 presents the second phase in the planning model, the event operational planning phase. The discussion on this phase encompasses the development of a network of event members who complete the written operational plans that provide action steps to guide the staging of an event. Chapter 6 discusses the third phase, the event implementation, monitoring, and management phase. This phase includes the key dimensions of concern when facilitating elements during the staging of an event. Chapters 7 and 8 present the fourth phase, the event evaluation and renewal phase. The discussion outlines theory, processes, considerations, challenges, and suggestions for facilitating this phase of the planning model.

Chapter 9 provides a review of the critical factors in the event bid process offered by the literature and then puts forth an argument on the key factor in the bid process. In addition, this chapter discusses bid tours and the all-important bid evaluations. Chapter 10 looks at the theories of quality and their application to event management and the role of the event manager. The discussion reveals the difficulties in developing quality events due to the three diverse event priority groups: the athletes or actors, the spectators, and the sponsors. Finally, Chapter 11 covers the theory of experiential learning and an application of the theory to event management practice. This chapter recommends experiential learning as a key element in the development of event management skills. Chapter 12 provides the conclusions and recommendations.

An overview of the focus of this text

This text focuses on sport, recreation and tourism event management and emphasizes the complex role of an event manager as a facilitator. In addition, emphasis is placed on defining traditional and niche events, the concept of knowledge, the planning phases when organizing components for staging an event, the critical factors for event bids, and the concept of quality and experiential learning.

Event elements outside the framework of this text

It is important to note that the event manager has a complex role in the staging of an event that necessitates managing a multitude of activities within a changing event environment. In performing this role, both depth and breadth of knowledge are necessary. Thus, an event manager's training needs to be diverse and extend to areas that are beyond the focus of this text. Examples of additional areas within the realm of event management are ethics, financial management, marketing, sponsorship, facility management, and law. Each of these areas of expertise can be applied to the organization and production of an event. Each aforementioned area is important enough to the staging of an event that they would require far more emphasis than a single chapter in this text could provide. However, a study of the above listed topics will provide a fuller understanding of the broad scope of requirements in event management. For example, understanding the application of law from the perspective of legal liability, risk management, dispute resolution, and contract development for athletes, facilities, entertainers, staff, and volunteers is a vital aspect of event management. In addition, marketing and sponsorship have a direct application to the viability of events. There are multiple texts on the market that discuss facility management, marketing, sport law, and other such subjects that relate to event management. There are limited resources on the event manager's role as a facilitator for the key phases that involve planning for an event. Therefore, this text is intended to concentrate on this gap in the literature.

Traditional and niche sport, recreation and tourism events

**Cheryl Mallen and Lorne J. Adams,
Brock University**

Photograph by Shawn Whiteley

This chapter defines two distinct types of events prevalent in the field of sport, recreation and tourism that are the focus of this text. These are *traditional* events and hybrid or *niche* events. The unique characteristics that differentiate traditional events from niche events are outlined followed by an explanation of the rise of contemporary niche events. The chapter ends with a statement concerning the demand for skilled traditional and niche managers in the burgeoning field of events.

Traditional events

This text defines a traditional event as a sport event staged for recreation, competition, or as a driver for tourism. Two key characteristics define a traditional event. The first characteristic requires that a governing body establish and enforce standardized rules and regulations that must be followed to produce the event. The second characteristic is that the activity is a recognizable and time-honoured sport.

A governing body, including an organization, association, or federation prescribes standardized rules and regulations that govern the traditional event. These rules and regulations specify elements such as the competition area (for example the playing field or court), the number of participants, their dress, and acceptable actions for participation. The governing body performs a sanctioning and overseeing role whereby the body ensures that the rules and regulations are followed by the event participants.

Exceptions to the rules and regulations can occur in a traditional event. The exceptions can be precipitated due to a range of pressures from areas such as a particular culture or country, and due to the need to adapt for new technologies or to the age of the participant population. A traditional event may undergo adaptations or transformations over time; however, the transformations do not give rise to an entirely new event. Change is limited. There is universality in the implementation of the rules and regulations. From generation to generation the event is conducted repeatedly in the same manner. The event is practiced to follow the rules and regulations, including the traditions, customs, and routines for a consistent, mature, respected, and recognizable event.

An example of a traditional event is what is called football in a large part of the world and soccer in North America. This sport event can be played as an elite level activity or as a local recreational activity. It can also be played with the use of a homemade ball and makeshift fields, as the players emulate the characteristics of the traditional event. The consistent use of rules and regulations at any level makes the event a time-honoured and recognizable game of football or soccer. Football or soccer events can be played in a single game, league, or circuit format.

The rules and regulations for the football or soccer events are standardized by the bodies that govern such elements as the playing field, number of players, their dress, and the conduct of each player. Multiple bodies all over the world govern football or soccer at the regional, provincial or state, national, and international levels. Some bodies adapt the rules for their particular purposes; however, the event itself resembles football or soccer that is played worldwide.

Each traditional sport event can be held within a defined market. Examples include netball in Australia, box lacrosse in Canada, hurling in Ireland, rodeo and jai alai in the United States, and sumo wrestling in Japan. These events are traditional events in their respective countries.

Traditional sport events can promote tourism as athletes and spectators travel to the event location to be involved with the spectacle. Examples of traditional events that promote tourism are the Olympic Games, the Arctic Games, the Canada Games, and the Asian Games. Each traditional event can encourage tourists to attend or to promote travel to see the area in the months before and years following an event.

Overall, a traditional sport event is regulated by a governing body and is recognizable as a time-honoured sport event. However, the purview of event management extends beyond the traditional events to include niche events.

Niche events

In contrast to a traditional event, a niche event is forged through innovations that alter or renew an event or create a completely new event. Many niche events are progressive hybrid events stemming from the roots of a traditional event.

There are three key characteristics of niche events. The first characteristic is that the event is created and adapted for a particular sport, recreation or tourism audience. The second characteristic is that there does not have to be a traditional governing body that has established time-honoured rules and regulations, although an organizing body exists that can provide rules and regulations. The third characteristic is that the event may exhibit recognizable traditional event components or may be unconventional in its form.

Niche events exist in many forms in the fields of sport, recreation or tourism. Examples include festivals, conferences, including media conferences, banquets, conventions, stampedes, shows, and charity events. The use of innovative designs can form new niche sport, recreational or tourism events.

Niche events can also be founded by altering or renewing a traditional event to produce the "next generation" of the event. This type of niche event may use a traditional sport event surface such as a rugby pitch or volleyball court or traditional equipment such as a lacrosse helmet or rugby ball, or rules and regulations that are derived from a traditional event such as basketball. A niche event has no requirement for the number of traditional components that could be utilized or the form in which they can be combined. Yet, a niche event can exhibit elements that are recognizable as those of a traditional sport event.

The niche sport or recreational event does not have a traditional governing body establishing rules and regulations, although an organizing body exists that does establish the rules and regulations for the particular event. The rules and regulations established are not expected to be traditional or passed down from generation to generation. There is always the potential for adapting the rules and regulations due to the influences of culture, the movement to incorporate new equipment technology, for a particular age group or type of abilities or the creative genius of the event manager.

A niche sport or recreational event may or may not remain consistent in its production. This type of event can be adapted to another generation of the event at any time. Whatever the focus, an individual event, a circuit of events, or a league at the local, regional, national, or international level, the possibility remains for full-scale changes to the event at any time.

A niche event can be continuously adapted for a particular audience. A niche tourism event of this type is the Niagara Falls, Canada *Winter Festival of Lights*. This annual event is tailored for a tourist audience intent on seeing the spectacular Niagara Falls during the winter months. There is no traditional governing body instituting rules and regulations, although an organizing committee exists. The Niagara Falls event is forged out of innovation and consists of lighting used to highlight the natural beauty of the falls and surrounding area along with the use of Disney characters in lights for an additional evening attraction. The event can be adapted at any time to meet the changing needs of the tourists, for example, moving the location of the light displays or adding or deleting lighted characters. Adaptations can be made to any individual element of the event, or the entire event can be adapted at any given time. Niche events involve the freedom to design an event with the use of conventional or unconventional components or activities.

Additional examples of niche events are springing up throughout the world. In the United States, basketball is being played on a series of trampolines instead of a traditional basketball court. Baseball home run derbies are being staged. In Canada, a niche event has extended snowmobile racing to the summer months by competing on grass instead of only a winter event on snow. Canada also hosts a World Outdoor Hockey Championship with adapted rules to award a goal for each penalty to avoid having a participant sit out in the cold when serving a penalty. In countries around the world niche skiing and snowboarding events are being conducted on hills of sand instead of the traditional mountains of snow. Football and soccer events are being staged in a three-on-three format on sand. Cricket events with adapted rules have been played in the West Indies, England, New Zealand, and South Africa. Skill testing events have sprung up, such as the golf long ball drive, putting, and hole-in-one contests. Niche adventure races involve trekking, horseback riding, or scaling mountains.

Events can start as niche events and then evolve to the traditional event realm. The triathlon is an example of a niche sport that has become a traditional event. This tri-activity sport event combines swimming, cycling, and running races. The combination of traditional sports established a niche event that grew from a local to an international phenomenon. The Ironman Triathlon, held in Hawaii, USA, is also an example of a triathlon that is a successful tourism event.

Over the course of time, the triathlon developed rules and regulations that were practiced in a consistent manner. The event was eventually accepted into the sports staged at the Olympic Summer Games. This acceptance meant participants were selected from a series of events conducted with standardized rules and regulations. In addition, there was recognition of the event as a triathlon at every level from local to internationally staged events. At this point, the triathlon entered the realm of a traditional event.

However, the triathlon continues to develop as a niche event. The niche triathlon event has been spurred on by continuing to adapt the multi activity event elements. This includes adapting to use two sport activities, such as walking and cycling, or adjusting to allow a team of three members to compete, each completing one of the sport activities. This continual use of adaptations to the triathlon keeps the event in the niche event realm; however, it is possible for an event to be produced in both the traditional and the niche event realms simultaneously.

Other examples of events that were born as niche events and evolved to the traditional event status can be found in the sport of skiing. Both skiing competitions on moguls and ski dancing started as niche events and then became traditional events. Volleyball is a traditional event, and then beach volleyball was developed as a niche event that has since moved to a traditional event. Today, both of these events have been included in major traditional events such as the Olympic Games and have standardized traditional rules and regulations.

Niche events continue to emerge. They may or may not move to the realm of traditional events in the future. Regardless, they are expanding the array of events, and event managers are needed to stage them around the world.

What niche events are springing up in your area? Consider the adaptations being advanced in your local traditional events that give rise to niche events. Also, what niche tourism events are, or could be, staged in your locality?

The rise of contemporary niche events

Why are niche events arising? This text proposes that niche events are arising as an outgrowth of our contemporary society that includes an environment of change.

We are living in a period of change that has been described as a postindustrial era (Bell, 1973; Zuboff, 1988). The impact of postindustrial change on contemporary society has produced an environment of complexity and unpredictability (Choo and Bontis, 2002). According to Homer-Dixon (2001), contemporary change impacts all aspects of contemporary society. This impact demands a process of active and continuous learning in order to accommodate change (Hirschhorn, 1984; Sproull and Kiesler, 1991). Individuals and organizations are encouraged to adapt to meet the challenge of change. A mindset to adapt and innovate has been stimulated in our contemporary society of change. Jensen (1999) stated that survival is contingent on the individual or group that "is most adaptable to change" (p. 16). This brings forth the question, are niche events being generated in a process of learning to react to change in our contemporary environment?

In the process of learning to accommodate change, a new concept has surfaced that Limerick, Cunnington, and Crowther (1998) call "collaborative individualism" (p. 103). This concept involves a group or a collective of responsible individuals being "held together by common cultures, shared world meanings and values" (Limerick et al., p. 128). This new form of collective encourages a mindset that one must "embrace individualism, collaboration, and innovation" (Limerick et al., p. 22). Each must be embraced simultaneously, and all members within the collective have a voice. As these individuals retain and develop their personal voice, they are encouraged to collaborate in order to develop innovations for managing in the contemporary environment of change.

Applying the concept of collaborative individualism to niche events requires a mindset, individual voice, and a push for groups of individuals to collaborate and to be innovative. With a voice at the grassroots level, collaborative individualism is occurring as groups are using innovative design to create niche events. Bound together by common threads from the event's culture, meaning, and value, they are capable of creating, sharing, and nurturing adapted meanings and values to create niche events. These niche events can be described as design experiments.

Cobb, Confrey, diSess, Lehrer, and Schauble (2003) describe design experiments as "test-beds for innovations" (p. 10). Cobb and his group of researchers indicate that design experiments offer the opportunity to complete a series of cycles of development and allow for regular revisions to an event.

The test-bed concept for events suggests that opportunities to design niche events abound. Niche event experiments can explore and reflect designs and activities that offer new understandings and innovations which create niche events. In sport, recreation and tourism event management, design experimenters are producing a growing body of innovative and creative niche events.

A need for skilled traditional and niche event managers

The sport, recreation and tourism industries have undergone phenomenal growth since the 1960s. The combination of increased traditional and niche events is changing the sport, recreation and tourism event landscape, in that each event needs one or more event managers.

Consider the potential number of event managers that could be needed in the world on an annual basis. Event managers are needed for local recreational and competitive events that extend to regional, provincial/state, national, and international events, including leagues, circuits, or tours for a variety of age groups and abilities. In addition, these traditional events can include a wide variety of sports ranging from archery to yachting. The numbers of niche events that are focused on are growing annually in the form of tourism-focused festivals, banquets, and shows. Add to this the number of sport and recreational events that are being altered or renewed to produce the next generation of events and the number of event managers required increases concomitantly.

The exact number of events held annually is unknown. Calculations are difficult due to the complex conditions in the sport, recreation and tourism industry. However, a general estimation is that millions of traditional and niche events are staged annually around the world. Hence, well-informed, prepared, and knowledgeable managers are in high demand.

Conclusion

A growing body of traditional and niche sport, recreation and tourism events drives the demand for experts who are knowledgeable and experienced in the field of event management. Today's event managers need skills to advance beyond using preestablished lists that dictate the replication of actions used to stage previous events. Contemporary event managers must be able to *think through* and self-determine the requirements of staging traditional or niche events. This requirement demands knowledge of, coupled with experience in, event management.

We now head to Chapter 2, where the concept of knowledge and a knowledge transfer race is discussed. Also, a uniquely formed definition of knowledge for sport, recreation and tourism event managers will be presented. Chapter 2 aims to guide event managers in their pursuit to assimilate knowledge for use in the event industry.

Chapter questions

1. List three traditional events and the two characteristics that make them traditional.
2. Describe three niche events that are being hosted in your area.
3. Can an event move from being traditional to becoming a niche event? If not, why? If so, what changes are necessary to make the transition?
4. Why are niche events growing in our contemporary times?
5. What does the dual growth of traditional and niche events mean for the field of event management?

The concept of knowledge in event management

Cheryl Mallen, Brock University

This chapter discusses knowledge and the concept of a *"knowledge transfer race"* (English and Baker, 2006) along with its application to event managers. To gain an understanding of knowledge needed for this race, common and advancement knowledge are discussed. Then, a unique definition of knowledge specifically designed for the field of event management is presented along with a strategy for assimilating event knowledge.

As far back as 1973, Bell noted that knowledge was situated as a "central" feature within our advancing society. Over the last several decades, the value of knowledge has continued to escalate. One reason for the explosive rise of the value of knowledge is the recognition that knowledge is a resource that aids productivity (Grant, 1996). Thus, productivity, and ultimately success in the field of event management, is in part contingent upon the knowledge that you acquire, share, create, and apply.

A knowledge transfer race

An emphasis on knowledge in society has stimulated what English and Baker (2006) call "the knowledge transfer race." In this race, each individual has the primary role of creating knowledge. Individuals and collaborative groups race competitively to continuously develop more knowledge. The key activity in the continuous development of knowledge is the sharing of this knowledge. There is a race to transfer or share knowledge in order to facilitate creating more knowledge.

The value of knowledge transfer or a sharing process was highlighted by George Bernard Shaw (1930) when he expressed the following in his play: *The Apple Cart*: "If you have an apple and I have an apple and we exchange these apples then you and I will still each have one apple. But if you have an idea and I have an idea and we exchange these ideas, then each of us will have two ideas."

An application of Shaw's exchange concept to knowledge implies that transference aids the development of all parties in the knowledge sharing process. This transference or sharing concept was expressed by Shaw decades ago, but it has become a requirement for participants in today's knowledge-based environment.

Knowledge has been described by Boisot (2002) as being personal in nature; yet, there is a critical dependence between the knowledge holder and the development of more knowledge with the use of a sharing process. Individual effort simply does not provide enough knowledge to fully compete in the knowledge transfer race. A connection to others is needed to further one's knowledge development.

For years transferring knowledge has been seen as a top priority because "the fast and effective transfer of knowledge is the only truly sustainable competitive advantage" (Drucker, 1994, p. 10). However, English and Baker (2006) posit that only those that acquire the appropriate knowledge to share can participate and gain additional knowledge through the transferring process. This is because you need to have knowledge to share with others so they will, in return, share their knowledge with you.

An application of this transference process indicates that those in sport, recreation and tourism event management must share knowledge in order to advance their own personally held knowledge. The development of knowledge through a process of sharing can facilitate understandings about the staging of events and can aid the development of innovations for the event industry and solving contemporary event problems.

To be competitive in event management in a knowledge transfer race, it seems logical that a strategy is needed for knowledge transfer. This strategy is a self-directed plan to develop the ability to become efficient and effective in the process of acquiring and transferring knowledge.

At the core of this strategy is the definition of knowledge as it applies specifically to sport, recreation and tourism event management. Once knowledge is defined, a strategy for participating in the knowledge transfer race can be developed. However, defining knowledge is not a clearly articulated process. Difficulties arise as one attempts to establish a definition of knowledge and the key characteristics that it entails.

Defining knowledge

How do you currently define knowledge? Think about your currently held definition of knowledge and record your answer. Next, review your definition of knowledge and be sure that you have listed at least three key dimensions, features, or characteristics of knowledge within your definition. Then, apply your definition of knowledge to the field of sport, recreation and tourism event management. The application includes recording the composition of the knowledge that you need to acquire specifically for the field of event management (Figure 2.1).

This is a difficult exercise. Researchers have been trying to define knowledge for decades, and the field attempting to define knowledge is growing even today. A single definition of knowledge for you to adopt does not exist in the literature. This singular definition of knowledge has been elusive. Researchers have offered multiple definitions and diverse statements on the meaning of knowledge, but

1. Record how you currently define knowledge.

2. List at least three key dimensions, features, or characteristics of knowledge within your definition.

3. Apply your definition of knowledge to the field of sport, recreation and tourism event management. If you have knowledge in the field of event management, what specifically do you have knowledge of?

Figure 2.1 Defining knowledge

Review the explicit statement you created to define knowledge in the assignment above. Does your definition guide you to participate in a knowledge transfer race in the field of event management? If so, how does it guide your participation? If not, what is missing?

Figure 2.2 Continue to define knowledge

instead of one concise definition, understandings of knowledge have been based only on various levels of scope, areas of emphasis, and a specific context. According to Edvinsson and Malone (1997), the difficulty in arriving at a consensus on a definition of knowledge stems from the intangible nature of knowledge.

In an environment where a knowledge transfer race is a key component to being competitive, how can you transfer knowledge if a solid understanding of the meaning of knowledge is elusive? Go back and look at the explicit statement you created to define knowledge in the assignment above. Does your definition provide you with enough detail to *guide* you to participate in a knowledge transfer race in the field of event management (Figure 2.2)?

If you do not know how to define knowledge, or what knowledge is comprised of, how can you obtain the necessary knowledge to be a valuable member of the event management field?

It would be helpful to have a definition of knowledge that expresses the multi-faceted current understandings of knowledge. This will enhance your participation in the event management knowledge transfer race. This is because the definition can then be used to develop a strategy to further obtain knowledge to share in the process of the knowledge transfer race.

Although researchers cannot agree on the definition of knowledge, there is no excuse for not articulating contextual understandings of knowledge. These understandings can be used to participate in knowledge production and, in particular, the event management knowledge transfer race. Basic definitions of knowledge do exist and express viewpoints that can aid your understanding.

In addition, the diverse articulations that attempt to further delineate the components within knowledge can also assist your understanding of the term. A definition of knowledge outlined below is an integration of a variety of researchers' definitions and their specific application to the context of event management.

Researchers have attempted to define knowledge by outlining the tangible components that mark one's knowledge. We will review several of these definitions as they relate to two categories of knowledge that we are calling: *common knowledge* and *advancement knowledge.*

Before we get into defining common and advancement knowledge, we need to discuss some terms that may create some confusion. The terms knowledge, information, and data have been used interchangeably in some contexts. However, in this textbook, the opinion of Boisot (2002) is followed and includes: "Think of data as being located in the world and of knowledge as being located in agents [within your mind], with information taking on a mediating role between them" (p. 67). In this view, knowledge, information, and data are considered to be three separate entities.

Common knowledge

Several researchers offer descriptions of common knowledge. To begin, Blackler (1995) indicates that common knowledge can be described as what one *does*. This implies that a feature or dimension of common knowledge includes an understanding of the activities completed by an event manager.

English and Baker (2006) describe common knowledge in terms of "know how" or the "thorough knowledge of the theory and actual practice of a process or procedure" (p. 4). This description implies that the dimensions of common knowledge include the understanding of contemporary theories (for example, complexity theory, contingency theory, systems theory, and management theory) and the application of those theories within professional practice, including the daily practices and procedures of managing events.

Gupta and MacDaniel (2002) describe common knowledge as the basic understandings of culture, politics, and personalities. This type of common knowledge involves being able to participate in the event environment in which we operate. This dimension of knowledge is based on basic understandings and how to conduct yourself in a social environment.

Nonaka, Toyama, and Konno (2000) indicate common knowledge is "conceptual" and "systemic." Conceptual knowledge is obtained as one develops understandings of information that is abstract in nature. Conceptual knowledge includes ideas that are expressed and can be visualized. Systemic knowledge is obtained through a general understanding of the organization, procedures, processes, schemes, and techniques involved in implementation. This type of knowledge includes methodological systems such as technological systems, manuals, or information packages.

For over a decade, common knowledge has been described as the components of *common sense* for a particular context or field, plus facts, concepts, and theoretical frameworks (Spender, 1996). This means knowledge includes the ability to discuss a field with a common language (including common terms used within the field) along with a basic awareness and understanding of the feelings and meaning within the language that is shared (Grant, 1996).

To obtain common knowledge, Spender (2002) indicates that it "grows-emerges-out of the interactions" (p. 160). Therefore, the development of your common knowledge is dependent upon the interactions that you have, including interactions with written material and with those knowledgeable of the event field. These interactions help to contextualize, interpret, and conceive options for using that knowledge.

Overall, common knowledge is explicit and provides the foundation that is necessary for your participation and judgment. This is because common knowledge is "the platform for everything else. It lies deep and brings together, in contextualized thought and action, all the other types of knowledge that are judged relevant – for it is the sources of such judgments" (Spender, 2002, pp. 157–158). The greater the common knowledge, the greater the foundational base that one can use to judge the value of new knowledge and to facilitate integration of knowledge within the currently held knowledge bank (Figure 2.3).

Advancement knowledge

Advancement knowledge is valuable as it is a higher level of growth and sophistication and can be characterized as an in-depth level of knowledge. This type of knowledge is conceived by an individual through personal perspectives and understandings that are conceptually held in the mind. Development of this kind of knowledge can provide a competitive advantage. This is because advancement knowledge is a product of a higher level of understanding that can lead to pioneering ideas, progress, and ultimately your success as an event manager.

A simple example of the difference between common knowledge and advancement knowledge can be expressed if you look at one's understandings. If you were to describe to individuals that have never been in a higher education classroom,

Stehr (1992)	Knowledge "is both a medium of social action and the result of human conduct" (p. 4).
Blackler (1995)	Knowledge consists of what one *does*.
Spender (1996)	Knowledge includes the acquisition of factual data, concepts, and theoretical frameworks – and – it includes "common sense."
Grant (1996)	Knowledge includes a basic understanding of a common language and the meaning within the language.
Nonaka, Toyama, and Konno (2000)	*Conceptual knowledge* is an understanding of concepts that are abstract in nature. *Systemic knowledge* is an understanding of the organization, procedures, processes, schemes, and techniques.
Spender (2002)	Common knowledge "grows-emerges-out of the interactions" (p. 160). Common knowledge "lies deep and brings together, in contextualized thought and action, all the other types of knowledge that are judged relevant – for it is the source of such judgments" (pp. 157–158).
Gupta and MacDaniel (2002)	It is the understanding of the basics of culture, politics, and personalities.
English and Baker (2006)	*Know-how* is having a basic "knowledge of the theory and actual practice of a process or procedure" (p. 4).

Figure 2.3 Features or dimensions of common knowledge

including stating the style and type of seating and technology found in a typical classroom, they could develop a common understanding of the classroom environment. However, these individuals do not have advanced knowledge concerning the variety of rooms and styles you have within the educational institution, and the different technology available in different classrooms. Those with advancement knowledge have an intimate understanding of the classroom context.

Advancement knowledge has been described in many ways. One description is that advancement knowledge includes "insight, intuition, and decisions based on gut feel" (Leonard and Sensiper, 2002, p. 486). Another is that advancement knowledge includes a movement beyond basic common knowledge to the intimate understandings of daily routines and practices (Nelson and Winter, 1982). Nonaka et al. (2000) indicate *routine knowledge* involves an in-depth understanding of the sequential order of events and includes insights on "know-how" in the industry concerning daily activities, processes, and procedures. In addition,

Nonaka et al. indicate *experiential knowledge*, acquired through the hands-on participation of practices, can move beyond common knowledge to advancement knowledge when subtle details of how to be efficient, effective, and successful are learned with practice. Due to the value of experiential knowledge in event management, this topic is discussed further in Chapter 11: An Integral Approach to Experiential Learning: A Foundation for Event Management and Personal Development.

Advancement knowledge can also be what Collins (1993) describes as *"enbrained knowledge"* and *"encultured knowledge."* Enbrained knowledge involves conceptual and cognitive abilities produced with practice. This includes developing awareness, thinking through requirements, and sensing needs. Encultured knowledge is the intimate understanding and awareness of the subtleties required for full participation in a particular culture.

Advancement knowledge also includes the creation of new knowledge. For years we have understood that creating new knowledge does not occur disconnected from current abilities (Kogut and Zander, 1992). Rather, new learnings in the form of innovations "are products of a firm's *combinative capabilities* to generate new application from existing knowledge" (Kogut and Zander, p. 390). This implies that to create new knowledge, it is the combination of what you already know and can do that is applied to a new situation to create new knowledge. Overall, the process of creating new knowledge requires individuals to synthesize their current knowledge for different applications or situations.

von Krogh and Grand (2002) indicate: "Knowing means holding certain beliefs about the world, this knowledge being justified in experience and current observations as well as conceptual reasoning and thinking" (p. 172). This definition of knowledge implies that beliefs of what constitutes knowledge are affected by experiences, observations, and abilities to conceptually reason and to think.

Obtaining advancement knowledge in event management is important as it can provide a real advantage when you are called upon to manage an event situation or issue, especially those situations that do not have well-defined parameters. However, advancement knowledge is difficult to obtain as it is tacit in nature (Nonaka and Takeuchi, 1995).

Tacit knowledge is what individuals hold in their mind and includes understandings, perspectives, beliefs, and models (Nonaka and Takeuchi, 1995). Polyani (1966) indicated that tacit knowledge is constructed through reasoning; while Ritchie (1998) and Winter (1987) stated tacit knowledge is constructed through personal experience. Due to the difficulty of getting an individual to articulate their tacit knowledge, it has been described as a type of "iceberg" (Schorr, 1997, p. 29).

It is intimate knowledge, but much of the knowledge is buried. Therefore, because of its hidden nature, acquiring advancement knowledge from someone else in an event knowledge transfer process can be a challenge.

The difficulty in acquiring advancement knowledge from someone else has been known for years to be due to the fact that generally the knowledge holder has never expressed the knowledge verbally or in writing (Spender, 1996). A solution to fully alleviate this issue has not been found. A person can have advancement knowledge, which is considered to be intimate and personal, and not realize that he or she possesses the knowledge. Therefore, participating in a transferring process and being able to express the knowledge in an exchange process is difficult.

To access common and advancement knowledge held by others, Leonard and Sensiper (2002) suggest the use of a process of socializing. The act of socializing helps to access knowledge that is entrenched within the environment or activities conducted while the advancement knowledge was developed. Socializing aids the development of common and advancement knowledge by probing, questioning, and stimulating discussions that relate to a particular context. Conducting interviews of key members in the field of event management can potentially give access to both kinds of knowledge. Shadowing an individual as they complete their daily tasks and asking pertinent questions relating to these tasks may reveal intimate details concerning their knowledge. Obtaining common knowledge is the starting point for gaining advancement knowledge, which may take significantly more effort to acquire.

The acquisition of common knowledge provides a foundational level of knowledge for participating in a knowledge transfer race. This is because common knowledge is "important for its ability to aid individuals to participate in exchanging and integrating knowledge that are *not* common among them" (Grant, 1996, p. 139). The exchange of knowledge begins with common elements which, in turn, can lead to uncovering uncommon elements. As you increase the amount of common knowledge that is shared, the process has the potential to synthesize the understandings and to create advancement knowledge (Figure 2.4).

Earlier in this chapter you were asked to record a definition of knowledge. Now … go back and review your initial definition of knowledge and the dimensions or features of knowledge that you were able to describe and compare them to the definitions and features of common and advancement knowledge described above. This review and the advance of your definition of knowledge are important for participating in the knowledge-based event environment.

Polyani (1966)	Knowledge is constructed reasoning.
Nelson and Winter (1982)	Advancement knowledge is intimate understandings of daily routines and practices without team members realizing the extent of the knowledge held.
Kogut and Zander (1992)	Advancement knowledge is "creating new knowledge ... from current abilities ... *combinative capabilities* to generate new application from existing knowledge" (p. 390).
Collins (1993)	Advancement knowledge includes *"enbrained knowledge,"* that is derived from cognitive and conceptual skills And *Encultured knowledge* that is derived by participating in culturally diverse situations to develop understandings of subtleties of the culture.
Ritchie (1998)	Knowledge is constructed through personal experience.
Nonaka, Toyama, and Konno (2000)	Advancement knowledge includes *routine knowledge* that involves an understanding of intimate knowledge within daily activities (know-how) And *Experiential knowledge* that involves the practice and experience provided by personal hands-on activity.
Leonard and Sensiper (2002)	Advancement knowledge is the basis for the production of "insight, intuition, and decisions based on 'gut feel' " (p. 486).
von Krogh and Grand (2002)	"Knowing means holding certain beliefs about the world, this knowledge being justified in experience and current observations as well as conceptual reasoning and thinking" (p. 172).
Conner and Prahalad (2002)	An advantage is derived from one's particular perspectives or a combination of knowledge that is available for creating solutions and innovations.

Figure 2.4   Features or dimensions of advancement knowledge

A definition of knowledge for the context of event management

To further aid your understanding of a definition of knowledge, a definition specifically for event management is provided. This definition was constructed by applying the multiple definitions and descriptions of common and advancement

> A definition of knowledge for the context of sport, recreation and tourism event management is:
>
> *Event Management Knowledge = The synergy of common knowledge and advancement knowledge that leads to perspicacity (quick insights and understandings) for competence (in actions and ability).*

Figure 2.5 Defining knowledge in event management

knowledge offered above. The ensuing definition of knowledge for the context of event management is presented in Figure 2.5.

A synergy of common and advancement knowledge involves more than just adding your knowledge to create a total level of knowledge. The synergy gives rise to combinations of knowledge that can be achieved through interactions. The combined effect of a synergy of insights and understandings is greater than just the addition of the insights and understandings. The synergistic combinations lead to personalized advancement insights and understandings for use in practice in the field of event management.

This definition of knowledge can now be used to guide the design of a knowledge transfer race strategy for event management.

A knowledge transfer race strategy

As mentioned at the beginning of this chapter, you are in a contemporary environment that describes knowledge as a valued asset. Further, a knowledge transfer race has begun that requires you to acquire more and more common and advancement knowledge. Although researchers cannot agree on a definition of knowledge, a definition of knowledge specifically for the context of event management was created above by applying multiple definitions of knowledge that have been delineated in the literature. This definition of knowledge can now be applied to develop a strategy for the pursuit of common and advancement knowledge in event management, or a knowledge transfer race strategy.

A knowledge transfer race strategy is a self-directed plan to assist you to become efficient and effective in the process of acquiring and transferring knowledge in event management. This strategy articulates a deliberate means to guide you to develop your capacity for knowledge for competitive use. In event management, a knowledge transfer race strategy aims to increase your understanding of categories of knowledge, to acquire common knowledge, to acquire advancement knowledge, to advance your perspicacity (quick insights and understandings), and to advance your competence (actions and ability) for use in the event management field (Figure 2.6).

A knowledge transfer race strategy involves recording categories that describe knowledge and extrapolating the meaning of this knowledge for the event industry. An example of a knowledge transfer race strategy is outlined in Figure 2.7. This written record lists a combination of common and advancement knowledge you can pursue for working in the event industry.

This author suggests you develop a personal written knowledge transfer strategy and that you revisit and update this document weekly throughout the semester of your event management course, and beyond. Every topic discussed in your class may aid you to better describe the knowledge you can acquire and transfer. Then, implement the knowledge transfer race strategy. To begin to implement the knowledge transfer race strategy, you require the development of a network to support the pursuit of knowledge.

A knowledge transfer race strategy is a deliberate means to act to develop your capacity for knowledge for use in the fields of sport, recreation and tourism event management.

Figure 2.6   Defining a knowledge transfer race strategy

Features of common knowledge	Application of the feature of common knowledge to the field of event management
Knowledge is an understanding of what they "do" (Blackler, 1995)	To develop and share understandings of the role of the event manager, including what they do to prepare for an event, activities during each phase of the event, including the development phase, logistical planning phase, implementation, monitoring, and management phase and evaluation and renewal phase.
Knowledge includes the acquisition of factual data, concepts, and theoretical frameworks (Spender, 1996)	An application includes understanding general deadlines and data requirements to host or bid for an event, concepts, and theoretical frameworks as mentioned above.
Knowledge includes "conceptual knowledge" (Nonaka, Toyama, and Konno, 2000)	An application includes developing general understandings of abstract concepts such as processes used to lead the development of ideas, understanding the concepts or ideas that have been used during events, and understanding the quality value of the ideas with respect to events.

Figure 2.7   A knowledge transfer race strategy for event management

Features of common knowledge	Application of the feature of common knowledge to the field of event management
Knowledge includes "systemic knowledge" (Nonaka, Toyama, and Konno, 2000)	An application includes understanding the systemic technological systems that aid events, the development of manuals, and information packages creation (such as production manuals and team packages) for events.
Knowledge is an understanding of the basics of culture, politics, and personalities (Gupta and MacDaniel, 2002)	An application includes learning the code of conduct of an event manager during all phases of an event. In addition, it includes understanding the organizations involved with an event, their current issues or problems and potential arising issues, and the impact of the organizations and issues on event decision-makers. Also, to be cognizant of a variety of personalities and understand how to deal with people that could subtly or overtly attempt to influence the event plan in a variety of manners.
Knowledge is an understanding of theory and practice (English and Baker, 2006)	An application involves a general understanding theory (for example, the features of contingency theory, complexity theory, and management theory) and how these theories provide the theoretical foundations for the planning phases in event management. In addition, the application involves understanding processes and procedures used in practice (such as communication requirements during each stage of the event planning model).
Features of advancement knowledge	**Application of the feature of advancement knowledge to the field of event management**
"Enbrained knowledge" (Collins, 1993)	An application includes developing cognitive and conceptual event skills by thinking through the logistical requirements to host a variety of events (that is, indoor and outdoor events) to adapt event activities based on the traditional and/or niche nature of the event.
"Encultured knowledge" (Collins, 1993)	An application includes learning the intimate details of a culture by being immersed in a variety of cultural situations.
"Routine knowledge" (von Krogh and Grand, 2002)	An application includes developing an intimate understanding of the routines in event management, including adapting routines for specific events and understandings of why certain routines are not conducive to successful event management.
"Experiential knowledge" (von Krogh and Grand, 2002)	An application includes pursuing practical experience in a variety of areas (such as event ticketing, scheduling, outfitting of the competition venues, accommodation, transportation, promotions and ceremonies).

Figure 2.7   (Continued)

Networks support the knowledge transfer strategy

A description from Castells (2000) indicates:

> Networks are *dynamic, self-evolving structures, which, powered by information technology and communicating with the same digital language, can grow, and include all social expressions, compatible with each network's goals. Networks increase their value exponentially as they add nodes. (p. 697)*

The combination of individual member relationships creates the structure of a network. The social nature of networks employs communication as their key characteristic of a network. Communication is a constant requirement for the formation and maintenance of the network. The key role of every member in the network is to communicate.

Each member within the network needs to develop the competence to be a valuable communicator. Harris, Coles, and Dickson (2000) indicate that network competence includes the ability to:

> *Share their understanding of issues and devise ways to relate to each other in carrying out the work necessary to bring about a shared vision of the future. This vision provides the context that orients all network activity. Retaining this orientation is critical to developing and maintaining networks. (p. 6)*

The sharing within the network provides opportunities for ideas to be generated and knowledge to be created (von Krogh and Grand, 2002).

To form an event management knowledge transfer network, core members or network activists are necessary to encourage the relationships in a knowledge sharing process. The network activists need to offer the necessary time, attention, and competence to develop and maintain the network relationships. A key component in a knowledge transfer race strategy is *network activism*. Network activism is a conscious effort to expand your personal network, to encourage contacts between the members in the network, and to advance the quality of the network relationships for exchanging knowledge (Figure 2.8).

If you cannot join a knowledge transfer network, you should seriously consider being a network activist and creating your own network for knowledge sharing. To develop a network, consider: Who would you contact to begin a personal network in order to pursue knowledge? What do you expect from each network member in terms of the transfer of knowledge, and what are you providing in return? How will you encourage a greater number of contacts between you

Network activism is a conscious effort to (a) expand the number of nodes within your personal network, (b) encourage contacts between the nodes, and (c) advance the quality of the network relationships.

Figure 2.8   Network activism

Your flexibility effect includes the use of personal perspectives, opinions, approaches, experiences, ideas and options to create knowledge differentiation, or one's "flexibility effect[s]." Differentiated ideas, interpretations, and responses provide a potential competitive advantage in the contemporary change-based environment (Zack, 1999).

Figure 2.9   Flexibility effect

and others in your network? Also, how will you advance the quality of the network relationships to gain more knowledge?

When developing a knowledge transfer strategy and a network to advance your strategy, it is important that you develop your own perceptions. The use of personal perceptions of knowledge and network activism can create a competitive advantage. The advantage is derived from what Conner and Prahalad (2002) call the *flexibility effect*. This effect includes knowledge that is personalized by intertwining one's personal perspectives, opinions, approaches, experiences, ideas, and options. In addition, personalization includes the impact of one's skill, personality, motivations, abilities, perceptions, and interpretations on those elements. This impact creates differentiation, or one's flexibility effect. According to Zack (1999), a flexibility effect includes differentiated ideas, interpretations, and responses that provide a competitive advantage. This advantage is produced through the personalization process that leads to insights, understandings, and the development of new knowledge (Figure 2.9).

The personalization of knowledge aids in the production of ideas and new knowledge. This is because differentiation ensures that ideas are varied and not limited to one particular person's viewpoint (Carney, 2001). Accepting and nurturing the personalization of your knowledge encourages the development of options, varied interpretations and solutions.

Conclusion

A knowledge transfer race has been declared. Those in event management cannot expect to be exempt from the knowledge requirements emphasized in contemporary society. To begin to participate in this race, a definition of knowledge is needed. This definition of knowledge can guide you to develop a knowledge transfer race strategy. This strategy guides your acquisition of the multiple dimensions of knowledge needed for the event management industry. Additionally, a network that encourages collaboration and sharing of knowledge aids in the effort to obtain more knowledge.

This chapter provided a definition of knowledge for the context of sport, recreation and tourism event management. In addition, a knowledge transfer race strategy was outlined by applying the features or dimensions of common and advancement knowledge to event management. The aim is to guide the pursuit of more knowledge to achieve perspicacity for use in the event industry.

It is the opinion of the author that you do not simply accept any of the definitions of knowledge presented. It is recommended that you review the definitions of knowledge and craft a personal definition of knowledge to guide your development of a knowledge transfer race strategy. In addition, you need to become a network activist to facilitate the implementation of the knowledge transfer race strategy. The implementation includes the search for knowledge with the expansion of your relations in event management, advancing the contact between the nodes and improving the quality of the network relationships. The combination of a knowledge transfer race strategy and the development of a network to achieve knowledge can position you as a valued asset within the industry.

To support the concept of a knowledge transfer race strategy, this text *does not* provide a list of elements that you can follow to produce a sport, recreation or tourism event. A list of elements is not conducive to the change-based times and the pursuit of knowledge. This is because all events are not alike, and the contemporary environment of change means that you will be working on events in the future that have not yet been conceived. In times of change it is important to be able to "think through" the particular requirements for the context and event. Thus, it is perspicacity that you are seeking. The quick advanced insights and understandings should position you well for the future. A planning model is offered to guide the development of your understandings of event management.

Chapter questions

1. What is a knowledge transfer race, and how do you participate?
2. Describe why you are in an event management knowledge transfer race?
3. What is common knowledge?
4. What is advancement knowledge?
5. How do you obtain advancement knowledge, and why is it so difficult to obtain?

The event planning model: The event development phase, Part I

Amy Cunningham;
Joanne MacLean, Laura Cousens,
Martha Barnes, Brock University;
Geoff Dickson, Auckland University of
Technology

The next six chapters discuss the event planning model and describe the role of the event manager in the staging of traditional or niche events. This model includes four phases as outlined in Figure 3.1.

This chapter examines the first phase in the planning model, the event development phase. In this phase, the event manager is positioned as a facilitator who guides the development of the event structures for governance, the event networks, policies, volunteer practices, and participation in corporate social responsibility.

Each of the five chapters that follow discusses the planning phases including the event operational planning phase, the event implementation, the monitoring and management phase, the event evaluation, and the rejuvenation or renewal phase.

Event development phase

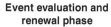

The event manager facilitates the development of event structures for governance, event networks, policies, volunteer practices, and participation in a corporate social responsibility program

**Event evaluation and
renewal phase**

The event manager facilitates the selection of event components to be evaluated, the completion of the evaluation tasks and the implementation of the evaluation recommendations

Event operational planning phase

The event manager creates and facilitates the development of written operational plans that are logical, sequential, detailed and integrated, along with contingency plans and the activation of a plan refining process

**Event implementation, monitoring,
and management phase**

The event manager facilitates the implementation of the written operational plans, monitors activities looking for deviations and manages all deviations from the plans

Figure 3.1 An event planning model

In the previous chapter we looked at the various meanings and definitions of the concept of knowledge. In this first imprint (section) of Chapter 3, the idea of facilitation is presented. A key role of the event manager is to facilitate the event processes to stage a traditional or niche event. This is followed by additional imprints that discuss facilitating event governance, policy, networks, volunteer practices, and corporate social responsibility.

The event manager as a facilitator

Amy Cunningham

One of the most exciting aspects of event management is the requirement to produce a team effort. The event needs a facilitator to guide the *knowledge sharing process* between members. In addition, the event manager is responsible for *facilitating* event processes. These are the processes that are found within the collaborative effort of planning and implementing an event, where all members of the group need to feel equally a part of the team effort.

The role of the event manager as a facilitator is established in the development phase of the planning model. This facilitation role will be discussed in more depth, but first let us take a step back and investigate the meaning of facilitation itself. The concept of facilitation is crucial to the role an event manager must play and provides the theoretical framework upon which we will draw our understanding within this section and the overall text.

What is facilitation?

Bens (2000) defines facilitation as "a way of providing leadership without taking the reigns" (p. 7). Facilitation theory assumes that learning will occur with the aid of one who facilitates the process of learning as opposed to one who simply provides knowledge to a group (Laird, 1985; Lambert and Glacken, 2005). Within this theory of facilitation, it is believed that since change is constant, the greatest teachers are those who have learned how to learn, and can lead others in self-directed learning and critical thinking (Lambert and Glacken; Peel, 2000). This style of leadership encourages the development of empowered learners and contributors to group processes, where the creation and dissemination of knowledge are dependent on all members of the group.

To be an effective facilitator and supporter of this theory one must subscribe to certain assumptions. According to Bens (2000), believers in facilitation theory and practice assume that:

People are intelligent, capable and want to do the right thing.
Groups can make better decisions than any one person can make alone.
Everyone's opinion is of equal value, regardless of rank or position.
People are committed to the ideas and plans that they have helped to create.
Participants can and will act responsibly in assuming true accountability for their decisions.
Groups can manage their own conflicts, behaviours and relationships if they are given the right tools and training.

The *process*, if well designed and honestly applied, can be trusted to achieve results (p. 8).

Now that we have a general understanding of what is meant by the theory of facilitation, the role of an event manager acting as a facilitator can be explored.

Role of an event facilitator

If we look back to Figure 3.1, the event manager has an important role to play as a facilitator throughout all of the planning phases. As a facilitator, your job is to *get others to assume responsibility and to take the lead*. Rogers and Friedberg (1994) expressed this facilitation leadership role as the following:

A leader is best
When people barely know that he exists,
Not so good when people obey and acclaim him,
Worst when they despise him.
Fail to honour people; they fail to honour you
But of a good leader, who talks little,
When his work is done, his aim fulfilled,
They will all say, "We did this ourselves." (p. 21)

The facilitator becomes the director of performance, where each participant plays a central role (Vidal, 2004). By the end of this performance, with the creation of group synergy, which should be one of the main goals of true facilitation, participants will have had "the pleasure of working creatively and collectively to

Describe the difference between *teaching* and *facilitating*.

Determine the *advantages* and *disadvantages* of teaching compared to facilitating.

Figure 3.2   Questioning the difference between teaching and facilitating

achieve some goals" (p. 394). Overall, facilitators aim to make specific processes easier during all phases of the event.

There are many specific skills, experiences, and knowledge that the event manager must possess to facilitate an event (Peel, 2000; Thomas, 2004). This array includes advancement knowledge which involves intuition about the processes which they are guiding. Intuition helps facilitators "act on their feet" and make quick decisions with regards to the needs of a group or process (Peel, 2000). By making these processes easier, specific tasks will be completed, goals will be met, and the team will feel a pleasurable synergy after a job well done (Vidal, 2004).

A good facilitator empowers the group and the individuals within it to rise to their own potential and have the confidence to be an equal player on the team so that no one becomes dependent on a "teacher." Everyone is shown to be their own developer of knowledge, and the strengths of each individual within the collective can be drawn out and their benefits maximized within the overall process (Peel, 2000).

Below is a comprehensive outline of some of the specific roles that a facilitator would play during the event managing process (Figure 3.3).

Facilitating the communication requirements

Greenberg (2002) explains, "Communication is the process through which people send information to others and receive information from them" (p. 217). This process can be a difficult one to facilitate, as it is made up of numerous interactions between various members of a team, all of whom bring their individual personalities, knowledge, skills and, communication styles to the table. It is an important job of the event manager, then, to act as a facilitator and to make sure that communication lines are open, that members of the team feel that they are being supported and that specific processes and requirements are articulated and managed throughout the overall process (Bens, 2000).

In organizational settings, the communication process can be extremely complex depending on the design of the organization. In many cases information may need to flow up or down through the "ranks" or be transmitted to certain individuals via other individuals (Greenberg, 2002). The complexity of these links

A facilitator
Helps the group define specific goals and objective.
Provides processes that assist members to use their time efficiently to make good decisions, and helps group members understand these processes.
Guides group discussion to keep things on track.
Keeps accurate notes that reflect the ideas of the group members.
Supports members in assessing their current skills and the building of new ones.
Uses consensus to help the group make decisions that take all members' opinions into account.
Supports members in managing their own interpersonal dynamics.
Helps the group communicate effectively.
Helps the group access resources.
Creates a positive environment in which members can grow and work together toward attaining group goals.
Fosters leadership in others by sharing leadership responsibilities.
Supports and empowers others to facilitate.
(Bens, 2000; Peel, 2000; Vidal, 2004)

Figure 3.3 The event manager as a facilitator

can lead to communication breakdowns and confusion if not managed properly. The wonderful thing about facilitating a group of individuals with whom you are considered a part of the team is that most of the communication in this process will move horizontally. As Greenberg states, "Messages of this type are characterized by efforts at coordinating, or attempts to work together" (p. 201).

In the previous section in this chapter, we learned that in the case of event manager as facilitator, one of the main roles is to create and support group dynamics (Peel, 2000). By focusing and guiding group members' communication and decision-making processes in a structured form, the facilitator can reduce the chances of engaging in faulty processes and harness the strengths of the group. If the proper communication requirements have been articulated and set in place by the facilitator at the onset of the event planning process, the facilitator should fade into the collective, only to be called upon to manage problems and situations as they may arise.

As a facilitator, the event manager is constantly listening, thinking, and reflecting throughout the process as problem solving and decision making are occurring between group members. In any group situation, decisions will need to be made, and any conflicts will need to be resolved. While the overall process of task completion is equally the responsibility of each member of the group, it is the

Be a supportive communicator.

Focus on the problem instead of the person.

Match words with body language and encourage group members to do the same.

Encourage the group to acknowledge each other's ideas.

Keep the conversation going.

Encourage open feedback.

Encourage the use of simple language.

Paraphrase to clarify; repeat what people say to assure them they are being heard and to make sure the group has understood and are clear.

Walk the talk; don't say one thing and do the other, and watch for this behaviour in group members.

Be a good listener and encourage the group to do the same; consider the use of a "talking stick" to ensure that everyone has a chance to speak and be heard.

Stay neutral, and avoid sharing your personal opinion unless it is requested; focus on your *process* role of communication.

Ask questions; this will invite participation, help to gather information, test assumptions, and get to the root causes of problems.

Synthesize ideas; encourage group members to comment and build upon each other's ideas.

Stay on track; set time guidelines for each discussion.

Summarize clearly.

(Bens, 2000; Greenberg, 2002)

Figure 3.4   Facilitation tips

role of an effective facilitator to guide the group to a synergy that is borne of effective communication (Vidal, 2004). In this regard, historically a facilitator would act as a neutral party who guides the group communication requirements, setting out specific strategies at the onset of the process, and interjecting as necessary to guide the group back into synchronicity as needed (Laird, 1985; Rogers and Friedberg, 1994).

Now that the importance of facilitating the communication requirements is understood, below are some helpful tips to consider (Figure 3.4).

Facilitating group communication requirements: the case of group rhythm and facilitation

According to the seminal work by Drucker (1946), "an institution is like a 'tune'; it is not constituted by individual sounds but by the relations between them" (p. 26).

An event can exhibit institutional characteristics and requires the facilitation of the relations between the many individuals involved to create a coordinated tune.

Lulu Leathley, an individual from Vancouver, British Columbia, Canada, is who specializes in facilitating group rhythm events (drumming circles) and promotes the importance of facilitated communication in group processes. The teachings of Leathley position the facilitator's role as beginning with the act of being a conductor. In music, the goal is to reach a moment in the facilitation of group music-making where everyone (despite their musical background and experience) feels empowered and collectively reaches a place of group synergy. It is her goal to slowly fade into the background and become a part of the group so that the music created is dependent upon each person and no one becomes dependent on her as a leader. To accomplish this goal, she sets certain communication requirements (both verbal and nonverbal) at the beginning of the group drumming circle. She very clearly articulates the importance of listening to each other, making eye contact, and getting in touch with inner intuitions and rhythms. In other words, she encourages and empowers group members to look inside of themselves for the knowledge that she believes they already possess in order to create something that is a sum of all parts of the collective. Throughout the facilitation, she encourages the group to bring their own inner rhythms and strengths forward in order to contribute to the collective song. She makes sure to keep the rhythm going, despite the ups and downs, and provides ample room and encouragement for feedback. At the completion of a successful event, there is the energy of connection.

In music collaboration, there is an overall feeling that is felt by the musicians when everything culminates in a satisfying "click" (Sawyer, 2006). This synergistic click is a challenge to attain as it takes the cooperation and ability of all group members working together to reach this goal. The facilitator's job is to communicate with the group both verbally and nonverbally in the beginning and then to reenter and guide the group and *sense* what is needed throughout the process.

As discussed in Chapter 2, knowledge allows you to become quicker with intuitive decision-making abilities gained through experience. In addition, your flexibility effect includes personalizing your knowledge, perceptions, and ideas for an advantage. A facilitator's role is to use their knowledge and flexibility effect to facilitate the event process. This facilitation includes recognizing when certain group members are overpowering others, when people are not listening to each other, or when the group is approaching a collective musical disaster. In this situation, Leathley responds and reacts to the needs of the group based on her own experience, knowledge, skills, and intuition: *the flexibility effect* she has acquired as a music teacher and facilitator.

If the group has succeeded in coming together and clicking, there is an overwhelming sense of empowerment, pride, and accomplishment as a collective at the conclusion of the event. As mentioned in the previous section, this is the sign that the event facilitators have been effective and successful in their role. Facilitating communication within the group process, then, can be seen as one of the most important roles of the event manager.

The sport, recreation and tourism event manager facilitates the communication processes. Their experience, knowledge, skills, and intuition: their flexibility effect, contributes to the ability to create a collective synergy in event production.

We have now reviewed the meaning of facilitation and the role of the facilitator, specifically regarding communication process requirements. Now let us revisit a concept addressed earlier within this text: the importance of the transfer of knowledge and specifically the role that the event manager as facilitator plays in this respect.

Facilitating knowledge transfer

Above, we have discussed the role of the event manager as a facilitator and what that entails during group processes in the organizing of an event. As a facilitator of a collaborative group effort, it is your job to make sure knowledge is transferred and built between group members. This, as we have discussed, helps to ensure that the best and most informed decisions are made in the pursuit of task completion, drawing on the collective knowledge of the group. But how does the facilitator go about ensuring that his/her own knowledge is transferred to inform the field as a whole?

The sharing of knowledge with others invites and assumes that other facilitators will in return share their knowledge, and as a result the knowledge apex will broaden and expand. This has very positive outcomes if we are to assume that the goal of sharing and receiving new knowledge is to continuously work toward honing our effectiveness and expertise as facilitators.

Within a practical setting, let us revisit Lulu Leathley's facilitation of rhythm-based events. As a facilitator within a network of other facilitators, Leathley engages in many specific knowledge transfer strategies which enable her to inform her field, contribute to the expansion of the knowledge pool, and broaden her own knowledge base. Some of these strategies include:

building relationships and sharing dialogue about experiences with other facilitators, attending rhythm facilitation conferences,

continuously attending training sessions with other facilitators with varying levels of experience,

joining discussion groups and posting information on various websites,

becoming an active member in the rhythm facilitator's guild, and

aiding others to develop facilitation skills by lending talents and experiences to mentorship programs.

The *network activism*, discussed in the previous chapter, is very strong within the drumming and rhythm facilitator community. There is a climate of cooperation and support that aids in the important transfer of knowledge. As a result of this enthusiasm and support, the community of facilitators continues to grow and individuals are able to develop their perspicacity (quick advanced insights and understandings) based on the knowledge that is shared.

Knowledge transfer, again, is extremely important in the broadening of the apex of a specific knowledge base. There are many ways in which an event manager may facilitate this knowledge transfer, and above we have examined various examples within one particular case. We have also outlined the specifics of facilitation, the role of the event manager as a facilitator, and the importance and ways in which communication requirements may be facilitated. Let us now begin a discussion on another area of interest in the development phase of the planning model: the facilitation of structures for governance when staging an event.

Facilitating event structures for governance

Joanne MacLean, Brock University

Let us consider an event of huge magnitude, for example the Olympic and Paralympic Games. In February/March of 2010 the communities of Vancouver and Whistler will welcome the world to Canada for a massive winter sporting festival. Competition in the Winter Olympics is conducted over a 17-day period, with another 10 days of Paralympic competition following. The event organizers, as their mission, have been inspiring the world through this event. The Vancouver Organizing Committee indicates "the mission is to touch the soul of the nation and inspire the world by creating and delivering an extraordinary Olympic and Paralympic experience with lasting legacies. The vision is to build a stronger

Canada whose spirit is raised by its passion for sport, culture and sustainability" (Vancouver, 2010, 2007).

This mission and vision is to be met through organizing an event that includes competition in 7 sports, with 15 disciplines. Thousands of employees and volunteers will stage the Games, and the images of athletes from hundreds of countries around the world will be televised and followed intently by fellow citizens. Organizing the Olympic Games requires an enormous planning process.

Now turn your attention to a smaller event run in your community, such as a community tourism event or a team sport provincial championship being hosted at your university. Even though it is of smaller magnitude and duration compared to the Olympics, it still involves many of the same components.

Event components can include elements, such as accommodation, accreditation, ceremonies, communications, food and beverages, hospitality services, media management, spectator services, and transportation. In sport, recreation and tourism events, the components list may also expand to include participant or competitor management, officials, drug testing or doping control, results, and awards. In each case, a considerable amount of work is devoted to planning and staging a successful event.

Events within sport, recreation and tourism have levels of magnitude, appeal, and complexity that require well-designed event structures that contribute to successful delivery. Often, the structure and governance of event management are "silent," somewhat behind-the-scenes of the main program of activities that are consumed or watched. However, in reality, the elements of effective structure and governance are foundations to success. Successful events simply cannot be achieved without a structure for planning and delivering the event that enables effective communication, decision making, and appropriate amounts of flexibility among event managers. In order to understand this in further detail, the purposes of the following sections include: Defining the concepts related to event structures and good governance of event management; outlining the theoretical dimensions of event structures that will enable the delivery of successful events, without identifying the specifics of that structure; identifying principles that result in the creation of effective event structures; and applying the theoretical dimensions and principles of event structures identified above to different types of events currently popular in the business of sport, recreation and tourism.

By following the topics identified above, students will gain an appreciation for two important fundamental principles about facilitating event structures for event management: First, different kinds of events require different event management structures that provide the best suited management for the particular event; and second, we believe that event managers are better served learning the *guiding principles* that will enable them to make decisions about the most appropriate and effective structure for the event being planned as opposed to duplicating the structure from another event. You may label these two fundamental principles *flexibility* and *specificity* regarding event management structures. The following sections will help you understand these and other principles and their application in creating effective event structures.

Event structures

So what exactly do we mean by the term *event structure*? The term event structure refers to breaking down the tasks associated with delivering the event such that employees or volunteers have specific roles and an understanding of how these roles interrelate. The structure involves individual positions or groups of individuals in committees that control tasks, understand the authority they have to make which decisions, and the reporting relationships between individuals and committees. Typically event leaders will publicize a management structure in the form of a chart with boxes and connecting lines outlining the task areas, with proximity between areas that need to cooperate and/or collaborate, and reporting directions.

Theoretically, the structure of an organization is usually examined from three points of view (Slack and Parent, 2006): The first viewpoint is *formalization* (the degree to which rules and regulations, policies, and individual and committee roles are defined to guide the activities of event managers). The second viewpoint is *complexity* (the scope and number of different individual committees and subunits required to deliver the event and the density of the hierarchy of authority involved). The third viewpoint is *centralization* (the degree to which decision making is controlled by those in charge of the event or delegated to individuals working at the level of committees or individual jobs). The event structure can be designed to be high or low in each of formalization, complexity, and centralization depending on the type of event.

Event structures are developed to aid the governance of an event. Governance refers to exercising the authority to define policy regarding how the event will be run, who does what, and when and how they do it. If an event is to be successful, then the structure created to deliver it must provide for effective transfer of knowledge and decision making. Facilitating event structures means that you have the knowledge and understanding necessary to create the most appropriate organizing structure for your event.

In addition to the theory discussed above regarding event structure, there are a number of other important theories that have been developed which aid in understanding effective event structures. These theoretical dimensions of event structures that we have chosen to include in this discussion involve systems theory, contingency theory, and complexity theory. The following sections will briefly introduce each theory in the context of understanding effective event structures for good governance and successful event management.

Theoretical dimensions of event structures

Event structures vary considerably. For concrete local examples, examine how your educational and recreational events are structured. Compare the recreational event structure to a local tourism event and a locally held elite sport championship. Each event can be unique in its structure. The structure dictates the hierarchy, which in turn influences the freedom to act in the process of making, relaying, and implementing decisions and actions when staging an event.

When creating an event, you will need to consider a structure that will lead to the most effective and efficient delivery for staging the event. In order to achieve this goal, there are several theoretical perspectives that relate information about effective organizations and event structures. The theoretical dimensions outlined next are largely complementary, in that parts of each theory may apply in specific ways to the event structure you develop.

Systems theory stresses that event management structures rely on the environment within which they operate for many of the materials that will be required for the event to run. Materials include a wide variety of items such as people, equipment, technologies, facilities, and knowledge to name a few. Systems theory suggests that the event will have three different systems working together: *input systems, throughput systems, and output systems.* In order to run an event, you must take in resources (inputs), create the event activities (throughputs), and generate end results for participants or others (outputs). The three systems interrelate and depend on each other for success. A change in one inevitably affects the other parts of the system. Any event you are organizing involves inputs or the acquisition of raw materials (competition facilities) and human resources (volunteers) to organize the event; throughputs might include the application of technology (website designed for managing communication and registration) and information (the number of teams that can be accommodated within the competition); and outputs include the enjoyment of competitors and the dollars raised for the charity of choice. The overall event system interacts within its

Systems theory suggests that event structures be created and managed by understanding the inputs, throughputs, and outputs required to deliver the event.

The organizing structure interacts with its environment to procure the materials required to run the event (inputs), create the activities of the event (throughputs), and generate end results for participants or other stakeholders (outputs).

Inputs-throughputs-outputs.

Materials-structures-products.

Human resources event activities experiences.

Figure 3.5 Systems theory

Contingency theory indicates that the most effective structure for managing an event is based on or contingent upon the contextual factors of the environment within which the event is being organized. Contextual factors of the environment include items such as the size of the event, competition with other like events, and the resources available to deliver the event.

Figure 3.6 Contingency theory

component parts and with its environment. Understanding the application of systems theory identifies the importance of component parts of the organization structure depending on and influencing one another (Figure 3.5).

A rational extension to systems theory in understanding the organizing structure and management of an event is *contingency theory*. This theory suggests that the effective structure of an organization is contingent on contextual factors of the environment within which it operates, such as size, competition, strategy, resources, and so on. As such, the design of the event structure and its units must "fit" with the environment and work well in coordination in order for the event to succeed. Therefore, there is no "best way" to organize an event structure, as it depends on factors within the environment of operation. For example, in a charity recreational event, the structure of the event organizing system will need to account for how many competitors register. However, the size of registration may be wholly contingent on how many facilities exist, how much time can be acquired within facilities, and how many referees are available. These factors may be impacted by other tournaments running proximal to yours in timing or location. Such factors are often termed constraints, and understanding event constraints and contingencies will lead to optimal organizing structure, decision making, and leadership (Figure 3.6).

In keeping with systems and contingency theories, *complexity theory* works to identify how organizations optimally adapt to their environments. Using this theory, managers focus on the required complexity of structure that can achieve the mission of the event while retaining the ability to adapt and make strategic

Complexity theory suggests that organizations can optimally adapt to their environment by creating an event structure which meets the needs of the event in terms of its overall complexity and does not become overly complex. Adapting to the environment within which the event is run allows the manager greater flexibility to make strategic decisions.

Figure 3.7 Complexity theory

decisions quickly. Complexity theory identifies the importance of complex adaptive systems, structures that commonly consist of a small number of relatively simple, partially connected structures. In our recreational charity event example, a simpler structure involving committees for scheduling, facility organization, registration, and volunteers that connect to each other via a tournament leaders' committee will be better able to communicate, make effective decisions, and adapt to its environment (Figure 3.7).

In academic study, the word theory is used to describe the logical explanation for a phenomenon that has been studied systematically and is thought to expand our understanding. The theories briefly described above provide a foundation for understanding why and how event structures may be optimally designed. How can we facilitate effective structures? What makes an event structure effective and another ineffective? How do event structures come to influence good governance, such that the decision making, policy development, and efficiency of the event are optimized? Understanding the above theories sheds some light on answering these questions. And from these theories, along with trial and error of what works in practice and the transfer of this knowledge, a variety of principles in event structures have been identified. Let's look at these in further detail.

Principles in event structures

Principles can be likened to rules or understandings that have resulted from theory and practice regarding how and why things work. In developing effective organizing structures for event management, a number of principles are identified that will help event organizers create the optimal structure for the particular event and environment within which the event is being delivered. Identified below are some of the major principles applying to event structure development.

Form follows function: This principle suggests that the type of structure created to manage the delivery of an event should be predicated on the purpose of the event and the definition of governance roles (for example, developing policy, managing, operating) within the event management design. Copying the event structure from a previously successful event does not necessarily result in a workable structure for another event. For example, using the structure developed to deliver the Olympic Games would be ridiculous when delivering a high school basketball tournament because the former event is much larger and more complex than the latter.

Operating specialization: Optimal event structures identify the activities required to deliver the event and cluster similar or like activities together into sub-units to encourage communication and decision making. By so doing, efficiency is created by maximizing interconnections among managers with responsibilities that impact one another, leading to more autonomous but interconnected work groups.

Increasing complexity increases both planning and time required for planning: The more complex an organizing structure, the more planning is required to ensure that the structure functions optimally. It stands to reason that this will take more time than with a simple structure. An example of this principle is with the organizing of the Olympic Games. Game operating committee structures are designed 6–8 years in advance of the competition at a minimum, and the extent of planning is exceptionally broad.

Communications efficiency: Planning does not take place in the brain of one person in isolation from others. Therefore, the structure for event management must create linkages and liaisons for individuals to communicate their activities and decisions, and this communication must be formally arranged in order to be efficiently enacted. The speed and number of communications can be enhanced depending on the type of event structure created.

Synergistic outcomes: Synergy refers to the phenomenon of greater efficiency and outcomes that occur when two or more agents work together than could be achieved had each completed the same effects in isolation. Event structures that create opportunities for synergistic outcomes are said to be efficiently lean and more effective for task accomplishment (Kilmann, Pondy, and Slevin, 1976). The accruing synergistic outcome results from the idea that the overall accomplishment is more than a simple summation of output, meaning that the whole is greater than the sum of its parts.

Understanding the theories and principles relative to facilitating effective event structures is very important, but knowing how to apply the ideas presented to create actual event structures is perhaps even more critical for the success of the event and its managers. Next we move to a discussion of the application of key characteristics of the above theory.

Application of theory and principles in event structures

The theory and principles outlined earlier in this chapter regarding the development of effective event structures apply to both traditional and niche events. In practice, traditional events may involve more formality of structure compared to niche events. This results from the dictates of the governing body and its established policy regarding how the event is to be organized. Systems theory suggests that the environment within which the event is hosted be considered for both traditional and niche events. The required resources needed to create the event, the anticipated outcomes of the event, and the event activities will also need to be considered. Contingency theory purports that the importance of fitting the event structure to both its purpose and environment, creating a structure that fits appropriately with the size, resources, and intent of traditional and niche sporting events is paramount. Complexity theory also establishes the importance of matching the structure for organizing the event to its environment and purpose, in order to create a structure that matches the strategy and adaptability that might be required in the environment. Being able to adapt to unforeseen problems, pressures, and changes is a fundamental requirement for traditional and niche event structure frameworks. This can be optimized when the structure created for the event is directly linked to its purpose (for example, form follows function). While it might seem precipitous to use another successful event structure when planning a new event, it is actually a risky proposition. Linking form and function or creating an event structure that identifies the intent and governance roles that most specifically meet the needs of the actual event is highly important. While this is critically important for traditional sport event structures, it may necessarily be stressed even further with niche events where the event structure is without the guidance of a governing body, established policy, or other comparable events. Similarly, creating a clear understanding of the operating specialization for the event and linking the activities of sub-units with common or dependent roles will encourage effective communication and create efficiency. This is the case with both traditional and niche sport events. The complexity of the event structure will surely impact the amount of planning that is required to enable effective communication and decision making along with the time it will take to make this a reality. Planning with the specific intent of ensuring coordination among the parts of the event organizing structure is an important role for event managers that can have a multiplied, synergistic outcome of much greater magnitude than the impact of the work of an individual or a committee. Event leaders need to take a role in creating synergy

Consider and understand the event environment;

Identify resources required to deliver the event;

Clearly define the goals and outcomes sought from the event, and create a structure that bears both in mind;

Create a lean structure, but one that is capable of completing tasks and adapting to change in a timely manner;

Build event structures based on the needs of the specific event;

Create linkages between operating sub-units so that area specialists share in decisions impacting their areas and communication is heightened;

Larger events will have more complex structures;

Activities of the whole working in a coordinated fashion can far surpass the contribution of any of the parts of the operating structure.

Figure 3.8   Practical dimensions in event structures

among the parts of the event organizing structure, where the impact will be a positive result in both traditional and niche sport event structures (Figure 3.8).

Creating event structures so that good governance will result is the ultimate goal of understanding and applying the theory and principles discussed above to the management strategies with your event. A structure that is flexible provides for effective levels of communication, decision making, and exchange of information among the individuals delivering the event. The structure created, while being specifically designed for the purpose of the event, will best serve the needs of event managers and contribute to overall success. Effective event structures for governance go 'hand in glove' with facilitating effective event networks that bring additional groups or constituent organizations relationships and resources to aid in the development of an event, our next topic of interest.

Facilitating event management using the network perspective

Laura Cousens and Martha Barnes, Brock University

Geoff Dickson, Auckland University of Technology

This section or imprint continues the discussion on the development phase of the planning model. In this phase the network perspective offers event managers a tool to identify the types of constituents, be they suppliers, competitors, buyers, or government representatives that are linked to an event. An event manager's role is to facilitate the exchange of resources within a web of interconnected constituents. Examining constituent organizations provides opportunities to gain a broad perspective of the potential types of relationships and resources available to ensure event planning efficiency and effectiveness. In this imprint we seek to provide an understanding of the network perspective, the nature of business networks, and the theoretical and managerial application in traditional or niche events. This imprint identifies concepts relevant to business networks to provide event managers with the building blocks to differentiate and to analyze their event network. Additionally, we will discuss the different forms of relationships that constitute a network and the importance of recognizing the value of social capital when facilitating relationships in a network. Finally, attention will be focused on the strategic role of networks, leveraging network relationships, and managing relationships in the context of an event network. Two examples are used to illustrate the value of business networks including the 2005 Montreal Aquatics World Championships (Parent and Seguin, 2007) that were canceled 5 months before the event and then reinstated by the Federation Internationale de Natation (FINA). The event managers failed to manage the relationships among the key stakeholders and then repositioned themselves to gain the event back. In addition, the case of the Sydney "green" Olympic Games (Kearins and Pavlovich, 2002) and the interactions among the environmental groups that constituted key stakeholders in a network will be discussed.

Building blocks: the concepts used to understand business networks

Each component in an event structure can establish business networks. *Business networks* are "the totality of relationships among firms engaged in production distribution and the use of goods and services" (Andersson, 1992, p. 50). Thus, webs of organizations become linked by a common purpose or set of objectives to produce an event. These networks may be constituted by a loose collection of firms, as in the case of one-off events which unite on a fleeting basis to achieve various goals through an event. In contrast, tightly linked networks are characterized by strong and enduring linkages that structure larger scale events that occur on a regular basis over longer periods of time. The nature of business networks varies depending upon the goals, longevity, magnitude, or location of an event. Each of these parameters surrounding an event will impact the number of constituents or organizations linked within the network, the types of relationships that bind the members of the network, as well as the structure that is the density, centrality, or strength of ties, of the web within the network. Importantly, a network is the sum of *dyadic relationships* among sets of linked organizations. A dyadic relationship describes two linked organizations, or "dyads," that are linked to one another. Importantly, the dyads do not reside in isolation from other relationships, and this embeddedness extends the focus of concentration from the two partners to those other relationships to which the organizations are also linked. Adopting a network perspective to understand the nature of relationships between and among collections of constituents involved in an event holds promise as a tool to manage the various groups or organizations with interests in the event. This network perspective also allows one to look strategically at how best to manage the resources and competitive advantages that exist within a network.

Viewing business networks as a web of relationships between linked organizations conjures a graphic representation of a spiderweb's star-like configuration. The arachnid's tightly woven silks create circular orb webs that extend from a central hub to various points. These webs may take various forms and serve different functions as necessitated by the spider's circumstances. Comparatively, the structure of business networks is reflective of the number of organizations, or *nodes*, together with the types of linkages that bind them together. Similarly, the number of connections between the nodes, or density of the network, also provides insight into the patterns of resource sharing across the network and the level of connectivity among network members. These and other concepts, such as centrality, periphery, and equivalency, describe the characteristics of networks. Significantly, each network is different and understanding its characteristics will enable event facilitators to leverage key facets of the network and exploit its many possibilities and opportunities.

Centrality captures a key concept of business networks that is suggestive of the proximity of nodes to one another, the presence of one or more hubs or central points among linked nodes in the network, and the power and dependence relationships among those linked in the network. In an event network, the hub or central point is typically the event organizing committee. It is to this central organization or group that most other nodes are linked. By way of example, the organizing committee is linked to the corporate sponsors, the facility provider, the local government, the media, and other organizations assisting with the staging of the event. However, an event manager must remain cognizant of the fact that the other organizations in the network may be linked to one another for reasons not related to this specific event network and are embedded within larger networks of organizations. Importantly, recognizing the centre or focal point of the web will enlighten managers to the structure of their network and the patterns of resource sharing it encompasses. According to Brass and Burkhardt (1992), centrality may be determined by counting the number of links connected to each node in the network, with the most linked organization falling in the central position. An organization's centrality may also be considered by looking at direct and indirect links. Here centrality may be increased by being linked to highly central others.

Understanding the relevance of an organization's position in the central or more peripheral areas of a network is vital given that linkages to powerful others, those organizations with access to valued resources resulting from their central position in a network, may provide access to communication and bargaining networks that have the potential to heighten an organization's power (Brass and Burkhardt, 1992). Contrary to central positions in a network are those on its periphery. *Peripheral positions* in a network are those that rest on the boundaries of the network and are typically not tightly linked to organizations in positions of power. While peripherally situated organizations may lack power, their location has been associated with heightened levels of experimentation and innovation (Porac, Thomas, and Baden-Fuller, 1989).

This discussion of centrality has focused attention on the impact of an organization's position, yet in event management the understanding of peripheral and central positions is vitally important on a daily basis. Event managers need to remain aware of the dynamic nature of networks given their propensity to shift as new resources, ideas, or governance structures impact one or more organizations linked to a network (Scott, Ruef, and Mendel, 2000). By way of example, the structure of relationships among collections of organizations that host an annual event may shift as new sponsors become linked to the event, or as the local government changes the policies for public safety at events. Continuing with this example, existing sponsors may be displaced from more central positions by the new sponsors, and emergency services may emerge as a primary partner. A crucial task for event managers is to recognize continual changes in the position of organizations in a network and to facilitate communication among those linked to the event (Figure 3.9).

Event managers need to be cognizant not only of the number of links to groups or organizations that are needed to ensure access to resources, but also of the different *types of linkages*, or relationships, that are needed to provide efficiency and effectiveness in the network. For example, a relatively small event may necessitate

In January 2005, the Federation Internationale de Natation (FINA) cancelled its contract with the Organizing Committee (OC) of the Montreal Aquatics World Championship. While the event was reinstated to the Montreal OC less than a month later, the factors contributing to FINA's concerns about the capacity of the OC to stage the event provide insight into the importance of identifying the key constituents or stakeholders of an event and managing relationships with them.

According to Parent and Seguin (2007), event organizers need stakeholders to provide events with valued resources, such as facilities, financial capital, equipment, human resources, or technical expertise. Partners also play a vital role gathering or disseminating information and dealing with political agendas or special interest groups. In the case of the Montreal World Championships, the stakeholders included FINA and the Aquatic Federation of Canada (AFC), athlete delegations and their support staff, three levels of government, the community (residents, businesses, schools, groups) and the media (Parent and Seguin). However, the failure of the original OC to manage the network of partners linked to the Championship resulted in the unprecedented move by FINA to cancel its contract with the event OC.

The stakeholders that unite for the purpose of hosting an event represent the network of linkages that provide the necessary resources. Central to enabling these partners to operate in a collaborative way are clear understandings of who they are, their interests in the event, their values, as well as their goals.Ensuring congruence in each of these elements is what Parent and Seguin (2007) refer to as *due diligence*. In the case outlined above, Parent and Seguin suggest that due diligence was not taken to adequately define the stakeholders that constituted the network and to agree upon the resource contributions and expectations of the stakeholders early on in the event development phase. It is suggested that the haste with which the event OC was compelled to attract potential stakeholders limited their capacity to ensure due diligence. As an example, the OC failed to adequately identify the partners and their roles, to establish the motives of organizations linked to the event, or to assess whether the partners complemented and fit with the event and other collaborators (Parent and Seguin, 2007).

Event managers that facilitate the network of organizational partners that provide the resources need to have an accurate understanding of the nature of resource contributions of each partnering organization. Resources may be facilities, finances, and in-kind contributions such as equipment, human expertise, or volunteer capacity. In this case, the facilitators failed to accurately gauge the financial contributions of the various partners in the network (Parent and Seguin, 2007). More specifically, confusion surrounding $1 million in rights fees and a limited understanding of the sponsorship commitments from partners were problematic. Misunderstandings surrounded whether or not the bid committee or the Aquatic Federation of Canada (AFC) or Montreal Sport International (MIS), the initiators of the bid process, held the "rights" to the event.

In this case, frequent personnel changes at the highest level of the OC caused disruption as relationships of trust and loyalty among stakeholders were disrupted. According to Parent and Seguin (2007, p. 198), "consistency in personnel was noted as a huge problem ... as knowledge transfer became a critical issue, as was the importance of building strong and positive relationships with key stakeholders such as FINA and sponsors." The high turnover among senior members of the OC resulted in a significant loss of social capital for the event OC.

Figure 3.9 Example of an event network in crisis: the case of the 2005 Montreal Aquatics World Championships

Finally, limitations in the communication and information exchange processes of the event also contributed to erosion of trust among organizations linked to the championship (Parent and Seguin, 2007). Managing relationships between the organizations linked to an event is fundamental, regardless of the size of the event. In this case, a general lack of communication between the OC and the stakeholders resulted in a growing lack of trust and the subsequent lack of decision making and conflict which undermined the relationships.

This case highlights key areas where failed efforts to identify partners, to build trust, and to communicate undermined the capacity of the event managers to adequately facilitate its network of stakeholders. Following FINA's decision to withdraw the event, new management, better relationships with funding agencies and corporate sponsors, and a transparent system of communicating were created (Parent and Seguin, 2007). Following these developments, FINA reinstated the event in Montreal. Importantly, this case highlights the importance of understanding the nature of relationships among those organizations or stakeholders linked to an event and managing relationships with this network of partners.

The role of facilitators of event networks in the development phase of the planning model is essentially to coordinate and manage the linkages of the various stakeholders in the event network. This type of coordination necessitates building a framework for collaboration that is underpinned by trust among the various stakeholders. Trust may emerge as a result of the social context that allows for the fluid exchange of ideas, knowledge, and information (Lang, 2004). Over time, the individuals representing organizations that link to produce a sporting event develop trust, mutual understandings, and share knowledge. The growing interdependence among the organizations provides a social context in which work efforts transpire. Thus, the social ties, or the *social capital*, among linked stakeholders provides a means through which valued resources may be accessed.

Managing relationships among stakeholders using various means of communication is crucial. This case demonstrates how a culture of mistrust and conflict may evolve if trust is undermined and collaborative efforts are stymied through the lack of transparency and communication management.

Figure 3.9 (Continued)

links with local clubs, schools, media, equipment providers, and event enthusiasts who may purchase tickets to the event. The event manager needs to determine the best type of relationship, for example a one-off exchange, a partnership, or a strategic alliance, to meet the needs of the linked stakeholder organizations. Relationships with schools may be ongoing linkages that require substantial amounts of time and energy to manage, whereas equipment providers are simply contacted on an as-needed basis with little or no communication in between. Managing relationships with the stakeholders is a key task, and thus those constituents considered to be the most important must be prioritized accordingly.

A firm's relative degree of centrality or more peripheral position in a network provides one indicator of power. So too are the types of interaction among organizations in a network. The *strength of ties* between organizations, those typically characterized as either strong or weak, are suggestive of characteristics such as the duration of a relationship (Weick, 1976). The indicators of the linkage's strength involve the amount of resources shared between partners, the level of mutual awareness of the constraints of partners (DiMaggio and Powell, 1989), and the frequency, or interaction between or among partnered organizations (Contractor and Lorange, 1988). The types of linkages available to event managers include, for example, one-off exchanges, partnerships, strategic alliances, joint ventures, interlocking boards of directors, and vertical integration. These relationships rest on a continuum of relationship strength that extends from weak relationships, exchanges that have no commitment or expressed intent to continue the relationship, to stronger forms of relationships that have increased trust, commitment, and loyalty such as interlocking boards of directors.

On this continuum, *partnerships* constitute a relatively loose form of relationship that has some level of commitment implied, yet the longevity of the linkage is a function of its usefulness rather than of its strategic value to the linked organizations. *Strategic alliances*, by comparison, are stronger forms of linkages characterized by increased resource commitments, heightened levels of trust and loyalty, and substantial links to the strategic objectives of both organizations (Doz and Hamel, 1998). These types of relationships are typically more enduring and are associated with key objectives, such as growth, organizational learning, or new product development (Doz and Hamel, 1998*)*.

Interlocking boards of directors result when members of the board of directors of one organization assume positions on another firm's board of directors. These types of linkages facilitate information transfers across the highest decision-making levels of the organizations. They provide an enduring link, as they may continue for years and they offer stability to both organizations through continuous involvement.

Vertical integration occurs when one organization purchases another or two organizations choose to merge to achieve strategic competitive advantages (Stotlar, 2000). The strength of ties between organizations linked in a network is suggestive of the *density of an event network* or degree of system coupling (Krakhardt, 1992). The level of density or degree of loose or tight coupling in networks is suggestive of the number of linkages between members of the network, whether few are linked or, at the other extreme, all members of a network are linked to one another. Tight coupling has been associated with heightened levels of connectedness among network partners and with more frequent interactions (Lang, 2004). In a dense network, all members are linked to the other members, albeit with varying types of ties such as partnerships or exchange relationships. Loosely coupled or fragmented networks are characterized by few connections among members, with little opportunity for the exchange of communication, ideas, or resources.

Event managers should evaluate the need for loose or tight coupling based upon their event characteristics. If the network members need to share substantial amounts of resources, to share decision making, to engage in joint strategic planning and in other ways cooperate in a highly integrated way over a lengthy period of time, a more integrated set of relationships among partners may be needed. Conversely, if one organization is guiding the decision-making process and few resources are exchanged over a short time period, little integration may facilitate the exchange of resources both efficiently and effectively. Thus, the overall magnitude of the event, the time frame required, and the level of integration in relation to decision making and planning may influence the need for a dense or more fragmented network.

Social capital: the intangible resource of networks

Networks of interorganizational linkages are *embedded*, or encompassed, within the social relationships that exist between individuals in the network. This social context has the capacity to facilitate knowledge and idea sharing, to provide stability to the network of relationships, and to ease the management of interorganizational relationships (Lang, 2004). However, not all event networks achieve or sustain the level of integration, or tight coupling, needed to provide for heightened levels of social integration that will facilitate knowledge or resource transfer. While the failure of event managers to adequately specify the structures or rules that will govern relationships has been cited as a key reason for unstable social interactions between stakeholders (Lang, 2004), steps can be taken to provide for formal information exchanges and informal knowledge transfers in a stable social context.

The context in which social relationships may evolve may range, according to Granovetter (1985), from high social *embeddedness* to low embeddedness. High social embeddedness is characterized by social interactions which are repeated over long periods of time and those that have heightened levels of trust and cooperation (Lang, 2004). Low social embeddedness is characterized by "arms length" interactions. In the context of an event, organizers may facilitate the development of *social capital*, the ability to access resources through social ties, by organizing regular meetings, social events, or feedback sessions that allow for personal interaction among individuals linked to the event. These types of encounters allow for the exchange of opinions and information to others in the network. Furthermore, opportunities for individuals to learn about others' values and to receive cues about important facets of events are important outcomes of frequent social interaction (Salancik and Pfeffer, 1978).

The knowledge integration necessary for efficient and effective interaction among partners in an event is dependent upon social capital. The shared understanding among partners, their convergence of world views, their shared routines, and similarities in norms and values provide the underpinnings for the diffusion of tacit knowledge that is grounded in life experiences or day-to-day routines and cannot be reduced to verbal or written codes (Badaracco, 1991). Thus facilitating the emergence of personal ties among individuals, and subsequently their organizations, provides event organizers with a means to enhance the overall capacity of the network to inform practices, implement plans, and operate efficiently.

Trust has been highlighted as a key component within social capital. According to Lang (2004), "It is trust that enables social capital to be created between people" (p. 93). For that reason, groups characterized by high levels of trust are able to accomplish more, to acquire more resources, and to facilitate action towards the goals of the network. Social capital is, in and of itself, a resource that needs to be nurtured and leveraged by event facilitators. Establishing the framework for social relationships to evolve, and by nurturing trust and cooperation among individuals, event facilitators will have at hand a unique framework for information sharing and a control mechanism underpinned by the norms and values of those linked to the event network (Lang, 2004). These types of strategic resources cannot be underestimated given their capacity to enhance the overall planning and delivery phases of the event being facilitated (Figure 3.10).

Conclusion

Managers must facilitate the cooperation of governments, the media, community groups and volunteer organizations, and corporate sponsors, among others, to share the necessary resources for staging the event. As such, these events, and the organizations linked to them, may be viewed as a network of interorganizational linkages that cooperate to produce a desired end. Facilitators of these events need to remain aware of the various components, or concepts, associated with networks to adequately manage a coherent and collaborative effort by all organizations within the web. Whether it is creating the means for social capital to evolve or assessing the strength of relationship necessary to ensure the adequate supply of resources from a partner, event facilitators need to view the interwoven set of relationships that constitute their network as a resource to be established, managed, and leveraged efficiently and effectively.

Whether event managers are facilitating an existing network of organizations or creating a network of collaborators to contribute to and benefit from an event, facilitating relationships among linked organizations is a crucial component of their responsibilities. In Kearins and Pavlovich's (2002) study of the role of stakeholders in Sydney's "green" Olympic Games, several tactics were discussed concerning managing interactions among the environmental groups that constituted key stakeholders in a network surrounding the Games. In the context of large-scale events, such as the Sydney Olympic Games, facilitating interaction among corporate sponsors, varying levels of government, impassioned environmental lobby groups, domestic and international sport governing organizations and the media among others, was fundamental to coordinating activities and managing the flow of information and communication across linked organizations.

In the case of the Sydney Olympic Games, efforts to provide structure to the network of environmental groups were made by creating a committee structure that enabled different stakeholders to work collaboratively. Draft planning documents, those outlining policies and procedures, were created and distributed in a timely fashion to stakeholders in the network. The organizations that would be involved preparing for and hosting the games were identified and co-opted into the network from the start. Communication was facilitated through the use of websites, audits, reports, and sharing of best practices and educational events such as workshops (Kearins and Pavlovich, 2002). Ensuring legitimacy for the network and its efforts was facilitated by engaging the general public and providing mechanisms for their representation in decision making and by ensuring that experts in various fields associated with the games were involved in the network. A focus on transparency, respect for the values and beliefs of various organizations linked to the network and enabling coalitions of organizations to emerge in the network were also highlighted as key mechanisms that eased interaction among members of the network of organizations involved in the Sydney Olympic Games (Kearins and Pavlovich, 2002).

Figure 3.10 Managing network relationships: learning from the "Green" Sydney Olympic Games

Chapter questions

Drawing from your understanding of all of the imprints in this chapter, please answer the following questions:

1. Describe what one does when they "facilitate," and how is facilitation different from teaching personnel involved in an event?
2. An event structure can be examined from three points of view including, formalization, complexity, and centralization. Describe these three points of view.
3. Describe systems theory, contingency theory, and complexity theory and relate these theories to the development of event structures.
4. What does the principle *form follows function* imply?
5. Provide an overview of your understanding of the network perspective, and how this perspective applies to the event manager in the development phase of the planning model?

The event planning model: The event development phase, Part II

Julie Stevens, Maureen Connolly, Lorne J. Adams, Cheri Bradish, Brock University

Photograph by Shawn Whiteley

This chapter continues the discussion on the first phase in the planning model, the event development phase. In this chapter, the event manager is positioned as a facilitator for the development of volunteer practices, and policies, and then participation in corporate social responsibility. We begin with an imprint (section) on volunteer management practices.

Facilitating volunteer management practices

Julie Stevens, Brock University

Staging a major sport event, whether it is a traditional or niche event, requires a significant number of personnel. The ideal scenario would provide a host committee with an endless stream of financial resources to enable hiring all the staff needed for staging a successful event. Unfortunately, event managers must deal with real as opposed to ideal circumstances, which means a majority of the work of event planning and staging is performed by a volunteer labour pool. In order to enable an event manager to facilitate a volunteer program for an event, the purposes of this section include identifying the contribution of volunteers, differentiating between the types of event volunteers, explaining the components of a volunteer program, and identifying the role of an event manager in facilitating an effective volunteer management program.

The contribution of volunteers to major sport events

"Volunteers are crucial to the success of the Games and we are sure that the experience gained by them will leave a lasting legacy"
(Gary Jakeman, General Manager of Shetland Island Games 2005 Ltd.).

Volunteers play a crucial role in major events (Fairley, Kellett, and Green, 2007; Ralston, Lumsdon, and Downward, 2005). International multi sport and single sport events as well as tourism events involve thousands of volunteers. By far, the Olympics present the most extensive demand for volunteers. The Organizing Committee for the 2008 Beijing Olympic Summer Games involved 100,000 Games-time volunteers. This represents about 70,000 for the Olympic Games and another 30,000 for the Paralympic Games. The 2010 Vancouver Winter Games Organizing Committee predicts 25,000 Games-time volunteers will be involved. Other major international and domestic multi sport and single sport events also rely upon a large number of volunteers. The 2002 Commonwealth Games recruited 10,345 volunteers who contributed 1,260,000 total hours of work. The 2007 Rugby World Cup included 6,000 volunteers to stage the 20-team competition, the 2007 Volvo Youth Sailing ISAF World Championships utilized 175 volunteers to service 226 competitors, and 4,000 volunteers were involved in the 2007 Canada Winter Games, a multi sport event that included 22 sports and 3,600 athletes, coaches, and managers. Each of these examples demonstrates the important role volunteers play in sport events.

The impact of event volunteering extends beyond the event and positively influences both the individuals who volunteer in the event and the host community in which the event is staged. Research demonstrates benefits from event volunteering, such as enhanced event volunteer adherence (Fairley et al., 2007), sustainable community tourism through event volunteering (Ralston et al., 2005), the opportunity to generate greater social capital within the community (Downward and Ralston, 2007), and improved public sector performance (Karkatsoulis, Michalopoulos, and Moustakatou, 2005). For example, the success of the 2002 Commonwealth Games in Manchester led to the creation of Manchester Event Volunteers (MEV), an organization that provides volunteer support for a range of community, regional, and national events. During the few years that followed the 2002 Games, MEV built a database of over 3000 volunteers and supported more than 400 events in the local community.

Event volunteers

Major events typically involve four volunteer tiers which reflect two main types of volunteers who serve different roles within the event organization (see Figure 4.1). The upper planning tier includes executive and managerial volunteers. *Tier one executive volunteers* develop a mission and vision for the host, typically serve on the Board of Directors, and are involved from the time the bid to host the event is awarded. *Tier two managerial volunteers* serve on the executive committee and usually plan and manage the major components within the host society. For example, within a Canada Games host society structure the executive committee includes Vice-Presidents and Associate Vice-Presidents for each functional area, such as Vice-President of Athlete Services or Associate Vice-President for Venues. The volunteers that serve this managerial role usually join the organization between 5 and 2 years prior to the start of a major event, and therefore are actively involved in the development phase of the planning model and beyond. *Tier three staging volunteers* are involved in the operational functions and primarily

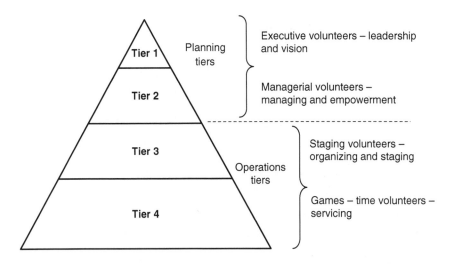

Figure 4.1 Volunteer tiers within a sport event organization

stage the event and fulfill short-term pre-event preparation or during-event servicing. These volunteers join the event organization up to one year prior to the event and are responsible for crucial short-term preparation. For example, multi sport events include many different sports, and each facility needs a venue team to organize the sport-specific competition. Members of a venue team are staging volunteers such as a Volunteer Representative, who manages the on-site volunteer lounge, and more importantly, contacts and schedules all the event-time volunteers needed to staff the venue. Finally, the bulk of the volunteer labour force is comprised of the *Tier four games-time volunteers*. Aside from attending briefing and orientation sessions, event-time volunteers start their duties when the event begins; hence their involvement is very brief. Some event organizations set a minimum commitment requirement for event-time volunteers. For example, the 2010 Vancouver Winter Games organization committee volunteer website states preference is given to candidates who are able to commit for the 27-day duration of the Games. Event-time volunteer roles can include services such as motor pool driver, parking attendant, and lounge hosts.

In order to ensure a successful event, host organizations need to properly service volunteers within each tier. In the case of large-scale events, this is achieved through a division specifically created to manage volunteers, whereas the volunteer program responsibilities may be designated to a small group comprised of planning volunteers and/or staff for moderate to small-scale events. The purpose of a volunteer division is to provide value-added service to the event. In other

The role of the Volunteer Services team was to:

Act as a *recruitment agency* for volunteer positions.

Find suitable candidates for the job roles including the process of *creating job descriptions*.

Set up interview areas within the *Volunteer Centre* and manage all administration surrounding the interview (including the database placement, paper work, and so forth).

Select Volunteer Leaders best placed to conduct volunteer interviews on behalf of the program.

Create database profile against job descriptions.

Develop a system for interviewing – questions, forms, exceptional issue resolution.

Provide training on interview process for all interviews.

Continually recruit volunteers with targeted skills for shortfalls.

Assist with reassigning any candidates unsuitable for their proposed role and *managing problematic issues*.

Manchester (2002) – emphasis added

Figure 4.2 Responsibilities of the volunteer services division for the 2002 Commonwealth Games

words, the volunteer division manages volunteers in order to enhance the event services to all stakeholders. Figure 4.2 outlines the responsibilities of Volunteer Services for the 2002 Commonwealth Games event organization. This example illustrates the extensive duties provided through a volunteer program and high-lights the comprehensive planning needed to properly manage the event's volun-tary labor force. Emphasis is added to show how volunteer services involve many fundamental personnel management practices such as recruitment, selection, resolutions, interviewing, and database administration.

Planning a volunteer program

Kemp (2002) refers to event volunteers as the "hidden workforce" and argues that event organizers must include human resources development as part of an event's plan. Volunteer management involves several human resource practices, but Rodsutti (2005) believes recruitment, orientation, assignment, and recogni-tion are the most critical. In combination, these practices comprise a volunteer life cycle that includes stages such as recruitment, registration, screening, orientation and training, assignment, accreditation and recognition (see Figure 4.3: Volunteer Life Cycle for Events). Planning and implementing effective strategies to manage the volunteer–event host relationship throughout each stage of the life cycle is crucial for success (Bussell and Forbes, 2007). However, it is important to consider

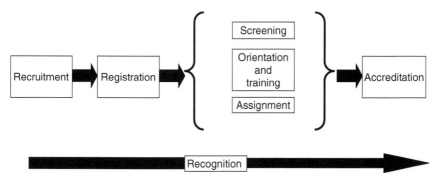

Figure 4.3 Volunteer life cycle for events

how personnel management practices, normally applied to employees, should be modified for a voluntary workforce that reflects disparate motives, commitment, aspiration, experiences, and skills (Wilson and Pimm, 1996). Further, Brudney and Nezhina suggest that the "greater number and variety of tasks performed, the greater the need for management practices to support, administer, and coordinate these human resources" (p. 306). This suggests that as an event volunteer corps expands so too should the complexity of the volunteer program. Hence, the event manager plays an important role in facilitating a volunteer program plan that services each stage of the volunteer life cycle.

The first and second stages of the volunteer life cycle involve recruitment and registration, respectively. Getz (1991) believes that the management of volunteers in short-term events must focus upon recruiting volunteers and building community support. Bussell and Forbes (2002) argue that the key to an organization's success in recruiting its volunteers is to understand its target group and suggest following the "4W's of Volunteering" – what (definition), where (context), who (characteristics), and why (motivation) as a means to develop this understanding. Shin and Kleiner (2003, p. 64) believe that planners responsible for the volunteer program must research several key areas about volunteers in order to develop an effective volunteer program. These include the following:

What are the responsibilities of the volunteer (job description)? What type of work is needed (short or long term)?

When will we need the volunteer (long-term commitment, one-time commitment, days, evenings)?

When and *how* will the organization benefit from using a volunteer?

Where is the volunteer needed?

Consequently, the event manager should use the "4W's of Volunteering" as a guide for the recruitment and registration program.

The timing of recruitment depends upon the scale of the event and the volume of volunteers needed for a successful staging. For major events, recruitment campaigns are developed and launched anywhere from 1 to 2 years prior to the event. For example, the application process for the 2010 Vancouver Winter Olympics began in 2008. In addition, recruitment may be staggered; that is, it may focus upon local residents first and then extend beyond the host city at a later stage. This strategy was used by the 2008 Beijing Summer Games host committee. Organizers started volunteer recruitment from the local area in August 2006 and opened registration to individuals outside the capital city in January 2007; enrollment closed in May 2008 for the August 2008 event. Smaller scale multi sport and single sport events may recruit within a shorter time frame.

Once a timeline for the recruitment campaign is formed, organizers must consider how registration will occur. Current strategies involve both electronic and hard copies submitted online, through the mail or in person. The 2002 Commonwealth Games received 24,000 volunteer applications (60% were submitted via the internet), which indicates that the volume of work involved in simply collecting and recording volunteer registrants can be very high. Registration is closely connected to assignment because event planners must understand what they need volunteers to do before they can be recruited. More specifically, application forms should collect information that is relevant for assignment such as availability, sport preferences, and skill sets. Although assignment occurs later in the life cycle, in the Operational Phase of the Planning Model, and will be discussed in the next chapter, it is intricately connected to the recruitment plan and volunteer application form.

The next stage of the volunteer life cycle includes three pooled tasks: screening, orientation/training, and assignment. The order in which these occur will vary among volunteers, but what is critical is that all stages are complete prior to a volunteer receiving accreditation for an event (Figure 4.3).

Screening volunteers involves conducting security checks on the criminal background of each volunteer. Given that police checks are costly and time intensive, event organizers must determine when a screening is necessary. Further, it must be decided who will assume the cost of the screening policy. Will volunteers pay for their own criminal checks or will the event organization pay the cost to conduct security checks after applications are submitted? Either way, the risk management policy of the host organization will provide direction to volunteer services regarding its screening procedures. In some cases, all volunteers may need to be screened, in which case volunteers are asked to submit a criminal records check with their application. Alternatively, a selection of volunteers may be screened, as was the case with the 2002 Commonwealth Games when event organizers conducted random security checks from its pool of volunteer applications. In other cases, organizers may decide that only high-risk jobs, such as those where a volunteer is in direct contact with a minor, need to be screened.

The training and orientation component of a volunteer program varies in scale from intensive, professional development experiences for executive and managerial volunteers to brief orientations for Games-time volunteers. The expanse of the program is related to the overall philosophy of the event; if organizers believe the mission of the event is to leave a lasting human capital legacy within the community, then training individuals for not only the current event, but future volunteer experiences may be an important underlying principle of the volunteer program. Training and orientation is also limited by the number of volunteers involved, as training 12,000 volunteers is much different from training 125 volunteers. For example, the 2007 Rugby World Cup organizers implemented a detailed training program for its 6,000 event volunteers. In total, 50,000 hours were spent preparing volunteers through one-day training sessions that addressed tasks and details specific to volunteer roles and event venues.

As mentioned previously, assignment is a critical stage in the life cycle because it directly influences a volunteer's satisfaction and as such impacts the overall success of the event. Gordon and Erkut (2004) stated that it is important to accommodate individual preferences when assigning and scheduling volunteers at events. More specifically, event organizers will enhance volunteer empowerment through tactics that ensure a fit between the volunteer and the task (Kim, Chelladurai, and Trail, 2007). Careful planning will ensure a volunteer's time, talents, and skills are utilized wisely and well (Murk and Stephan, 1991). Therefore, the event manager must consider first, what information is needed about each volunteer, and second, how to utilize the information in deciding where to assign a volunteer. A key planning component of assignment involves designing job descriptions. Planning and staging volunteers need to conduct a needs analysis for each unit in order to identify the necessary tasks and numbers. In this way, volunteers can apply to specific positions that meet their personal preferences, while at the same time the event organization can effectively meet all volunteer requirements.

Once recruited, trained, and assigned, a volunteer is finally ready for accreditation. At this point, volunteers should be well informed of their role, duties, and schedules. Plans for accrediting volunteers should be well developed to manage the number of volunteers involved. For example, it took the 2002 Commonwealth

Games organizers 42 days to distribute 12,000 uniforms to its volunteers. Recognizing all volunteers, regardless of type and length of commitment, is a major challenge for event managers. The volunteer life cycle diagram indicates recognition as an ongoing service that begins immediately when the volunteer is recruited and ends after the event is over. Recognition programming meets the "care and comfort" needs for the volunteers and must suit the volunteer. Volunteers need to be thanked in a manner that makes them feel truly appreciated. Event-time volunteers may simply like event clothing, refreshments, and a comfortable place to rest during a shift, while the long-term commitment of the event organization Board of Directors justifies a more formal recognition. Overall, ongoing recognition of the volunteer corps is needed to celebrate its contribution to the event.

The event manager plays an important role in cultivating a positive volunteer environment within the event organization. The volunteer program needs to be a priority and as such, be a separate component in any event structure. This volunteer component cannot exist in isolation. Consequently, event managers need to align the volunteer program with the overall event and educate everyone involved in the event about the purpose, practices, and policies of the volunteer program. As Murk and Stephan (1991) state: "Successful volunteer experiences hinge on the mutual satisfaction of meeting volunteer and organizational needs" (p. 73). By cultivating a two-way appreciation of the event and the role of volunteers within an event, the event manager will ensure that "volunteers are engaged and involved appropriately in achieving the mission and purpose of the organization" (Volunteer Canada, 2001, p. 49).

In addition to facilitating a volunteer management program in the development phase of the event planning model, event managers must concern themselves with policies that support all elements of an event. The concept of policy development is discussed next.

Facilitating event policy development

Maureen Connolly and Lorne J. Adams, Brock University

As an event manager, you will come face to face with both established policy and the need to develop new policy. Sometimes you will feel constrained or limited by policy and other times you will wish that you had a policy in place to help you deal with one of the contingencies that has arisen from an event you are managing. Such is the life of an event manager. You have to negotiate a world that is at once well defined and perhaps restrictive in some matters, but ill defined and fluid in others. As these issues arise, you will need to ask yourself whether existing policy helps with the present situation or does it need to be modified? You might also need to ask whether new policy needs to be developed or can the issue be dealt with without a formal policy?

Graff (1997) has done much work with volunteers and has identified that there are four general purposes or types of policies. She has put them in the context of volunteer programs but they are germane to your role as an event manager. She has described the four functions of policy as:

1. Policy as a statement of belief, position or value.
2. Policy as a method of risk management.
3. Policy as a rule.
4. Policy as an aid to program effectiveness.

The Brock University web site at: http://www.brockku.ca provides a document entitled: The Administration of Board Policies. This document extends the above concepts a little further and indicates that:

Policies follow a prescribed format for consistence and ease of reference.

Policies state the position on a particular subject that has institutional implications.

Policies mandate or restrict actions to ensure compliance with governing principles, laws and regulations.

Policies provide guidelines, alternatives and limits to decision makers.

Policies promote operational efficiency and/or minimize risk consistent with the objectives.

Similarly, the University of Alberta indicates on their website (http://www.common-ualberta.co/stellent/groups/public) that: "Policies need to be clear and concise statements of expected behaviours, practices and standards. As policy reflects the values of the institution it is important that new and existing policy be developed or revised using an effective and consistent approach."

It should now be clear that policy forms the foundation on which your event should unfold. While that may seem self-evident, as Graff (1997) has indicated, policy decisions are made on a regular basis; however, they might not be called policies nor may they be committed to paper. In her terms then, writing policy is formalizing decisions that may have already been made for an event. Doing so will provide clarity and indicate the importance of the matter. Further, the fact that a policy appears in written form may encourage people to be more compliant with the written rule rather than an unspoken expectation. Written policy also ensures that decisions are not made on an ad-hoc basis (Graff, 1997).

It is true that many policies are written in response to crises or problems (Graff, 1997). When there is deviation from the plan or something goes wrong you will see the gaps in existing policy. The need to develop new policy to deal with what is going on now and/or to prevent it from re-occurring in the future will be evident.

The process of policy development, then, is yet another responsibility that must be facilitated by an event manager. While it might seem to be a daunting task initially, you have already been exposed to the processes required to create effective policy. To this point in the text, you have been advised to understand the nature and intent of your particular event, as well as the audience, the participants, and the stakeholders involved. This will provide the context for writing policy. However, as we now point out, many times effective policy can only be written if it is in response to clearly written and realistic goals and objectives. When conceived in that context it is possible to achieve the goals that Graff (1997) has authored for policies, namely that responsibility is clarified and lines of communication and accountability can be established. In her terms, policy then can ensure continuity over time from manager to manager, and event to event.

A source that has summarized some of the policy literature is The Ontario Health Promotion Resource System. They concluded that policy development is not a linear process but does consist of four stages: *initiation, action, implementation*, along with *evaluation and reformulation*. This indicates policy development is an ongoing cycle of activity without a final end point. They also provide a series of key questions that are very helpful as you begin to develop policies:

> Have you identified and analyzed the issues your policy needs to address?
> Are your policy goals reasonable, and your policy objectives measurable?
> Does your policy specify who is responsible for what?
> Have you identified the barriers to implementation you are likely to encounter?
> Do you have a plan for dealing with barriers? (http://www.ohprs.ca/hpror/mod5).

Consistent with the theme of this text, what follows is a theoretical orientation by Dr. Maureen Connolly on the development of policy. This author has focused her theoretical lens on the development of policy using a variety of perspectives.

As you will see, these theoretical perspectives allow you to position the practical elements we have discussed above, in a much larger context that will guide your behaviour as an event manager. While Dr. Connolly makes her theoretical framework clear, it is by no means the only way to approach policy development. You should, as she encourages, explore and think through how you would establish your theoretical framework for a practical and tacit approach to policy development in event management. The theoretical orientation and practical scenario by Dr. Connolly is now presented.

First, I want you to realize that there is no such thing as unguided or unpremised action. That is, there is always a policy at work. It is up to you (and me) to be aware of the forces, values, and beliefs guiding our actions, or we can behave in the absence of that awareness, and be unconscious about what is guiding our actions. Either way, it is a decision. Second, I cannot have you walking away from this imprint without something different to think about; so, when I present you with the theory or model that I propose as a dignified approach to policy development, I will be adding a slight twist to it. Given the thematic of much of the work written in this text, contingency theory will be guiding my discussion of policy development. This involves adding consideration of bodily contingency to the human relations considerations typically associated with contingency models. Third, my pitch then, is this: there really is nothing more practical than a good theory if you want to do the right thing in the right moment, know what guides your action and be able to step back in the midst of the confusion and connect with that guiding principle. I will provide an example and will offer you an opportunity to think, learn, and reflect.

Human relations models of organizational behaviour seem to be the appropriate models to apply when examining events which are dependent on interpersonal relations. Human relations models recognize professionals and clients as complex persons who make choices about how to act and what to believe based on their perceptions of a number of interrelated personal goals and organizational/event characteristics. Given the endless array of variables that are free to vary or "contingent" on peoples' choices and subsequent actions, human relations models are frequently referred to as contingency models (or theories).

Contingency models indicate that individual satisfaction and performance and overall organizational effectiveness depend more on an appropriate "fit" among an array of situational, technological, environmental, social, relational, cultural, and personal variables than on the use of any single approach. Contingency models are also concerned with the processes by which people manage ambiguities, uncertainties, and complexities.

An important task in the development phase of a planning model involves facilitating the creation of policies for the particular structure, network, staff, and volunteers in an event. Event policy development involves the generation of statements or premises that direct personnel involved in an event. Policies direct (or guide) expected approaches, actions, accountability, and the consequences of actions. The combination of event policies provides the foundational framework for all actions and desired outcomes. The goal of policy development is to guide event personnel by providing direction in those key areas: approach, procedures, and actions/protocols.

According to Webster (1985), policy is prudence or wisdom in the management of affairs, sagacity. Sagacity means discernment or the ability to do the right thing in the moment. Planning with discernment requires that I ask myself the following questions:

What are the intentions?

What are the assumptions?

Who or what are the resources, how will they be distributed and under what authority?

What are the relationships necessary for things to work and what is the authority structure for advancing the relationships?

What has or has not worked and how do I know?

What or how shall I learn from this and what is the process for adapting for the learning?

These questions can also be used to initiate the development of policies. Answering questions such as those posed above can aid in revealing topics that can be used to develop policies for an event. For example, if the event program includes multiple committees, then the intention of the relationship between committee members might be that these committees are to work in tandem as an efficient group approach. Policies are needed to provide the foundational framework of how committee members are to interact to be efficient. Procedural policies are needed to guide actions during the interactions. Protocol policies are necessary to provide rules of behaviour during the interactions. The intertwining of policy between and among these factors increases accountability.

Complementary concepts in policy development

The complementary concepts which follow are paradigm citizen, hidden curriculum, cultural atanement, and the lived body. We shall consider each of these in turn. Wendell's (1996) "paradigm citizen" (p. 41) is an idealized, young, ceaselessly productive individual who can keep a technological and machine pace and whose body does not make visible the inability of event planners and policy developers to come to terms with contingency and diversity. Wendell also articulates what she refers to as "the myth of control," that is, "the refusal to come to terms with the full reality of bodily life, including those aspects of it that are rejected culturally, which leads people to embrace the myth of control, whose essence is the belief that it is possible, by means of human actions to have the bodies we want and to avoid illness, disability and death" (p. 9).

A key concept at work here is the reality of the body. Events and policies which do not take seriously the bodies of the organizers, resource people, support staff, and volunteers as well as the eventual participants or attendees are doomed to the vagaries of unacknowledged but usually foreseeable contingencies.

Bain's (1990) work on the hidden curriculum in physical education is highly applicable to event contexts, and resonates remarkably well with contingency models and bodily contingencies in particular. By "hidden curriculum" Bain refers to what is taught to students by the institutional regularities, by the routines and rituals of teacher/student lives. The dynamics of power or expectations are not explicitly or didactically promoted, but rather are lived as normal, familiar, and unquestioned. Three themes which emerge from Bain's work in hidden curriculum are meritocracy, technocentric ideology, and construction of social relations. Meritocracy is the use of a standard to regulate goal-directed behaviour through the myth that hard work will get what it deserves, or put another way, compliant behaviour will be rewarded accordingly. The emphasis is actually more on order and control rather than on achievements, and usually creates a two-tiered system of workers, one group who believe that they will be rewarded, but who seldom get the resources or training they require in order to achieve a higher level and the other group consisting of talented and/or clever individuals who get resources and continue to achieve regardless of how hard they work. Technocentric ideology constructs ends or goals as taken for granted and unexamined. Emphasis is then placed on the development of increasingly effective and efficient means of achieving these goals. In such an ideology, existing social arrangements tend to be reproduced rather than challenged and the body tends to become a commodity to be exchanged for admiration, security, or economic gain (Bain, 1990, p. 29). Construction of social relations is also a reproduction of power dynamics through unquestioned patterns of interaction, exemplifying a cavalier lack of awareness to diversity and contingency.

If as an event manager you want to enact an authentic meritocracy, build into the event and its policies accountability and consequences structures that can make it so. If the ends justify the means, then expect short cuts and various other forms of "hacking" in the name of efficiency rather than holistic and innovative problem solving. If reproducing inequitable power differentials goes unchecked, then expect apathy and lack of commitment in the realms of respect, courtesy, and public relations.

Lanigan's (1988, 1992) notion of cultural attunement is a strategy for meta-analysis, or understanding the big picture. He gives us three things to think about – normative logics of a culture (the implicit and explicit rules), the signs or indicators that those rules are important (how people behave to uphold or break or stretch the rules), and the larger overarching codes that keep all of this working. Taking this structure to an event and the policy development that guides it we would see protocol policies as the normative logics, procedural policies as the signs or indicators, and foundational framework policies as the larger systemic or code level.

Merleau-Ponty's (1962) concept of the lived body finishes off our complementary concepts section. The "lived body" is an actual body in the everyday world of time, space, and relationships of people, places, objects, and happenings. Here is an example which I hope allows you to distinguish between the lived body and the abstract or disconnected body. We are in a space together and I am too hot, you may be too cold. It does not matter what the measured temperature reading is; my lived experience is "too hot." Likewise, we might have different lived experiences for things, such as chair comfort, lighting, sound, odours, chemical sensitivities, and so forth. *It is the lived bodies who fill out the event evaluations and decide to hire you for their next* event, so taking lived bodily contingencies into account in your planning and policy development is more than a courtesy – it is an economic and reputational necessity. These concepts are discussed and expanded upon in great detail in Chapter 10: Facilitating Quality in Event Management.

Application: policy becomes praxis

As you read the following example, make a note of which policies need to be made more explicit, and where gaps may appear in written policy. The example makes clear the link to contingency theory. Once you have completed reading the example, based on your knowledge and thinking through the issues and how they affected the participants, you should be able to indicate the type and the context of policies that you would need as an event manager.

This example is an annual meeting and conference for a national organization based in active living for citizens with a disability. Approximately 120 participants,

65 youth with disabilities, an organizing team of 10–12, a conference services team of four, various support staff, and 65 student volunteers. There was also significant liaison with the surrounding city and region.

As far as sport, recreation or tourism events go, a 5-day, 350-person event is hardly extravagant; however, the contingencies were intriguing, to say the least. Chief among these were the heavy construction projects scattered across the area hosting the event, making entrances, exits, way finding, and overall access a challenge for nondisabled participants and a nightmare for participants with disabilities.

There were obvious explicit rules. Safety and dignity of all participants was a priority. People with disabilities were consulted on how needs were to be met. No effort was spared to make spaces accessible. Planning began 15 months in advance of the event. Unspoken rules were more subtle: everyone has good intentions; all stakeholders get equal credit; no one argues or fights … we have mature disagreements; reputational impact is significant; promised activities will unfold as they have been described; all volunteers and support personnel will show up and know what they have to do. Deeper subtexts were anxiety over injuries, ignorance of the disabilities, fear of saying the wrong thing or being inadvertently offensive, food allergies, getting lost on the way to activities, missing buses and planes, and no shows. The larger system at work for this event to be successful was an authentic meritocracy; that is, a code of conduct where people did indeed work hard for the good of the event, felt a sense of pride in that work ethic and were publicly appreciated for that work ethic.

Within the conference there were several prominent happenings including opening ceremonies, various receptions, excursions to the surrounding region's tourist sites, closing banquet, annual general meeting, the conference sessions, keynote and plenary speakers, activity and, social program for youth delegates. One youth delegate activity was sailing. The sailing activity had been organized months ahead of time with numbers of kids who needed special seats or partners being discussed, number of boats available along with the number of support personnel needed to be present on site. There was one-to-one volunteer support for the delegates, even though none of the volunteers had expertise in sailing. The city provided free bus transportation for the delegates, their volunteers, medical support, and coordinators for the free buses. Directions to the site were in hand. The weather was perfect. We had mistakenly assumed that the weather was our only uncontrollable contingency, and at the outset, it was cooperating. As one contingency after another presented itself we realized in hindsight, and in spite of our commitment to authentic meritocracy, that we had not taken seriously enough the lived experience of body, space, time, and relation. The saga unfolds.

The greater than typical numbers of persons using wheelchairs and ambulatory assists meant that boarding the buses took an hour longer than we had planned. Although we had phones, there was no phone contact at the site, so we could not inform them of the late arrival. This is an example of nondisabled people underestimating the time it takes for a person with disabilities to access a transportation vehicle. Further, the delegates on the buses were experiencing the hour of waiting in a hot space in close quarters with other bodies, so the lived experience of that hour probably felt much longer and the bodily experience of sweating on vinyl seats with 30 of your close friends was also a less than exhilarating start to the activity.

Finally, the buses departed and air-conditioning and motion dismissed the previous frustrations. Directions to the site were excellent; getting from the site entrance to the boats was more complicated as there was no signage, no familiar humans; there were no obvious signs of a sailing activity for youth with disabilities. Thanks to innovative and observant volunteers, we were able to make our way to the dock where three boats and three sailing support personnel awaited 65 children and youth as the weather developed into the hottest day on record.

Results included dehydration leading to adverse medication reactions in several delegates (unanticipated lived body responses); numerous nonevent people in the general area volunteered their boats, drinking water, and a variety of play objects (balls, frisbees, kites). This was an unanticipated but welcomed experience of lived relation. Once again, lived time reared its ugly head as waiting for turns felt endless; however, volunteers maximized the waterfront site, thereby utilizing lived space in an innovative and safety conscious fashion. The coordinators learned from the earlier lived time bus loading adventure and began a phased return to the campus once groups of delegates had completed their recreational sailing and tourism experience. As a planning team we had woefully underestimated lived time and lived bodies and had overestimated the lived relation preparedness of our sailing program team. Our volunteer and citizen lived space and relation contributions were pleasant surprises.

This one happening within a larger event is a dramatic example of how considering lived body allowed us to plan, adapt, and evaluate our behaviour. However, it did not allow us to turn back the clock and pretend that all was well and that our planning and policies had been adequate to the challenges of our highly (bodily) contingent population.

It must also be said here that even if our group had not been a group of children and youth with disabilities, several significant errors occurred long before the sailing day happened. I challenge you now to revisit these earlier posed questions in light of the event just described.

What were the intentions?

What were the assumptions?

Who or what were the resources?

What materials were needed?

What were the relationships that are necessary for it to work?

What did not work and how did I know?

What/how shall I learn from this?

What can be done better next time?

Now, add to your reconsideration of these questions one final reflective activity: Assume that your overall approach is a contingency-based model with a serious consideration of bodily contingency. Suggest one procedure and one protocol, along with required policies that might have made a difference for the sailing day. Embracing contingency will allow you to anticipate and respond in ways that make your policies coherent and your events memorable for all the best reasons, including actions that promote dignity and respect.

One challenge in event management is the facilitation of the generation of policy statements that direct personnel in their expected approaches, actions, accountability, and the consequences of actions. Overall the practice of generating policies is used to guide activities within the structure of an event, including the multiple staff and volunteers.

Another important area for consideration in the development phase of the planning model is corporate social responsibility. Participation in corporate social responsibility can enhance an event, and a discussion on this valuable area in event management is now provided.

Facilitating corporate social responsibility

Cheri Bradish, Brock University

"Being a responsible corporate citizen in today's sports marketplace means being a vigilant steward of the emotional and financial investment made by individuals, companies and community groups into your sports organization. It is recognizing, valuing and nurturing the partnership that is fundamental to that investment"

(Sport Executive, Maple Leaf Sports and Entertainment, 2005).

Corporate Social Responsibility (CSR) is a re-emergent and important strategic concept for modern managers and professionals. As such, it is important for event managers to understand the importance of "giving back" through their respective organizations and events. Whether through charitable links, employee wellness programs, or even international outreach, event managers need to appreciate the importance of community well-being and to firmly commit themselves and their organization to taking an active lead in positive community actions.

Broadly defined and interpreted, CSR is regarded as an all-encompassing commitment of an organization to sustained community well-being both in theory and in practice. More generally, CSR can also be interpreted as an organization's commitment to behave ethically. A sound commitment to CSR may be accomplished through a number of means, including discretionary business practices, empowering accountability, corporate resources, as well as community development and input (Kotler and Lee, 2005). CSR in principle can also be referred to as *corporate citizenship*: the obligation that an organization has to be ethical and accountable through positive action.

As greatly interpreted, CSR has come to be known and associated with a number of "giving back" concepts and practices, which provides for sport, recreation, tourism, and event managers a number of different possibilities for demonstrating a commitment to community well-being. As its core, a *true dedication to CSR must exist to make the commitment relevant and authentic.* Managers can adopt a number of related strategies under the greater CSR umbrella. Doing so will facilitate sound and ethical business practice which includes the principles of corporate reputation, cause-related marketing, strategic philanthropy, community relations, and even sport for development.

Corporate reputation is a complex mix of characteristics which identifies an organization's public "personality." Corporate reputation is a measure of the public and corporate perception of the organization, which is hinged to its practice of responsible business action and commitment to community well-being. It is important for sport, recreation, tourism, and event managers to understand and interpret corporate reputation. A company which has a highly regarded reputation will find considerable favour with stakeholders, employees, and consumers.

Cause-related marketing is, as the name suggests, primarily a marketing strategy which, when executed properly, can be positioned as a true commitment to community well-being. Cause-related marketing could be considered another important link to a company's CSR practice. By way of example, cause-related marketing is the support of a social cause by a firm through a developed affinity program for its consumers. A simple way to create a link then would be for "Recreation

Organization A" to donate one dollar to the National Cancer Society for every registrant at a local event. There are many such programs in existence today. These programs are most effective when practiced authentically and when demonstrating a true commitment to the cause by having company leaders and employees actually participate in the event in large-enough numbers to be recognizable.

Strategic philanthropy is understood simply as strategic giving, most commonly in the form of financial support. An organization adopts a cause (or causes) to support, which is in line with their mission and objectives, and supports that cause financially throughout the year. Again, like cause-related marketing, it is important that there is a true commitment (for example, money and time) to these causes and the partnership is authentic in wanting to improve the position of the cause.

Community relations as part of the greater marketing umbrella is also an effective outlet for CSR practice. Here, through community outreach programs, a sport, recreation or tourism organization can develop greater relationships with the community. The opportunity then exists to highlight the positive actions of both the company doing the supporting and the community services receiving the benefit. Community relations, media relations, and public relations can all work together to develop and execute sound CSR programs.

Sport for development is a concept whereby organizations understand and interpret sport and recreation as a vehicle for development, be it economic and/ or community, and even as is indicated in the International Olympic Code of Conduct, peace for all nations. Partnerships with Sport for Development organizations, such as "Right To Play" (Figure 4.4), add a global element and more international focus to an organization's overall CSR commitment.

As an event manager, understanding CSR gives you an advantage in terms of enhancing whatever event you may be organizing. Being aware of companies that have a well-developed CSR plan is another tool you can add to your tool box. Matching the right company to the event is your challenge, but once a match has been found, everyone, including you, stands to benefit.

On one level, if the company has been matched with the event, you may have access to resources, including human, technical, financial, and materials that you might not otherwise have. On another level, the prestige or visibility of your event may be enhanced by being able to link with a company that is highly respected. On yet another level, there may be a "trickle down" effect where some will say: If X event is involved then we should be involved as well.

The notion of giving back to the community creates a symbiotic relationship. The event gains support and recognition from the community, and the

The organization *Right To Play* uses specially designed sport and play programs to improve health, build life skills, and foster peace for children and communities affected by war, poverty, and disease. Working in both the humanitarian and development contexts, Right To Play has projects in more than 20 countries in Africa, Asia, and the Middle East.

Right To Play is a global-scale implementer of Sport for Development and Peace programs and takes an active role in driving research and policy development in this area and in supporting children's rights.

Right To Play focuses on four strategic program areas including: Basic Education and Child Development, Health Promotion and Disease Prevention, Conflict Resolution and Peace Education along with Community Development and Participation.

Working with partners, funders, and the local communities, Right To Play tailors every program to meet identified needs. Each program has specific goals, impacts, and outputs. To build each program they draw upon specially designed sport and play-based resources, as well as the expertise of program development, research, monitoring and evaluation, policy and country office teams.

The principles of the Convention on the Rights of the Child underpin Right To Play, and they ensure that their programs benefit the most marginalized children including girls, street children, former child combatants, refugees, and children affected by HIV and AIDS.

Right To Play's Team of Athlete Ambassadors is supported by an international team of top athletes from over 40 countries. These athletes inspire children, are role models for healthy lifestyle choices, and help raise awareness and funding for Right To Play projects. Led by four-time Olympic gold medalist and Right To Play President and CEO Johann Olav Koss, Athlete Ambassadors include Wayne Gretzky, Martina Hingis, Dikembe Mutombo, Haile Gebrselassie, Michael Essien, Frank Lampard, Anja Pärson, Chelsea Football Club, and many more.

The global reach of Right To Play is extensive as they work in Azerbaijan, Benin, Chad, China, Ethiopia, Ghana, Indonesia, Jordan, Lebanon, Liberia, Mali, Mozambique, Pakistan, Palestinian Territories, Rwanda, Sierra Leone, Sri Lanka, Sudan, Tanzania, Thailand, Uganda, United Arab Emirates, and Zambia.

For further information on Right To Play see http://www.righttoplay.com/site/PageServer?pagename=overview

Figure 4.4 "Right To Play"

community stands to gain both tangibly (such as economic infusion) and intangibly (such as reputation as a tourist destination). Events that have a well-defined CSR plan, and a commitment to the plan, can increase market share, strengthen their brand position, improve the corporate image, and enhance employee morale. It may also lead to increased attraction from stakeholders.

While it has been recommended that you be aware of companies that have a well-developed CSR plan, it also would behoove you to promote CSR to targeted partners or stakeholders. By doing so, you can enhance the reputation and success of the event and create a win-win situation for the event and community.

Chapters 3 and 4 have outlined the development phase of the planning model. We now move to Chapter 5 and the event operational planning phase of the model.

Chapter questions

Drawing from your understanding of all of the imprints in this chapter, please answer the following questions:

1. Discuss the impact of volunteers in the field of event management and the need to properly service the volunteers.
2. Describe practices within a volunteer life cycle.
3. Describe a minimum of three strategies outlined in this chapter that are used to reveal areas that require the generation of policy statements that direct personnel involved in an event.
4. What is Corporate Social Responsibility (CSR)?
5. How can CSR be instituted within events, and what value to you place on CSR?

The event planning model: The event operational planning phase

Cheryl Mallen, Brock University

Photograph by Shawn Whiteley

This chapter focuses on the second phase in the event planning model, the event operational planning phase. This phase involves the creation of written operational plans. These plans are created for each component established in the event structure. Examples of components include accommodation, accreditation, ceremonies, communications, drug testing or doping control, food and beverage services, hospitality services, media management, officials' management, participant management, volunteer management, results and awards, spectator services, and transportation. Also included in this phase is the assignment of the staff (volunteers or paid employees) responsible for creating the written operational plans that outline the action steps required to stage the event. Linkages between the staff members assigned to separate components of the event create an intraorganizational network. This chapter details four key mechanisms for network and operational planning success. These mechanisms include the cultivation of the operational planning network, the creation of logical, sequential, detailed and integrated plans, the inclusion of contingency plans, and the activation of a plan refining process. In addition, this chapter outlines key issues in operational planning and provides practice scenarios.

Mechanism 1: the cultivation of the operational planning network

The formation of the operational planning network requires an event manager to have the sensitivity to facilitate the assignment of the best possible number and combination of individuals with planning expertise to meet the event operational planning requirements. The task of creating operational plans for each component requires an intricate combination of talented planners. There is no single formula for assigning the network of individuals correctly, as each situation is unique. However, if individuals are assigned incorrectly, problems that influence the efficiency of plan development may arise.

A simple exercise will demonstrate the complexity of assigning individuals to tasks. Consider subdividing the members of your class to complete a number of components that could be in a traditional or niche event. How would you subdivide the class? What elements would you consider in subdividing the group? There are many ways to assign network members including: dividing individuals into groups that have similar expertise; creating groups that offer a wide variety of expertise which could broaden the knowledge base or groups that are devised based on whether they work well together. Individuals could be placed in groups based on their personal interest in the component. There is not one particular way to subdivide the group that can be applied to every situation. It is important for an event manager to develop an understanding and sensitivity to the elements of assigning individual members of the network based on the particular context in which they are being assigned.

Individuals assigned to each event operational planning component make up a node. A node may be further subdivided into constituent nodes. For example, those planning the accommodation component can be subdivided into constituent nodes whereby each is responsible for the accommodation plans of a separate part, such as those for the event participants, another for the officials, and a third for the organizing committee members. Linkages between constituent nodes foster the interactions required to complete the overall accommodation planning tasks.

The linkages between nodes (including linkages within a component and between components) create a network of multilateral intraorganizational alliances. These linkages determine how members interact to establish plans, manage planning decisions, and cope with issues or problems. Each linkage is part of the structural design creating a network alliance that can be unique in its application.

The design of the network alliance is crucial to the effectiveness of the development of successful operational plans. There are many influences that impact the design of a network alliance. To illustrate examples of some of the influences, the characteristics found within contingency theory and complexity theory can be applied to a network design. These two theories were initially introduced in the development phase in Chapter 3 and are also applicable in the operational planning phase of the planning model.

The characteristics of contingency theory indicate that there is no single correct way to structure the alliance linkages between the planning nodes. This is because, as contingency theory states, the search for one correct structure is simply not available in the world, as one system of organization cannot be found that "is superior to all others in all cases" (Owen, 2001, p. 399). The structure of each operational planning alliance must be efficiently designed for the specific needs of each event.

An application of this characteristic of contingency theory during the event operational phase implies that an operational network design that worked for a previous event may not work for any other event. So, what guides the design of each network in the operational planning phase?

Wijngaard and deVries (2006) indicate that it is the authority and responsibility assigned with the tasks that determine a configuration or structure. Therefore, it is the expected behaviours of the event operational network members and the event planners that guide the network design. This implies that an event manager needs to be sensitive to the event context in order to effectively configure the multilateral positions, the role of the members, the power, approvals, subdivisions, and overall autonomy required for event operational planning. Hierarchical structures in event operational planning may simply be too inflexible for a complex event environment. In addition, one multilateral design may not be best when applied to all of the components. Different intraorganizational network designs may be needed for the various event components.

Another theory, complexity theory, is also applicable in the event operational phase. Complexity theory indicates that a basic condition of our contemporary environment is that it is in a pivotal state (Doherty and Delener, 2001). This means that the environmental conditions include levels of "uncertainty, diversity and instability" (Stacey, 1996, p. 349). A stable state in the environment is not achievable because the "world is primarily made of dissipative structures" (Keirsey, 2003, p. 4). Dissipative structures involve a constant evolving of structures as they are being pulled apart and refitted by several forces, and this means one cannot be expected to be in a state of "equilibrium" (Keirsey, p. 4). Complexity in the environment includes evolving structures, which means we cannot expect to work in an environment void of change.

An application of the characteristics of complexity theory indicates an event manager must efficiently design the operational network alliance to be adaptable for conditions of change. An understanding that change is expected implies that once the network alliance is designed and instituted, the work of the designer is not finished. The network must be managed to cope with new or changing conditions.

A state of equilibrium cannot be expected within the event operational network. Change may involve the movement of network members within the nodes, the replacement of some members, or the reconfiguration of how the nodes interact. Multilateral intraorganizational network alliances are made over time, and adaptations must also be made continuously to ensure the design meets the flexibility demands for developing operational plans to stage an event. This requirement can be a constant and time-consuming task for an event manager.

Mechanism 2: the creation of written operational plans

The event operational network members are assigned the task of creating the written operational plans that constitute the documents that provide guidance for staging of each component within an event. This task compels the members of the operational network to produce the directions for the delivery of the event which cannot necessarily be developed automatically by technology (Wijngaard and deVries, 2006). These written plans establish the goals, control, and direction functions for staging the event. Generally, multiple operational plans are created in tandem. All members of an operational network within each node are required to have the expertise needed to meet the scope of responsibility for the planning function. This scope includes designing the written format for the operational plan and creating logical, sequential, detailed, and integrated plans.

The written event operational plan: establishing a design format

To begin the task of recording the step-by-step instructions for the operational plan, a format is needed to achieve consistency and control (Wijngaard and deVries, 2006). This format guides how all written operational plans are to be laid out. Multiple formats have been used for sport, recreation and tourism events. Again, there is no one correct format that shall be used. The general rule for selecting a format is to ensure that all requirements of the plan can be expressed. These requirements can include providing an executive summary, the objectives, the timing of each planned activity, a detailed list of planned tasks, the authority for each planned element, and event diagrams illustrating activity sites and the placement of key event items. Any format selected must take into account the complexity and fluidity of event operational planning along with the requirements of what must be recorded within a specific plan to ensure the elements are communicated in an easy-to-use manner.

An example of a design format that illustrates the timing, a detailed list of activities, and the authority is found in Appendix A: Example of an operational plan for the National Collegiate Athletic Association (NCAA) men's basketball championship, round 2, San Jose, California: The hospitality component.

Logical operational planning

To create logical written operational plans, all members of the operational planning network must learn to consider the individual activities or tasks necessary to complete their particular component. Goals are established and then members "think through" and record each task to be enacted; a coherent and logical step-by-step written list of reasoned event activities is developed.

Many events that have previously been held have information, either electronically or in hard copy, that provides lists or outlines of event activities. This reference information may provide guidance for developing logical operational plans for an event. However, the reference information is contextually specific and does not take into consideration the numerous nuances that exist in another specific event. The information is tied to the structure of the operational network, the components, and detailed actions that were designed for that event. Reference information is valuable only for gaining common knowledge about an event. The reference material does not replace an event manager's responsibility for thinking through each activity. There are no shortcuts to the thinking through process.

Event operational planning with a "thinking through" process is not a simple activity. The process necessitates concentration on every element within each component and delineating the logical steps to be recorded in the operational plan documentation. Operational planning includes the deliberate creation of suppositions, assumptions, and conclusions of the logical steps necessary to stage a successful event.

Sequential operational planning

Each operational plan must itemize the event tasks in an ordered and reasoned sequence. The most common method used to achieve this end involves using the concept of time. For example, an operational plan can be subdivided to record all of the tasks that must be completed three, six, or twelve months prior to an event, the activities during the week prior to the event and a minute-by-minute list of tasks for each day of the event. As a parallel activity, separate sequential plans can be created to outline the specific items needed from the venue (such as rod and drape, tables, chairs), including the time and site at which they are required.

To aid in the development of sequential operational plans, the concept of *weaving* is used. Weaving involves conceptually thinking through all of the requirements for one element of an event at a time. For example, a network member can conceive and record the tasks necessary to complete the media management operational plans by conceptually weaving the potential requirements of one media member from the moment of arrival at the event parking lot until they depart. This weaving process is followed repeatedly to develop the multiple logical and sequential steps that must be recorded in the operational plan. A planner can *weave forward* or *weave backward*.

Weaving forward involves recording elements as they will happen, in a progressive, unfolding process. In contrast, weaving backwards requires conceptually thinking of the end product and then backtracking to determine the step-by-step activities that were completed.

It does not matter if a planner conceptually thinks through the planning requirements by weaving forward or backwards. The aim is to develop a process that aids in determining the sequential steps to stage the event.

Detailed operational planning

The amount of detail required in an operational plan differs from event to event. The plans need to be written in a clear format to ensure other members in the network can read, understand, and be guided to complete the tasks as outlined. The plan must provide clarity, limit emerging questions, and reduce the potential for improper interpretations concerning the actions needed to produce the event. A detailed account of each task is necessary, with the difficulty being in determining the appropriate threshold for detail.

There are three threshold levels of detail in operational planning. Each level requires a different amount of detail in the written record concerning each event task. The three levels are referred to as level 1, level 2, and level 3 planning. The higher the threshold level, the greater the detail provided within the operational plan.

Level 1 planning provides the lowest level of planning detail. A level 1 plan exhibits a minimal level of detail to explain each task. Level 1 planning is open to questions concerning clarity of the event tasks and does not provide a detailed step-by-step list of directions to avoid misinterpretations should others enact the plan. Consequently, level 1 planning is open to interpretations that may alter the planned activities. For an example see the level 1 planning column in Figure 5.1 at the end of this chapter.

Level 2 planning requires a medium amount of planning detail. This level of planning provides general clarity and offers more detailed step-by-step directions to enact the plan. Level 2 planning answers the majority of questions one would have if implementing the plan. However, the plan is still open to some interpretations that may alter the planned activities. For an example see the combination of level 1 and level 2 planning columns in Figure 5.1.

Level 3 planning demands the highest level of detail. The level 3 plan provides clear instructions and includes the intimate requirements to complete the tasks. Level 3 planning is open to a limited number of questions and potential plan deviations, as minute details for the completion of each task have been provided. For an example see the combination of level 1, level 2, and the level 3 planning columns in Figure 5.1.

Plan objectives:

1. To develop an operational plan to manage the anthem singer for the event.

2. To ensure the operational plan includes the integration of the anthem singer's plans with other event components and includes contingency plans and undergoes a refinement process.

3. To ensure an effective communication system to disseminate the plans for managing the anthem singer to each individual responsible for elements in the plan.

Timeframe	Person(s) responsible	Level 1 planning (basic level of planning detail provided)	Level 2 planning (intermediate level of planning detail added to the basic level)	Level 3 planning (highest level of planning detail added to the basic and intermediate levels)
4 months prior to the event	Anthem coordinator	Confirmation of singer: – telephone confirmation with singer, indicate: – date – time of technical check – time of the performance – venue – performance requirements (such as a bilingual version and must attend a technical check 1.5 hours prior to the event) – fee to be paid – that they are to drive their own vehicle to the event and – one-night accommodation for evening before event to be provided	Follow-up confirmation in writing with singer (for example, e-mail), include all level 1 planning details in the letter plus: – directions to the venue – where to park (cost of parking) – which entrance to enter – number of tickets they have been allotted for the event	Confirmation letter also states: – if the event will pay the parking (if a parking pass will be forwarded or the process to be reimbursed for parking fees) – how to confirm the number of tickets they will use for the event and where to pick up the tickets – name of person to meet upon arrival and site to meet them – contact name and number should questions or issues arise

Figure 5.1 An example of an operational plan format and the three levels of detail for a volunteer anthem singer at a televised sport, recreation or tourism event

Timeframe	Person(s) responsible	Level 1 planning	Level 2 planning	Level 3 planning
3 months prior to the event	Anthem coordinator and accreditation coordinator	*Confirm singer's accreditation pass:* – anthem singer name is placed on the accreditation list	– Review of access the anthem singer requires in the venue and double check that the accreditation to be provided allows the access	– Accreditation is completed and the arrangements made so the accreditation pass is in the hands of the person assigned to meet the anthem singer at the venue entrance (accreditation provided upon singer's arrival, avoiding standing in line for the accreditation pass)
	Anthem coordinator and host hotel coordinator	*Confirm singer's accommodation, food and beverages:* – book 1 room for the anthem singer in the event host hotel – arrange to have bill paid by the event – determine what will be placed in the room (such as a fruit basket and bottles of water) and the person responsible – arrange for singer's breakfast and lunch to be at host hotel – call singer to confirm room and meals provided – provide name and contact information for host hotel should questions arise	Follow-up confirmation in writing with singer (for example e-mail), include all level 1 planning details in the letter plus: – directions to the host hotel – directions from the host hotel to the venue – inform singer to charge breakfast and lunch from host hotel dinning area on the room and the event will pay the charges	Confirmation letter also states: – if the event will pay the host hotel parking (and how to get reimbursed or if a parking pass will be forwarded) – indicate incidental charges are to be paid by the room occupant (for example, room service, in-room movie, laundry, and minibar)

Figure 5.1 (Continued)

Timeframe	Person(s) responsible	Level 1 planning	Level 2 planning	Level 3 planning
2 months prior to event	Anthem coordinator and event coordinator	*Confirm singer's introduction:* – create and provide introduction information to the event coordinator (for the PA script and television)	Call singer to confirm information prior to submitting introductory information	– Confirm pronunciation of name with anthem singer and provide phonetically spelled name for use in the PA script and for use by television
	Anthem coordinator and event coordinator	*Arrange for a technical check:* – call and arrange for a venue technician to be at the singer's technical check verbally confirm event date, time of technical check to be 2 hours prior to event, exact site within the venue (for example, at centre field)	Follow-up confirmation in writing with anthem singer and technician (for example, include all level 1 planning plus: – the type of microphone and sound equipment to be available – the number of microphones required – CD of anthem provided as back-up if singer cannot perform)	– Confirm how the technician and singer can communicate just prior to event should any issues arise – confirm how singer will be given the microphone and ensure they know how to turn it on – confirm where singer will stand after anthem until they depart at the end of opening ceremonies
	Anthem singer and event coordinator, anthem	*Contingency meeting:* – meeting held to discuss potential anthem issues and to predetermine how they will be managed	– Contingency meeting is open to all suggested potential deviations from the plan that could occur	– Contingency suggestions are recorded, and all result in a written predetermined response

Figure 5.1 (Continued)

Timeframe	Person(s) responsible	Level 1 planning	Level 2 planning	Level 3 planning
		Issue 1: anthem singer does not arrive or cannot sing for any reason Response to Issue 1: Anthem CD to be ready to be played immediately	– CD to be played during the technical check to ensure it is available	– communication available to allow dissemination of anthem issues – for example, audio technician at telephone landline ext. 2222 and anthem coordinator on their cellular phone
		Issue 2: anthem singer begins to sing and technical issues arise Response: CD of anthem to be in place and ready to be played	– arrange for CD of anthem to be played during the technical check to ensure it is available	– arrange for CD to be loaded and ready to be played for event
1 week prior to event	Anthem coordinator and event coordinator	*Refining production meeting:* – all anthem singer operational plan details reviewed – checklist of requirements created for use on event day	– Communication with host hotel to confirm accommodation and meal arrangements made	– Final telephone call made to anthem singer to confirm all details
Event day TIME	Anthem coordinator	– Anthem singer arrives on site and parks their vehicle	– Attendants in parking lot informed to expect anthem singer and where to direct them (which gate)	– Parking attendant calls anthem coordinator to let them know the singer has arrived and is heading to the correct gate

Figure 5.1 (Continued)

Timeframe	Person(s) responsible	Level 1 planning	Level 2 planning	Level 3 planning
13:00		– anthem singer enters venue gate	– singer met at gate and accreditation provided – singer escorted to the holding lounge	– singer shown change room & washroom area upon arrival – told where they can leave their valuables while they perform
13:15		– singer in holding lounge – coat rack, coffee/tea, etc., provided	– briefing provided on the role and timing of the anthem singer activities	– reconfirm the anthem introductory information, name pronunciation, titles, and so on.
13:30	Anthem coordinator	– technical check occurs – singer to walk to their spot to sing and test the microphone and sound system	– venue sound technician stays on hand throughout the entire technical check to manage any equipment issues – backup anthem CD tested	– singer informed where they will wait for their cue to sing, the cue to sing, who will give and retrieve the microphone, the direction they are to face for the television camera, the exit they are to use to leave the area after singing the anthem and route to watch the event (tickets provided)

Figure 5.1 (Continued)

Timeframe	Person(s) responsible	Level 1 planning	Level 2 planning	Level 3 planning
		– singer escorted to wait in the holding lounge	– reading material provided	
13:50 15:00 15:07 15:07:30 15:12:30 15:13		– singer escorted to staging area – introduction of singer – anthem singer sings – anthem singer departs from field – singer thanked – singer escorted back to change area to get their valuables & then seated to watch the event – they depart at end of event		

Figure 5.1 (Continued)

An event manager must facilitate an understanding of the sensitivities of the detail required for a particular event to the members of the operational planning network. Once the detail has been recorded, integrating the multiple plans for the various event components is necessary.

Integrated operational planning

The development of the operational plans for each event component creates a separate entity, but a key to successful event management is the integration of the details between plans. Integration, interlacing, or intertwining event elements creates multiple coherent, cohesive, and smoothly flowing plans for the overall event.

An example of integration for an accommodation plan is the interlacing of elements from the transportation plan within the accommodation plan. This integration can help to coordinate elements, such as the transportation drop-off and pick-up sites at the accommodation venue. The integration can also ensure transportation coincides with the accommodation check-in time arrangements. Integrating elements from the accreditation plan can also assist in the distribution of accreditation and room assignments all in one coordinated effort.

All separate event component operational plans require the integration of key elements from other plans. An integration or exchange process must be created and facilitated.

A successful integration process is reliant upon two key operational factors. The first involves the establishment of integration exchange opportunities for the operational network members. The integration process must be designed to provide an adequate number of exchange opportunities between the nodes. The nodes must have exchange opportunities that occur on a regular basis and must be adaptable to allow intermittent integration exchanges to meet the integration workflow requirements. An event manager facilitates this integration process and ensures that additional exchange opportunities are arranged if required.

The second key factor involves shared understandings of the need to exchange or to cooperate to share planning data. The large amount of planning detail and the need to determine how the data can interact make the activity of integration complex (Matusik, 2002). Time and facilitation are required to ensure operational network members understand the structures and strategies established to aid the integration process.

Successful integration is a function of sharing data between the operational network nodes. Network theory indicates operational network members can exchange planning data without the use of a hierarchy. Opportunities to integrate can include a process consisting of elements such as messages, bulletins, announcements, charts, drawings, diagrams, sketches, maps, reports, formal and informal meetings and briefings.

Overall, the strength of the logical, sequential, and detailed operational plan is in its integration. Each member of the operational network must work cooperatively to integrate key elements between plans. The success of an event may indeed be contingent upon the extent to which the event manager can facilitate the transfer of operational data across the planning nodes. The flow of the operational planning knowledge is contingent on the structure and strategies established to disseminate the transfer.

Another mechanism that aids the development of excellent event operational plans is the inclusion of contingency operational plans. Contingency operational plans or contingency plans are developed simultaneously with the event operational plans.

Mechanism 3: the inclusion of contingency plans

To enhance planning preparedness, contingency plans involve determining potential deviations from the operational plan that could occur and predetermining action steps to reduce the chance of the deviation or should it occur, to manage each deviation. The outcome of contingency planning is a backup plan.

Contingency planning can help to develop a greater level of preparation for any event. However, contingency planning cannot ensure that all deviations will be foreseen. There will always be unexpected deviations from the operational plans due to the complex nature of events. The more contingency situations predicted and planned for, the more time the operational planning members provide to the network members to manage deviations that were not predetermined.

Generally, to begin contingency planning, a contingency meeting is held. The objective of a contingency meeting is to host an open forum for operational network members to express their ideas concerning potential deviations from the plan that could occur. Each event component or sub-component hosts a contingency meeting to discuss the potential plan deviations for that specific component. Examples of contingency issues include concerns about equipment malfunction, should a hot water pipe unexpectedly burst or should a protest for a social issue be staged at the venue on the day of your event.

Facilitating a contingency meeting requires an event manager to keep members on the task of determining deviation ideas and to prepare a written record of these ideas (and not moving into how to manage each deviation). Contingency meetings allow members to be creative about what could potentially go wrong at an event. It is important to facilitate the meeting to allow the ideas to flow and hold the assessment of practicality concerning a potential deviation until the next step of contingency planning.

After a contingency meeting, the next step is to determine which of the deviations suggested will be managed prior to the event. The operational network members develop action steps for coping with each deviation should it occur. Contingency action steps are created in the weeks and months after the initial contingency planning meetings have been completed. Each contingency issue can be integrated within the operational plan or can be added as a supplementary or contingency operational plan.

Mechanism 4: the activation of a plan refining process

Once a logical, sequential, detailed, integrated operational plan is developed along with the contingency plans, it must be refined for use. One method to achieve that goal involves hosting a meeting with key representatives from each component and facilitating a production meeting for refining the plans. In this meeting, the representatives review the integrated plans and refine the details into a coordinated and efficient effort.

Another refining process is intended to add detail to the plan and eliminate any questions that may arise if the plan is implemented. An example of a refining process was illustrated by the 2002 Salt Lake Olympics Organizing Committee (SLOC). This Committee instituted a peer review process as a refining technique along with what they called an "Executive Roadmap" (Bowen, 2006). The peer review process included an exchange of operational plans for consideration by others within the event operational network. Reviewers searched for gaps in the detail provided in the operational plan, ensured clarity in the planning statements, and determined any arising questions when reading the operational plans. The roadmap consisted of an executive summary of the key timelines that needed to be met and was used for quick reference. Skilled event planners completed the refining process to meet the goal of planning excellence.

The operational plan refining process is the last step in the operational planning phase. An example of an operational plan that illustrates the different level of planning detail that can be recorded is found at the end of this chapter in Figure 5.1.

Contemporary issues in the event operational phase

There are three key issues in contemporary event operational planning. These issues include time, communication, and an environment of cooperation for coordinating operational plans.

Time is an issue for an event manger. Event management involves struggling to facilitate the completion of all operational plans within the time frame available. Time impacts the level of planning detail that can be completed, the contingency plans developed, and the refining process. An event manager must be continuously cognizant of the pace of planning and facilitate the completion of operational plans within a set time frame.

Communication is vitally important in event management. Facilitating excellent communication is the role of the event manager. This role involves ensuring that the operational network exchange opportunities are utilized and encouraging interactions between nodes in the operational network. Encouraging greater communication is vital to the outcome of the event.

Facilitating an environment of cooperation for coordinating operational plans can be the greatest challenge an event manager faces. According to Grant (2001), the foundational issues in operations include problems of cooperation and coordination. Cooperation problems stem from the variety of personalities involved in the operational network. Coordination problems stem from the skills, abilities, and knowledge of the operational network members that are required to integrate the plans.

In addition, coordination issues emerge due to the advancing virtual or dispersed work environment. This environment allows you to work from anywhere in the world with the use of communication technology. Coordinating activities from off site requires additional communication and demands clarity within the communications.

Additional issues in operational planning practice are provided in Appendix B: Facilitation Issues and Suggestions for the Implementation, Monitoring, and Management Phase of the Planning Model by Scott McRoberts.

Practice operational planning scenarios

Key knowledge on how to develop operational plans can be acquired by practicing planning. The practice can involve individual planning, a small team planning exercise, and a changing team format scenario. Individual planning may allow you to advance your personal ability to move from level 1 to level 3 planning; however, it does not provide key knowledge on working within an operational network, which is the norm in event management. Therefore, a small team and a changing team format are recommended when practicing event operational planning.

A small team format involves working in groups of two to four people. The team members brainstorm in a collective to construct knowledge on the creation of logical, sequential, detailed, and integrated operational plans from level 1 up to level 3 planning. Learning advances as multiple individuals discuss, think through, and determine the details to be recorded in the operational plan. Symes and McIntyre (2000) and LaDuke (2004) indicated that the key to creating knowledge was the ability to question. In event management, posing questions in a small group is used as a key mechanism to guide development of knowledge in the areas of the planning detail required, decisions on what is important and what is incidental or unimportant along with how to manage the recording process.

A changing team format involves multiple groups with 2–4 members in each group. Every group completes the same practice operational planning task; however, halfway through the planning process two members from each team switch to work with another team. In this format, team members must use their knowledge to determine how to get to know the new members, how to update the new members on the planning status, how to integrate their knowledge into the plan, and how to make progress when members change.

Working in a changing group format simulates the realities of an operational planning team in the industry environment. Previous discussions on complexity theory indicate that the environment is pivotal (Doherty and Delener, 2001). A stable state is not achievable due to "dissipative structures" (Keirsey, 2003, p. 4). A changing group format moves the group from a state of equilibrium to a changing or evolving environment. It is common in event management for operational planning to take months to years to complete, and the team does not remain in a state of equilibrium during this time period. Practicing in an environment that is affected by change forces may provide an advantage for the development of operational plans and ultimately working in the event industry.

Mallen and Adams (2006) provide evidence that practicing event operational planning in a changing group format encourages a consciousness of multiple planning strategies, management of differing opinions on the direction of the plan, to explain, interpret, intertwine ideas, establish the assignment direction, and create conclusions every time the group evolves.

To aid in developing your operational planning skills, three practice scenarios are provided. In the industry, you will receive a general overview of your operational planning task. No one can give you all of the directions on every detail that must be completed for the planning task. You will need to think through the planning elements and break them down to determine the specific planning details and requirements. These scenarios have been established to encourage you to think through the details required. If you cannot determine the answer, posing and recording the question illustrates your understanding of the requirements.

To complete the scenarios follow the following five-step process:

1. Design the planning framework (consider the example of an operational plan format above).
2. Develop two to three planning objectives.
3. Create level 3 planning detail in the logical and sequential operational plan (include a time line for all activities and assign responsibility for tasks). For example, assign volunteer A or B.
4. Include a separate contingency plan for a minimum of five potential contingency issues.
5. Record the process selected to refine the operational plan.

Remember ... small details make a difference in your operational plan. Once the first draft of the operational plan has been completed, review the plan as if you were a participant that had to follow the steps in the plan. Look for arising questions. Any unanswered question leaves the opportunity for interpretation of the plan, and that is how deviations can occur.

Three operational planning practice scenarios are now presented.

Practice scenario 1

Thin microchips could potentially be placed on multiple sites on the body of athletes, such as figure skaters, gymnasts, divers, or free style skiers to aid the judging function of many sports. The microchips could transmit a microwave signal to a wristwatch size computer and feed the information onto a screen for the judges to view. In theory, the information provided would indicate the body position of the athlete at all times during the competition, including the number of rotations, whether a rotation was a full 360 degrees, and the exact body position upon landing or entry into the water. This technology could eliminate the qualitative component of judging, as the computer program could provide feedback on the level of difficulty of the move and the completeness of the actions.

Create an operational plan for the outfitting of athletes with the microchips for an event of your choice (for example, gymnastics or figure skating). In the operational plan consider the management of the microchips once they are brought to the competition area and are ready to be outfitted onto the athletes, the ball, and the judges' screens provided to game officials; include the process of the required security to ensure a fan does get access to the microchips and wear them and show up on the system; and include the process to return the micro-chips after the competition and the storage of microchips for multiple date use. Prepare contingency plans for at least five potential problems with the micro-chip system (for example, a malfunction of a microchip, the theft of microchips and an attempt to break into the computer program and override the athletes' microchip record).

Take time to think through each step required in the operational plan and how you will organize the work. In your mind, think through the requirements as if you are an athlete or judge utilizing the microchip system. What are the needs of the athletes? What are the needs of the judges or officials? What questions would you have concerning setting up and using the system? Complete a logical, sequential, and detailed plan to illustrate your skills in event operational planning.

Practice scenario 2

You are responsible for managing a major tourism event media conference (event of your choice). The media conference is to be held midmorning, one day prior to the launch of the event and is at a major hotel in the downtown area of your city. You want to have print, radio, television, and web-based media personnel in attendance.

Create an operational plan for managing key elements of the media confer-ence, including the invitations for four key media outlets to attend, one of each from the newspaper, radio, television, and a web-based media outlet. The opera-tional details must include the details for setting up the media conference in the hotel including the process to manage the media as they arrive, have their cre-dentials checked, receive accreditation, and participate at the media conference. Remember the operational plan must include all communication requirements (for example, communicating to the venue staff the requirements for tables, chairs, microphones, platforms, rod and drape, the hanging of signage, and security).

Build into the plan the speakers representing the event along with the media opportunities, such as personal interviews and photo opportunities. Assume you have the funding to support all of your activities.

Practice scenario 3

You are to invite and manage the transportation and accommodation requirements for three key sponsors attending a major recreational event with over 500 participants. You can select the recreational event activity. Then, begin the plan with invitations to the sponsors (again, the sponsors can be selected by you). Assume the sponsors are from out of town and develop transportation plans for one representative of each sponsor company to arrive at the event venue to participate in the opening ceremonies (one to arrive by car, another by train, and a third by airplane). Develop accommodation plans for a local hotel. Remember that the operational plan must include all communications with the VIPs concerning the developing plans and an information package to provide the VIPs with all of the finalized information concerning their transportation, accommodation, event participation at the opening ceremonies, and their viewing of the recreational event activities. Assume you have the funding to support all of your activities.

Conclusion

In the second phase of the planning model, the operational planning phase, network members complete intensive operational plans that include timed activities for each event component. The strength of an event operational plan is determined by the logical and sequential process, the amount of planning detail provided, the integration forged between the planned components, the extra preparedness based on the contingency plans, and the process of refining the plans prior to their use. Facilitating quality operational plans can be developed with practice. The concept of quality in event operational planning is discussed further in Chapter 10: Facilitating Quality in Event Management, after the event planning phases have been presented. Overall, the operational plans are created in preparation for the next phase in the planning model, the implementation, monitoring, and management phase.

Chapter questions

1. How are contingency theory and complexity theory applied to the operational planning phase of the planning model?

2. Describe the difference between level 1, level 2, and level 3 planning.
3. What do contingency plans provide, and why are they important in event management?
4. What is a plan refining process and how does it assist an event manager?
5. What are three key issues in the event operational planning phase, and how can an event manager overcome these issues?

The event planning model: The event implementation, monitoring, and management phase

Lorne J. Adams, Brock University

Photograph by Shawn Whiteley

This chapter emphasizes the role of the event manager in making the operational plan work when it counts the most – at the event itself. While many may be aware of the details within the operational plan, no one knows it as well as you. That is why you will be called upon to facilitate the work of the people who implement the plan, monitor the activities, as well as manage and provide guidance for the unforeseen problems that arise. How you manage all of this will determine not only the success of the event but also your success as a manager.

A lot will be asked of you as the event unfolds. Understanding yourself and your role is critical to the success of the event. You cannot be a dispassionate observer; you will be totally immersed in the event and all it entails. You will also bring your unique set of skills and abilities, predispositions, and biases with you. They are as much a part of the event as the people and systems that you are attempting to manage.

Implementation: executing the plan

Implementation involves the execution of the plan by moving the planned operational concepts and processes from the members who completed the planning to a myriad of event staff and volunteers who are tasked with executing the plan (Bowen, 2006). Facilitating the implementation of the operational plans does not take place in a passive world; it is purpose driven, goal oriented, and dynamic. The environment does not wait for us to act. We live in a unique change-based time (Mallen, 2006), and the forces of change demand that we react and manage the repercussions of that change. In this environment, implementation is not easy. The first step entails coordinating and getting all the people implementing the plan on the same page.

Disseminating implementation requirements and production meetings

A much broader group or team will be responsible for implementing the plan than that which created the plan. They need an opportunity to hear, understand, and assimilate the plan in their unique area of responsibility and in the larger context of the overall plan. Production meetings are held to provide this opportunity. There are several key elements required when hosting production meetings: the invitees, agenda, supplementary materials, ensuring understandings of goals, objectives, roles and responsibilities, and facility tours.

Who is involved in these meetings? In some cases when the event is small, it is possible to involve everyone in the production meeting. However, as the size and complexity of the event increase, it is less practical and possible to involve everyone. Your plan should have determined managers at each node. It is essential that these people are in attendance. They, in turn, will be responsible for holding implementation meetings with the staff and volunteers who make up the network members associated with their unique area of responsibility.

What does hosting an implementation meeting entail? To begin, a detailed agenda needs to be developed. This will help you prescribe an adequate amount of time for the meeting and an agenda. You want to maximize the use of people's time and keep them focused. A detailed agenda with some general guidelines allotting time for each item helps to maintain attendees' focus and will allow a flow to occur in the meeting.

Be considerate of people's time and send the agenda out with enough time for participants to review and analyze the material. This is a subjective guideline. If you send it too early, you risk having it set aside and forgotten; if you send it too late, people may be reviewing materials as the meeting unfolds. This will lead to needless discussion and can derail a meeting quite quickly. As a rule of thumb, a week to 10 days of advance notice is a reasonable time frame for many people.

Supplementary materials should also be provided with the agenda. This includes providing the written operational plans. Once again, as these are the people who are going to train others and keep them on track, a high level of detail is required here. Throughout the plan, each member's personal responsibilities should be highlighted in some way. This can be as simple as a bolded text or a coloured highlighter. This personalized plan takes time, but for each member it is a focusing agent. Also, the addition of an executive summary can minimize questions. In addition, providing an organizational flow chart will help delineate responsibilities and establish a context for each node involved in the plan. Finally, a diagram of the facility with detailed and accurate instructions will further the development of understandings of locations and placement of equipment. The pictorial representation will save a lot of verbal explanations that can be misinterpreted.

When members attend production meetings, never assume that everyone has read the material provided in advance. People don't intend to derail a meeting, nor do they deliberately attempt to hold up the process by shirking their responsibility to review the material. However, they may have busy, complex lives, and sometimes even the well-intentioned have to deal with issues not associated with your event, no matter how important it may seem to you. As the facilitator, it is your responsibility to provide a verbal review to ensure they understand the material for which they are responsible.

Production meetings provide opportunities to ensure that each member implementing the plan understands the goals and objectives of the event. They must also know their responsibilities, including required actions. Creating specific responsibilities limits the possibility of someone thinking that someone else was responsible for a particular task and thereby increases accountability.

It is also important that team members understand the interrelatedness of their role with other elements of the plan. They need to see how what they are doing contributes to the larger plan and that what they are doing is valued. When it becomes clear that what they are doing is not an end in itself but an important part of a much larger whole, commitment and motivation are enhanced.

In addition to the written materials and their discussion at the production meeting table, a tour of the facility or facilities to discuss elements at the site in the context of the operational plan is essential. During a tour, node managers may be able to assess specific needs or problems, such as access to electrical outlets, sound system, running water, internet access, and so on (Figure 6.1).

At the end of production meeting(s) and facility tour(s), component managers and the constituent node managers within each component should be aware of the specific goals of the event, their unique responsibilities, and how they fit into the overall plan. They should also be familiar with the venue(s) and be prepared to motivate and train those who will report to them. Their questions should have been answered and, if you have done a good job, they will be excited about getting started.

Monitoring the dynamic and fluid operational environment

During implementation, you as the facilitator need to focus on the details of the plan using a "zoom lens." Two key areas of focus are monitoring the issues of timing and progress. For example, you need to monitor whether enough time has been allotted for getting essential materials to the venue in a timely manner so that people are not sitting around waiting to do their work. Also, have you allocated enough time for the setup and testing of the equipment? If people need to be at two or more venues at specific times, is there enough time for travel? Monitoring involves questioning to determine if people are attending to the task that will lead to a successful implementation of the plan in the time scheduled.

Orienting new staff (paid and volunteers) requires event organizers to effectively and efficiently transfer the required knowledge to the new personnel. It is extremely important to recognize that overloading staff with knowledge that is irrelevant to the scope of their positions will create confusion and will ultimately utilize valuable time. Therefore, event organizers must determine the scope of each position, the timeframe the staff will be required, the information that is required to be transferred, and the most effective means of transferring that information based on each individual's *previous experience*.

The previous experience that an individual can bring to the event can be extremely beneficial if the individual is placed in a position where they can utilize their own tacit knowledge. When determining effective techniques for transferring knowledge the preferred method of choice is "job shadowing" or "train the trainer." For example, if you were to hand an individual a 30-page manual on how to create the credentialing or accreditation passes for all staff at an event, the manual might not make any sense to the individual based on their previous experience. Therefore, the event organizer should facilitate their knowledge development by working with the event member by walking through the entire process with the individual as many times as required for the individual to be comfortable to perform their duties. Once they have reached that stage you can provide the manual for them to refer to, as they will now understand all of the knowledge that has been captured in the manual. It is imperative that event organizers recognize the skills that the staff bring to each position and target the knowledge based on that experience. In the previous example it may take four or five hours for an individual to be comfortable performing their required duties; however, if you have an individual who has been involved in previous events working with accreditation, the manual may be a sufficient means of transferring knowledge, followed by a brief tour and orientation of the accreditation office.

The event manager has a key role in facilitating processes for the transfer of knowledge from the event operational planning phase to members involved in event implementation. The event manager then facilitates the completion of this process. The facilitation may require adaptations in the process for those with more or less skill to manage their tasks. It is the responsibility of the event manager to have the sensitivity to determine the adaptations required for the transfer of knowledge processes to effectively assist each network member with the process.

Figure 6.1 Effective methods for facilitating transfer of knowledge by Melody Rioux

Clearly, operational implementation performance cannot be fully controlled (and the concept of control may even be a misnomer) in a dynamic and fluid environment. However, as an event manager you will be looking for *scope control*. Scope control asks that people stay within the confines of the project and not add or introduce elements that are not part of the overall plan. However, while we attempt to control as much as we can and operate within the parameters of the plan, "basically the system is not 'closed'. That is, the system is open to all kinds of unexpected influencers" (Wijngaard and deVries, 2006, p. 395).

One main source of influence to the plan implementation is from the network members themselves. These members need some level of autonomy. Yet, "this autonomy adds also to the unpredictability and ambiguity of the system of control" (Wijngaard and deVries, 2006, p. 395). Also, maintaining control is a complex issue in events, but it is your job to ensure that quality is a part of your event. Refer to Chapter 10 Facilitating Quality in Event Management. Chapter 10 provides definitions of quality and suggests you create a personal quality statement to guide your work as a facilitator implementing, monitoring, and managing an event. Examples of quality statements for facilitating events are provided.

As a facilitator, it is important that you see and be seen by network members. You should employ an operating principle that involves "the five Ps of implementation." Use your *presence* and *profile* to support *positive* and *productive performance*. Presence is the concept of management by walking around. When you are present it is easier for dialogue to occur. Implementers can ask you questions and you in turn can question them. This will reduce ambiguity in the first instance and, in addition, provide the sense that what they are doing is important and a worthwhile contribution. Your presence also reinforces your perception of attention to detail. Ultimately you will have a working knowledge of all phases of the plan.

Your presence also raises the profile of the specific components. If it is deemed important enough for you to visit them, it raises the value of that unit to the people completing the task. Like it or not, as an event manager you have a profile and you can use that profile in positive, productive ways. When you have taken the time to visit, ask and respond to questions, a subtle process of accountability has been introduced. If you have addressed the concerns of the front line workers, listened to their suggestions, and provided your vision of the project or event, people will be more committed to doing the work and doing it well. They are people and you are seen as a person, not an object. If workers have the sense that we are all important to the eventual success of the project, they will be more committed to ensuring that success with their productive performance.

Managing operational plan implementation

As the event manger, it is your responsibility to facilitate the management of deviations from the operational plan that may happen for any reason. This will be a tough task. According to Wijngaard and deVries (2006), tacit knowledge is required to make judgments on the precision of performance. Tacit knowledge, you will recall, is related to advancement knowledge. As the text has pointed out, tacit knowledge has been acquired through personal experience. It is the know-how you have acquired over the years as a student, as a volunteer, as an emerging professional. It is that "job sense" that comes from having been there. Schön (1983), in his book *The Reflective Practitioner*, refers to professionals being able to work "in the indeterminant zones" that their training has not explicitly prepared them for. This requires an application of knowledge. Several tips can aid you to keep implementation on track:

- Determine deviations from the operational plans through a variety of mechanisms such as periodic progress reviews, anecdotal reports, and direct observation.
- Create a climate in which people are not afraid to report implementations in a timely way, including arising problems and issues.
- Do not wait for progress reports; be out on the front lines of implementation, observing and asking questions.
- Every implementation plan contains risks, some unforeseeable. Create a contingency plan for all foreseeable issues and be prepared with a strategy to assess and manage unforeseeable issues (adapted from "How to stay the course: sensing and responding to deviations from plan," 2006).

Once you have noted that there is a deviation from the plan, you will need to develop a strategy for bringing things back on track. A skilled and knowledgeable event manager is needed to handle issues, to create a decision-making process, and complete the adaptations to ensure that the planned activities conform to timelines and acceptable levels of completeness. The decisions on how to manage issues must be aligned with the overall objectives and priorities of the event. You will need to determine ahead of time the process to be used, who will be involved, a strategy to resolve conflict, and an implementation stage; you will also have to be mindful of time constraints and the need to act quickly.

Overcome foreseeable failure when managing deviations from the plan

You need to be conscious of the fact that managing deviations from the operational plan can invoke a predictable response that can be a negative for the event. You need to overcome this predictability to improve your decision-making abilities during event implementation. This predictability was revealed by Dörner (1996) as he outlined in great detail how well-intentioned, intelligent people can experience difficulty in complex, dynamic systems. He developed a game with a hypothetical population and simulated the real world environment and found participants responded in a consistent and patterned manner.

His research indicated that participants tended to *act without prior analysis of the situation*, that is they accepted things at face value without much consideration of prior events or history that were germane to sound decision making. The lack of an immediately obvious negative effect of an action deluded them into thinking that their decision had solved the problem. Participants *failed to anticipate side effects and the long-term consequences of a particular course of action*. In addition, participants *failed to take into account the lag time between action and consequences* and were forced to react quickly at a future point as a consequence of their prior decision. This "domino effect" was repeated in the simulations and in most cases compounded the problem or created new ones that needed to be handled with increasing urgency. In his terms, problems increased exponentially, not in a linear fashion, and created a catastrophic conclusion. In his words, participants demonstrated "an inadequate understanding of exponential development and an inability to see that a process that develops exponentially will, once it has begun, race to its conclusion with incredible speed" (p. 33). Dörner (1996) concluded: "People court failure in predictable ways" (p. 10).

When you consider that events are run under strict time constraints, Dörner's (1996) work is worth remembering. Certainly, no one intends to fail, nor would you actively court that outcome. However, if you do not understand yourself or the system (event) you are dealing with, the possibility exists that your desired outcome will not be achieved. In addition, when called upon to make decisions, it's worth noting that decision making is not a single activity, something that takes place at a particular time. Decision making is best described as a process, one that takes place over time and is "replete with personal nuance and institutional history" (Garvin and Roberto, 2001, p. 1).

It would behoove you to go back and look at the material on complexity theory, contingency theory, and systems theory presented earlier in this text. An understanding of the theories will help you make the decisions that will need to be made during the implementation of an event. In addition, consider how you will analyze situations (including taking into consideration the history, side effects, and consequences of actions).

Predetermine the decision-making team and process

When managing deviations from the plan, the decision-making team must be predetermined. Basically, you are answering the questions, who's in and why? There is no magic formula for this or guidelines for answering these questions. There will be key players that your advancement knowledge will make obvious. Certainly, anyone who will be directly impacted should be considered.

The process that the decision-making team works within must be predetermined. Who gets brought into the issue? How are they informed? How much time is needed to assemble or obtain a decision? How quickly must the decision be disseminated? Is there a need for a dispersed decision process (teleconference)? How will the decision-making process unfold (consensus, simple majority, majority, advisory to an ultimate decision maker)? How will conflicts in the decision-making process be handled?

As we have already indicated, any response to a plan deviation needs to relate to the vision and goals of the event. Mintzberg, Raisinhani and Théorêt (1976) described a process model as a situation whereby the goals are clear but the methods to attain them require decision making. These researchers indicate that decision making in a process model includes an environment whereby "the entire process is highly dynamic, with many factors changing the tempo and direction of the decision process" (p. 263). In a process model, the decision-making process has historically been divided into three areas: *identification, development,* and *selection* (Mintzberg et al., 1976). Identification provides the recognition of the situation and communication through the system that a decision is required. Development involves the search for options as solutions. Selection includes the evaluation of options and the finalization of the chosen decision for implementation.

Once a decision is rendered, a decision-making implementation process must be followed. This process determines how decisions will be implemented. Who will implement the decision? What processes will be put in place to ensure that the decision is being acted upon? What monitoring will be put in place to ensure that the decision is achieving its desired outcome? The process to implement decisions must be facilitated for efficient and effective application of decisions. To help to achieve this state, preprogrammed decisions are created.

Preprogrammed and not preprogrammed decisions

As you have spent many hours developing the plan for your event, you will have asked yourself the question, "What if?" on many occasions. In event management, a large portion of decision making in the operational network is prescribed and automatically implemented at a designated time. The prescribed decisions are stated in the contingency operational plans. When the situation(s) arises, the decisions are enacted. These decisions are considered to be preprogrammed.

In contrast, there will be situations when the decision making is not preprogrammed. During these situations, the communication system that was preestablished becomes vitally important to achieve operational network membership negotiation, coordination, decision making, cooperation, and for the integration of actions within the overall operational plan. According to Wijngaard and deVries (2006), when completing operating plans outside of the preprogrammed decisions, a pattern of decision making and work functionality is established that requires support from the system. Facilitating the communication system is a priority to manage not preprogrammed decisions.

Inherent implementation, monitoring, and management issues in operational network practice

In operations management, network members "contribute significantly to the performance of the system" (Wijngaard and deVries, 2006, p. 408). Network members are positioned within the planning and control framework to implement tasks and manage arising issues and problems. Although the planning and control elements eliminate as many potential situations as possible, they "can never be complete; there are too many tacit elements in the situation to control" (Wijngaard and deVries, p. 405). If planning and control frameworks can never provide full control, then the system is open to providing inadequate planning and control (Konijnendijk, 1994). This inadequacy includes ambiguity, which in turn provides opportunities for individual interpretations of planned tasks (Wijngaard and deVries, 2006). Without the possibility of full control, the planning and control frameworks can offer what Wijngaard and deVries call "perceived control" (p. 405) and a base line from which deviations can be determined. This implies that full control is not possible and the event environment will involve facilitating arising issues.

Issue: operational plan detail and implementation performance

If the operational plans are not detailed in nature or if circumstances arise that require deviations from the operational plans, then there is a necessity for a degree of operational freedom, and the need for decision-making increases. In order for members to be effective in their decision making, the operational network members implementing the plan need "a good understanding of the system to control, the specifics of the actual situation, as well as of the underlying rationale of the planning and control framework" (Wijngaard and deVries, 2006 p. 398). In addition, the operational network members adapting to the plan need a solid understanding of the event goals and expected outcomes.

If the operational plans are detailed in nature, the operational network need only initiate the steps as prescribed. A detailed plan limits the degree of decision making and operational change or freedom to make changes.

Issue: implementation knowledge and performance

One of the issues that may impact implementation performance is the knowledge level of the operational team members. You will need to ascertain if the implementation network members understand and have a working knowledge of the overall event requirements and objectives. Obviously you can't give a test to ensure that this has happened, but they should be given a number of opportunities and forums to facilitate this objective.

An initial way to help ascertain if the level of knowledge has been transferred to the implementation network members is simply to check the attendance records in the minutes of production meetings. Have the members attended the meetings regularly so they can learn the requirements and the objectives? If they have missed meetings, what steps have they taken to obtain the information provided? What steps have you taken to assist those who have missed access to the information?

Another issue that arises is the implementation team's knowledge concerning their role(s). As the event manager, this might be a good time to look in the mirror and ask yourself questions. The questions may include: How well did I facilitate the process to ensure every member understands their role? Did I make assumptions because of my own deep familiarity with what is required? Did I use language that is clear and understandable? Was a time frame allotted to every task and was it realistic? Was the integration process completed?

Issue: deviations from the plan

There are any numbers of reasons that an activity may not be completed as planned. Some of the issues that may contribute to that outcome are now highlighted. One of the most obvious problems is that an operational team member(s) adapts to the role or the event due to an individual's level of understanding, or lack thereof. Further, sometimes people take it upon themselves to alter the activity for reasons known only to them. Perhaps prior experience; it's the way it's "always" been done; it's not the way we used to do it; they can make it better, and so on.

One of the main contributors to activities not being completed as planned is the communication system and the communication skills of the members.

In addition, communication is a key factor in the capacity of the intraorganizational network members to function as a team. Communication assists in increasing the level of cooperation present to complete tasks. Your role is to facilitate the communication process to ensure general communication problems are overcome. These problems can advance if information is withheld, if information is available to only a select few, or if decisions that affect a particular role or task are not communicated.

Issue: implementation conflict

Conflict may not be inevitable, but any time you bring a group together to work towards a common goal the potential exists for conflict to occur. "Ironically, one of the important characteristics of a well structured team – diversity of thinking, backgrounds and skills – is itself a potential source of conflict" (Keeping on Track, HBR, 2006, p. 8). One of the purposes of bringing people together is to examine options, to engage in critical and collaborative thinking, and ultimately to embark on the best course of action. Obviously, this kind of focus can engender great debate; people can have widely divergent thinking. As meetings unfold, there may come a time when, in trying to decide between two alternative positions, people become entrenched in one camp or another. The longer this goes on, the greater the likelihood that conflict will result. Garvin and Roberto (2001) point out that conflict comes in two forms – *cognitive conflict* and *affective conflict*.

Cognitive conflict is the kind of healthy debate that is focused on the task at hand. It is substantive in nature, open to other alternatives, and ultimately designed to solve problems. The exchanges can be quite intense, but they are not personal; they are about the exchange of ideas with the ultimate goal of coming up with the best possible plan.

Affective conflict, on the other hand, is personal. It may arise from a clash of personalities, a visceral dislike for someone, or a defensive reaction to criticism. When you have interpersonal conflict, people are less likely to cooperate, to listen to new ideas, to move the project forward. They may become entrenched in a particular position, as noted above, and are less accepting if a decision is made that is at odds with their firmly held stance. To promote cognitive conflict and to reduce affective conflict, Garvin and Roberto (2001) provide a framework comprised of the "three Cs" of effective decision making, including *conflict, consideration*, and *closure*, and, as they point out, each of them needs to be handled carefully. The conflict portion has been outlined above but bears repeating. As an event manager you want to facilitate as much cognitive conflict as possible while at the same time minimizing affective conflict.

The second "C," consideration, is a fairly simple concept but one that in practice is often ignored. As we have pointed out, when there are two sides to an issue, one side will be chosen and the other set aside. Obviously, then, some people are going to have to support and implement a course of action that they did not, at one point in time, prefer. The concept of consideration is sometimes referred to as due diligence or procedural justice. At its heart, it refers to a sense of fairness. It is a far different thing to be heard, to express your views and ideas, than it is to be considered. Considered indicates that your ideas have been listened to carefully, been weighed in the context of what must be, and are clearly understood.

Consideration requires the facilitation of members who listen actively, ask questions, take notes, ask for explanation, are patient during explanations of positions, and keep personal positions to themselves. At all costs, avoid looking like you already have made up your mind.

Consideration also means that once you have decided, you communicate what the final choice is and why it is the best course of action. Making reference to the input you have received and how it impacted your choice will go a long way to providing acceptance.

Providing closure is also a balancing act. Debate cannot go on incessantly, nor should it be halted prematurely. In many cases, the event itself will dictate the time frame in which a decision is to be rendered, but even if that is the case, there is a need for closure. It is a skillful facilitator who knows when to "call the question." The skilled know when enough information has been gathered, when repetitiveness is apparent, and when to avoid the trap of paralysis by analysis.

Issue: implementation communication

Throughout this text you will find both explicit and implicit exhortations to communicate frequently and effectively. Effective communication is essential at every stage for an event manager. So much has been written about communication that it is beyond the scope of this text. However, we encourage you to constantly work on the development of your communication skills. Be an active listener and all that it entails, including eye contact, bridging, paraphrasing, body language, asking the right questions, being non-judgmental, not personalizing issues, and so on.

Finally, be generous with your praise. Publicly acknowledge the accomplishments and successes of those who are carrying out the plan.

Additional implementation, monitoring, and management issues

Additional material on issues in the implementation, monitoring, and management phase are provided in the appendix. See Appendix B: Operational Issues at the National Collegiate Athletic Association (NCAA) Round 2 Basketball Championship, San Jose, California, by Scott McRoberts.

Conclusion

Clearly, a lot is expected of an event manager facilitating the event implementation phase, and your skills will be tested. Event managers need to understand themselves and the complex systems that are part of any event. It is also quite clear that careful preplanning and well-articulated goals and processes are essential to a successful event.

You need to be aware that decisions you make will have both short-term and long-term effects on the eventual success of the event. Event managers have the ultimate responsibility of monitoring and managing the implementation effort. You will be called upon to use direct observation and tacit knowledge. As you will be responsible for getting things back on track, you will also be responsible for putting in place the processes to do so. Be cognizant of the two different types of conflict that were discussed (cognitive and affective) during your facilitation activities. Also, remember the importance of improving communication skills.

We now move to the next phase of the event planning model, the evaluation phase. This phase actually begins in the development phase and advances through each phase of the model; however, we will discuss this phase overall in the next chapter.

Chapter questions

1. Describe a production meeting (including why the meeting is held, who participates in the meeting, and what is accomplished at the meeting).
2. What are two key areas of focus when monitoring an event?
3. Describe the 5 Ps of implementation.
4. What can you do to overcome foreseeable failure when managing the implementation of events?
5. There are inherent issues when implementing an event; what are the issues and how do they influence an event?

The event planning model: The event evaluation and renewal phase, Part I

Scott Forrester, Brock University

This chapter focuses on the evaluation and renewal phase of the event planning model. The goal is to equip the event manager with the necessary knowledge in order to effectively negotiate this phase, properly evaluate the event, and make data-driven decisions regarding renewing the event. In so doing, this work is broken up into two chapters. This chapter discusses the background knowledge in evaluation and renewal for the event manager and the decisions required before evaluating. Next, Chapter 8 presents the development of event evaluation tools and using knowledge from event evaluations to inform the event renewal phase. It is important to note that preparation for the evaluation and renewal phase begins in the development phase of the planning model and continues through all of the phases.

Background knowledge for the event manager

Earlier, in Chapter 2, the author defined common knowledge as basic foundational knowledge. In order for event managers to be able to successfully facilitate the evaluation phase of event planning they need to develop a foundational level of understanding with respect to both the concept and application of evaluation. Managers need to understand what evaluation is, why evaluation is necessary, and how evaluation is different from research or assessment. One needs to know the key evaluation questions, general steps in evaluating the event and decisions required by the event manager in order to successfully facilitate the process of conducting event evaluations.

What is evaluation?

The definition of evaluation typically depends on the reason and the context in which it is applied. The term *evaluate* is a verb, implying action required on the part of the event manager, and is defined as "to determine or fix the value of" or "to determine the significance, worth, or condition of, usually by careful appraisal and study" (Merriam-Webster's Dictionary, http://www.m-w.com/, n.d.). Similarly, *evaluation*, a noun, is defined as an "act of ascertaining or fixing the value or worth of" or "an appraisal of the value of something." (Webster's On-line Dictionary, http://www.websters-online-dictionary.org, n.d.).

For the purposes of this text, a more specific definition of evaluation, suitable in the context of sport, recreation and tourism events, is: the systematic collection and analysis of data in order to make judgments regarding the value or worth of a particular aspect of an event. The particular aspect of the event may relate to the satisfaction of attendees, the worth of volunteers, the effectiveness of the advertising or promotion, or the economic impact of the event as measured by the number of tourism dollars generated by the event. Regardless of what is being evaluated, the goal is to systematically collect data which can then be used to make decisions during the renewal phase of the event planning model regarding the improvement of the event.

Henderson and Bialeschki (2002) indicate that there are three components that are necessary in order to conduct evaluations. The first necessary component is the *purpose*, the second is the *data*, and the third involves *decisions*. The purpose refers to why the evaluation is being undertaken in the first place or what specifically about the event is being evaluated.

Identifying the purpose of the evaluation involves establishing evaluation questions that determine the framework in which to evaluate the event. As Henderson and Bialeschki (2002) suggest, "it is essential to clearly identify what questions are to be addressed or what criteria to evaluate before data are collected for an evaluation or research project" (p. 18). The data refer to the information that will be systematically collected in order to address the purpose. Last, the decision-making component involves determining the "significance," "value" or "worth" of the event based on the analysis of the information (data) collected in relation to the purpose of the evaluation. These decisions come in the form of both conclusions, interpretations stemming from the data analysis, as well as recommendation-proposed courses of action regarding what needs to be done or could be done based on the conclusions. These findings often suggest how the data might be applied in practice and subsequently inform the renewal phase of event planning.

Why is evaluation necessary?

Evaluating the event is a necessary step in the event planning model so that data-based decisions can be made regarding the merit, worth, value, or significance of the event, which then allows the event manager to make informed decisions regarding the disposition of the event. The event manager can also use evaluations to justify the allocation of resources, scrutinize the competing interests, and analyze the finite budgets that most events operate under. Results from well thought out, carefully and systematically executed evaluations are essential to sound decision making. Event managers are increasingly being held accountable for numerous aspects relating to the production of an event such as human resource and volunteer management and security to name a couple. In general, regardless of what aspect of the event is being evaluated, the purpose of evaluating the event is to measure the effectiveness of the event in terms of meeting its stated goals and objectives and to measure the quality of the performance of the event such as whether or not the event was profitable. Henderson and Bialeschki (2002) in their summary of evaluation identified five key purposes:

1. *Determine accountability*: This involves establishing the extent to which the allocation of resources, revenue, and expenses, marketing, promotion and sponsorship efforts, activities and processes "effectively and efficiently accomplish the purposes for which an [event] was developed" (Henderson and Bialeschki, p. 25).

2. *Assess goals and objectives*: Events can be evaluated in terms of whether or not the goals and objectives were met for the event. This may also help determine the appropriateness of the stated goals and objectives and whether they need to be modified for future events.

3. *Ascertain outcomes and impact*: The extent to which festivals, conferences, conventions, or local, regional, national, or international sporting events have encouraged tourism can be measured by the economic impact of the event through examining the direct and indirect financial benefits through tourist expenditures on a local economy. Or the event manager may wish to determine the impact that a local festival has on the quality of life in a community.

4. *Identify keys to success and failure*: Evaluating the event may also serve the purpose of identifying what worked well and why, what didn't work well, why it didn't work well, and how that could be avoided or improved upon in the future.

5. *Improve and set a future course of action*: Evaluations can also help identify ways that particular aspects of an event can be improved as well as assist in the process of making decisions regarding the implementation, continuation, expansion, or termination of an event.

In addition to these five key purposes, evaluation can also identify and solve problems, find ways to improve management, determine the worth of the event or its programs, measure success or failure, identify costs and benefits, identify and measure impacts, satisfy sponsors and authorities, or help the event gain acceptance/credibility/support (Getz, 1997). Another summary, this one by Chelimsky (1997), outlines three key functions of evaluation. The first is the development or the provision of evaluative help to strengthen the event and to improve event performance. The second is accountability or the measurement of results or efficiency, which provides information to decision makers. The third key function is knowledge or the acquisition of a deeper understanding surrounding the factors and processes underpinning the event contributing either to its success or its failure. Regardless of the specific purpose, evaluation is a key component in the event planning model.

Differentiating between evaluation, research, and assessment

Before proceeding further, it is important that the event manager is able to distinguish between similar but different terms in order to be able to effectively facilitate the event evaluation process. The terms assessment, evaluation, and research are often mistakenly used interchangeably. While there are similarities between the three terms with respect to the systematic methods used to collect data, their purpose and outcomes are very different.

Assessment is oriented toward practice and can be defined as "any effort to gather, analyze, and interpret evidence that describes institutional, departmental, divisional, or program effectiveness" (Schuh and Upcraft, 1998, p. 3). Evaluation has been defined as the systematic collection and analysis of data in order to make judgments regarding the value or worth of a particular aspect of an event. While both assessment and evaluation may share similar systematic methods of collecting and/or analyzing data, assessments have a *descriptive* purpose, while Schuh and Upcraft observe that "evaluation is any effort to use this evidence to improve effectiveness" (p. 3). Evaluation moves beyond just a descriptive function and is used to make decisions regarding the value, worth, or improvement of some aspect of an event.

Meanwhile, research is generally defined as a systematic inquiry designed to establish facts and principles, generate and test hypotheses, test or generate theory, contribute to a body of knowledge, or develop a deeper understanding of a particular phenomenon, the results of which may, or may not, be generalizable. Erwin (1993) differentiates between research and evaluation in that "research may contribute new knowledge, but it may not suggest that programs need improvements or are functioning well" (p. 231), and similarly Schuh and Upcraft (1998) observe that "it [research] may or may not have anything to do with determining effectiveness or bringing about change" (p. 3).

An event manager must be able to distinguish between these terms so that their understanding of the purpose of evaluation and how the information generated from evaluations is used to make decisions about the worth of the event. Subsequently that information can be utilized in the renewal phase of the event planning model.

Key evaluation questions

In addition to ascertaining whether or not the event was successful in achieving its goals and objectives, there are a number of other questions that evaluations can answer. Evaluation questions typically fall into one of five recognizable types according to the issues that they address (Rossi, Freeman, and Lipsey, 1999):

1. *Questions about the need for the event* (needs assessment): Needs assessments are often used as a first step in determining the initial ability to host an event or when designing a new event or restructuring an established event.
2. *Questions about event conceptualization or design* (evaluating program/event theory): Evaluating the conceptualization or design of an event involves explicitly stating in written or graphic form the theory guiding the event and then measuring how appropriate it is. This is most essential when planning brand new events and when pilot testing events in their early stages.
3. *Questions about event operations, implementation, and service delivery* (evaluating event processes): Process evaluation provides information for monitoring a specific procedure or strategy as it is being implemented so that what works can be preserved and what doesn't can be eliminated.
4. *Questions about the outcomes and impact of the event* (impact evaluation): Impact evaluation examines both the intended and unintended impacts of the event.
5. *Questions about event cost and cost-effectiveness* (evaluating efficiency): Evaluating event efficiency involves examining the benefits of the event in relation to the costs incurred by the event. Cost-benefit analysis can be used to evaluate the relationship between event costs and outcomes/impacts (benefits) by assigning monetary values to both costs and outcomes/impacts. Cost-effectiveness analysis also uses event costs and outcomes but examines them in terms of the costs per unit of outcome achieved.

Facilitating the process of evaluating the event

In order to effectively facilitate and manage the event evaluation process, there are a number of questions that the event manager has to consider before undertaking such an endeavour. The following questions are adapted from McDavid and Hawthorn (2006) in order to better fit within the context of evaluating events.

What type of event is it, and where is the event in terms of the program life cycle?

Is it a traditional or niche event? If traditional, what type of sport (see overview on traditional events in Chapter 1); staged for what reasons (recreational, competitive, and/or tourism), and at what level (local, regional, provincial/ state, national, or international)? Or, what type of niche event is it (festival, banquet, conference, convention, stampede, or other type of show)? Also, if niche, what is the history of the event, how did it evolve, and is the event growing, remaining stable, or declining? Regardless of whether or not the event is traditional or niche, the event manager should consider where the event is in relation to its life cycle. That is, has the event lost its impact or freshness; does it appear to have gone flat or lost its appeal?

Who are the key stakeholders of the evaluation?

Stakeholders refer to all individuals, groups or organizations having a significant interest in how well an event operates. For example, those with decision-making authority over various aspects of the event, sponsors, administrators, personnel, participants, clients, visitors, political decision makers, members of governing bodies, community leaders, or intended beneficiaries all have a vested interest in the event. As most evaluations are typically user driven, the event manager should identify early in the process the stakeholders and consider their information needs when designing the evaluation project.

What are the questions or issues driving the evaluation? That is, what is the goal or purpose of the evaluation?

Before evaluating the event, McDavid and Hawthorn (2006) recommend that event managers should know: who wants the evaluation done and why, are there any hidden agendas or concealed reasons for wanting the event evaluated, and what are the main issues that the evaluation should address (need, event design, event operations and delivery, outcomes and impact, cost and efficiency). While different stakeholders will have varying views and agendas, it is important that the event manager be aware of these groups and views when designing the event evaluation in order to avoid contaminating the data.

What resources are available to evaluate the event?

Most resources are typically dedicated to the production of an event. There is typically a scarcity of resources available to evaluate the event. When planning the event evaluation, the event manager should consider what resources will be required in order to effectively evaluate the event. These resources could be related to money, time, personnel, necessary expertise required, organizational support, or any other resources that the event manager would need in order to effectively evaluate the event.

Have any evaluations been conducted in prior years?

Evaluation projects are different each time they are conducted. In order to reflect the uniqueness of the situation and the particularity of what is being evaluated, event managers can take advantage of evaluations of similar events in other settings or evaluations conducted in previous years. Rather than simply accept evaluations that have been previously conducted, the event manager should take into consideration the following questions: What issues did the evaluation address? What was evaluated, and how similar is it to what is currently being evaluated? Who conducted the evaluation? Who were the stakeholders? How credible is the evaluation? What measures were used, and what aspects are applicable to the current evaluation effort?

What kind of environment does the event operate in?

You will recall that complexity theory suggests that organizations adapt to their environment by creating event structures that are not overly complex and are also contingent upon the contextual factors of the environment. Questions relating to size of the event, competition with other events, available resources or the degree of formalization, complexity, or centralization in the event structure all need to be taken into consideration when preparing to evaluate.

Which research design strategies are suitable?

While the details of different quantitative or qualitative research designs are beyond the scope of this chapter, "an important consideration for practitioners is to know the strengths and weaknesses of different designs so that combinations of designs can be chosen that complement each other" (McDavid and Hawthorn, 2006, p. 30). As a result, differences between quantitative and qualitative research, different research designs, and different research approaches will be briefly touched upon in Chapter 8 or Part 11.

What sources of evidence (data) are available that are appropriate given the evaluation issues, the event structure, and the environment in which the event operates?

Given the research design of the evaluation project as well as the approach to evaluating the event, what data should be collected in order to address the evaluation questions? Event managers should consider whether there is any existing data that can be used to serve their evaluation purposes as well as whether quantitative or qualitative data will best meet the needs of the evaluation effort.

Which evaluation approach seems appropriate?

The event manager will likely not be able to answer this until they have a foundational understanding of the strengths and limitations of different evaluation approaches, which are discussed in Chapter 8 or Part 11.

Should the evaluation be conducted?

After reviewing the previous issues, the event manager must still decide whether or not to evaluate the event. While it is a step in the event planning model outlined in Chapter 3 of this textbook, "it is possible that after having looked at the mix of evaluation issues, resource constraints, organizational and political issues, research design, and measurement constraints, the [event] evaluator ... recommends that no evaluation be done at this time" (McDavid and Hawthorn, 2006, p. 32). There is no sense in wasting the significant amounts of money, time, and resources needed to evaluate the event if the results of the evaluation are not going to be used.

General steps in evaluating the event

So far, this chapter has defined evaluation, explained why evaluation is necessary, and elaborated on the purpose of evaluation. We have differentiated between evaluation, research, and assessment as well as identified several key questions that evaluation studies are designed to address. Further, an overview of a number of questions that the event manager has to consider before undertaking such an endeavour has been provided.

If the event manager decides to proceed with the evaluation, the following five steps are common to most evaluation projects.

First step: Determine what is being evaluated and specify the evaluation questions.

Second step: Identify sources of evidence; develop appropriate measures and data collection strategies.

Third step: Collect and analyze the data.

Fourth step: Prepare and disseminate the evaluation report.

Fifth step: Make decisions regarding the improvement of the event and modify as necessary.

In order to complete the fifth step or to make recommendations regarding the improvement of the event and to modify or renew the event as necessary, a number of decisions must be made. These decisions are outlined below.

Decisions required by the event manager before evaluating

In order for event managers to be able to successfully facilitate this phase of event planning, there are a number of elements that must be determined regarding evaluation. The evaluation should be conducted in the context of a theoretical framework and might include the following: informal versus formal evaluations, formative versus summative evaluation, what to evaluate, quantitative or qualitative, approaches to evaluation and dealing with political, ethical, and moral evaluation issues.

Role of theory in evaluating events

Earlier in this chapter, research was differentiated from evaluation. It was stated that research is conducted to develop or test theory, whereas evaluations are conducted in order to make decisions about the value or worth of something. While evaluations are not intended to develop or test theory, theory can be used to guide the evaluation project and determine what is being evaluated. When evaluating an event it is important to view the event from a systems theory perspective. Recall that systems theory suggests that event structures can be created and managed (as well as evaluated) by understanding the inputs, throughputs, and outputs required to deliver the event. While it may not be feasible to evaluate all the resources (inputs), activities (throughputs), and outcomes (outputs) of the event, it is important to view the event from a systems perspective.

Process theory involves using the overall event plan to describe the assumptions and expectations about how the event is supposed to operate. These assumptions and expectations should be examined before evaluating the event in order to determine whether or not the expectations for the event were met and if aspects of the event operated as they were supposed to.

Contingency theory can also help event managers realize that the choice of organizational structures and control systems depends on, or is contingent on, characteristics of the external environment in which the event operates (Jones, George, and Langton, 2005). That is why no two evaluation studies are identical. Even if the event has not changed dramatically from previous years, aspects of the external environment likely have. This in turn influences the operation of the event, which needs to be accounted for when evaluating the event from year to year. So, while evaluation projects are not designed to develop or test theory, systems theory, process theory, and contingency theory can help event managers develop a deeper understanding of the event and help focus on what aspects of the event to evaluate.

Informal versus formal evaluations

Event managers need to continually evaluate aspects of the event informally. This may be through watching others or the processes of the event or through talking and listening to clients, participants, staff, or volunteers. This informal evaluation may also occur by making comparisons based on past experience, common sense reasoning or through intuition. Regardless of how it is occurring, informal evaluations, while serving a purpose, do not result in systematic, reliable, and credible information that can be used as the basis for improving the event. Formal evaluations, on the other hand, are based on systematically gathered data through structured questions or surveys. This allows event managers to make informed, data-based decisions that are reliable and can be used as the basis for improving the event. While informal evaluations are likely a part of every event evaluation, and should be as the event manager needs to understand the pulse of the event, formal evaluations are also needed in order to make judgments regarding the value or worth of a particular aspect of an event.

Formative versus summative evaluations

One of the early pioneers of evaluation distinguished between formative and summative evaluations based on the *timing* of the evaluation (Scriven, 1972). Formative evaluations occur while the event is in progress and are used to evaluate what is happening while the event is being implemented. Summative evaluations occur at the conclusion of the event and typically examine the impact or effectiveness of the event. They are often used for accountability purposes in terms of whether or not the event achieved its goals and objectives. The benefit of formative evaluations is that they can occur at any stage, and feedback is provided while the event is still in progress so that changes can be made while the event is happening. Summative evaluations usually provide the evaluator with information relating to merit or worth and result in making decisions to improve the event. The next time it is run, summative evaluations can examine changes: immediately following an event (such as the economic impact of a regional sport tournament on a local community), six months to a year after the event (for example, increased tourism to cities after hosting the Olympics), or 5–10 years after the event (for instance, increased human rights in China after hosting the 2008 Beijing Olympic Games).

In addition to differences in timing, McDavid and Hawthorn (2006) distinguish between formative and summative evaluations based on their *intended uses*. In this regard, formative evaluations are intended to provide advice and feedback regarding the processes of the event, and the intent is to improve those processes and their effectiveness during the event, whereas summative evaluations focus on the "bottom line" regarding whether the event is achieving its intended goals and objectives. Both formative and summative evaluations are important. The event manager needs to make evaluative decisions during the developmental stages and implementation of the event. Once the event has concluded, decisions must be made in order to judge its merit or worth and to make disposition decisions regarding the renewal of the event.

What to evaluate?

Before deciding whether to conduct a formative or summative evaluation, the event manager needs to determine what exactly is being evaluated. Henderson and Bialeschki (2002) discuss *"five Ps of evaluation"* in relation to what aspects of an event could be evaluated. These include *personnel, policies, places, programs,* and *participant outcomes.* They further suggest that programs can be evaluated based on inputs, activities, or outputs of the event. The inputs are the resources used to implement the event. Activities are the organizational processes within the event, and outcomes include such items as the economic impact of an event.

McDavid and Hawthorn (2006) observe that evaluating program effectiveness is the most common reason for conducting evaluations. They also suggest several other aspects of events that can be evaluated, such as event efficiency (including a cost-benefit analysis of the event), cost-effectiveness of the event, or how well the event was implemented. Event managers should be aware that basically any aspect of an event can be evaluated including: the development and implementation of the event plan, outfitting of the venue, ticketing and accreditation, security, communications, information and signage, transportation, parking, and so on. Before making any decisions with respect to evaluation approaches or data collection strategies, the event manager must clearly determine what aspect of the event is being evaluated, why it is being evaluated, and the criteria to be used to evaluate it.

Quantitative evaluation versus qualitative evaluation

Numerous textbooks have been devoted to both quantitative and qualitative research methods. There has also been considerable discussion over the years as to the appropriateness of both. To recapture that discussion and describe in detail the canons of both approaches is beyond the focus of this chapter. Event managers should consult the myriad of books, both academic and/or professional, available on the subject. However a brief thumbnail sketch is provided for your review.

Although there are many differences between quantitative and qualitative research methods, both have a place within evaluation. Before making decisions with respect to research designs and evaluation approaches, the event manager should have a basic understanding of the differences and similarities between quantitative and qualitative frameworks. A quantitative framework is an "inquiry into a social or human problem, based on testing a theory composed of variables, measured with numbers, and analyzed with statistical procedures, in order to determine whether the predictive generalizations of the theory hold true" (Creswell, 1994, p. 3). Qualitative frameworks, on the other hand, are defined as "an inquiry process of understanding a social or human problem, based on building a complex, holistic picture, formed with words, reporting detailed views of informants, and conducted in a natural setting" (Creswell, pp. 2 and 3). Based on these definitions, the event manager should see that quantitative approaches to evaluation typically emphasize measurement procedures that generate data in the form of numbers, whereas qualitative data are generally expressed in the form of words and provide a means for developing a deeper understanding of a particular phenomenon within a specific context. Event managers need to decide which framework and type of data should be collected or whether a blend of both is required to produce the most complete analysis. In so doing, event managers should be "creative thinkers and problem solvers and remember there is more than one right answer" (Riddick and Russell, 1999, p. 90). Ultimately, the choice of the framework and type of data should depend on the purpose of the evaluation as well as what is being evaluated.

Approaches to event evaluation

Goal-based approach: Although two main types of evaluation, formative and summative, have previously been distinguished based on the timing and intended uses of the evaluation, numerous evaluation models have been developed over the years. Among the first was the goal-based model developed by Tyler (Isaac and Michael, 1981) in the 1930s. The purpose of this goal-based, goal-attainment (Henderson and Bialeschki, 2002) or evaluation by objectives (Worthen, Sanders, and Fitzpatrick, 1997) approach is to determine whether or not the event is achieving its goals and objectives. In this approach, goals and objectives are used as the criteria by which the event is evaluated. Goals are a broad statement about what is to be accomplished (Rossman and Schlatter, 2003), whereas objectives are specific statements that describe how the goal will be accomplished. Goal-based evaluation can be used with either outcome or organizational objectives. Outcome objectives examine the impacts or effects of the event on individual behaviours in one of four behavioural domains: cognitive (such as thinking, knowledge), affective (such as feeling, attitudes), psychomotor (such as movement, acting), or social (such as how people relate to each other). Organizational objectives refer to internal processes within the event and relate to both the operation of the event and the amount of effort to be expended in the delivery of the event. In order for this approach to be effective, the goals and objectives for the event have to be well written. As Rossman and Schlatter recommend, objectives should be: specific, clear, and concrete for understanding, measurable for objective assessment, pragmatic (attainable and realistic), and useful for making programming decisions. In addition to being one of the most common approaches used, the advantage to goal-based approaches for evaluating an event is the objectivity that this approach provides for establishing accountability. The drawback to using this approach is that the event needs to have well-written goals and objectives.

Goal-free approach: In response to the criticism of goal-based approaches to evaluation, namely that they do not take unintended outcomes into consideration, Scriven (1972) developed the goal-free approach. This approach seeks to discover and judge effects, outcomes, and impacts of the event without considering what they should be. When facilitating the use of this approach, the event manager should begin with no predetermined idea of what might be found. The overall purpose of this approach is to find out what is happening with the event. According to Henderson and Bialeschki (2002), in this approach the evaluator will "usually talk to people, identify program elements, overview the program, discover purposes and concerns, conceptualize issues and problems, identify qualitative and/or quantitative data that needs to be collected, select methods and techniques to use including the possibility of case studies, collect the data, match data and the issues of audiences, and prepare for the delivery of the report" (p. 72). The advantage to this approach is that it examines actual effects of the event, regardless of whether or not they were intended and allows for in-depth analysis, usually through the collection of qualitative data. The drawback to this approach is that it can be very time-consuming and some effects may be difficult to measure.

Responsive approach: In response to criticisms that evaluations were not being tailored to the needs of stakeholders, Stake (1975) developed the responsive model of evaluation. This approach stresses the importance of being "responsive to realities in the program and to the reactions, concerns, and issues of participants rather than being preordinate with evaluation plans, relying on preconceptions and formal plans and objectives of the program" (Worthen et al., 1997, p. 159). Stake suggested that an evaluation is responsive if it "orients more directly to program activities than to program intents; responds to audience requirements for information; and if the different value-perspectives present are referred to in reporting the success and failure of the program" (p. 14). The purpose, framework, and focus of a responsive evaluation "emerge from interactions with constituents, and those interactions and observations result in progressive focusing on issues" (Worthen et al., p. 160). When taking a responsive approach, the event manager must continuously interact with individuals from various stakeholder groups. The manager needs to determine what information is needed and must present it in a way that it results in understanding.

Empowerment evaluation: Fetterman, Kaftarian, and Wandersman (1996) developed the empowerment evaluation model. This model uses evaluation concepts, techniques, and findings to foster improvement and self-determination. The focus of empowerment evaluation is on programs. It is designed to help program participants evaluate themselves and their programs in order to improve practice and foster self-determination. The evaluator–stakeholder relationship is more participatory and collaborative than Stake's responsive evaluation. As a result evaluators taking this approach work toward building the capacity of the participating stakeholders to conduct evaluations of their own. This approach enables managers to use the results from evaluations for advocacy and change and to experience some sense of control over the event being evaluated. The process of empowerment evaluation: "is not only directed at producing informative and useful findings but also at enhancing the self-development and political influence of the participants" (Rossi et al., 1999, p. 58).

The Content, Input, Process, and Product (CIPP) Model, A Systems Approach to Evaluation: The CIPP model (Stufflebeam, 1971) is intended to provide a basis for making decisions within a systems analysis of planned change. The CIPP model defines evaluation as the process of delineating, obtaining and providing useful information for judging decision alternatives. This definition, in effect, incorporates three basic points. First, evaluation is a continuous, systematic process. Second, this process includes three pivotal steps: the first is stating questions requiring answers and specifying information to be obtained; the second is acquiring relevant data; and the third is providing the resulting information as it becomes available to potential decision makers. The manager can then consider and interpret information in relation to its impact upon decision alternatives that can modify or improve the event. Third, evaluation supports the process of decision making by allowing the selection of an alternative and by following up on the consequences of a decision.

The CIPP model of evaluation is concerned with four types of decisions: planning decisions, which influence selection of goals and objectives; structuring decisions, which ascertain optimal strategies and procedural designs for achieving the objectives that have been derived from planning decisions; implementing decisions, which afford the means for carrying out and improving upon the execution of already selected designs, methods, or strategies; and recycling decisions, which determine whether to continue, change, or terminate an activity or even the event itself. In addition, there are four respective kinds of evaluation: context, input, process, and product, hence the acronym CIPP.

Context evaluation yields information regarding the extent to which discrepancies exist between what is and what is desired relative to certain value expectations, areas of concern, difficulties, and opportunities in order that goals and objectives may be formulated. *Input* evaluation provides information about strong and weak points of alternative strategies and designs for the realization of specified objectives. *Process* evaluation provides information for monitoring a chosen procedure or strategy as it is being implemented so that its strong points can be preserved and its weak points eliminated. *Product* evaluation furnishes information to ascertain whether the strategies, procedures, or methods being implemented to attain these objectives should be terminated, modified, or continued in their present form.

Event managers can use the CIPP model of evaluation as a framework for ensuring a complete and comprehensive evaluation of any event or aspect of it. Utilizing the CIPP model as a guideline, event managers can evaluate not just the outcome of the event but the entire planning process, the event itself, and the intended and unintended outcomes of the event. The CIPP model is designed to evaluate: the selection of goals and objectives, optimal strategies or program designs for achieving these objectives, methods to improve the execution of already selected program designs, methods or strategies and whether or not to continue, modify, or terminate the event or aspects of it.

Professional judgment approach: Should the event manager feel that s/he does not have the necessary expertise required to facilitate the event evaluation, one option, and another approach, would be to hire an outside professional consultant. If a high degree of objectivity is required or if the evaluation requires expertise beyond that of the event manager, then s/he may want to consider hiring an external expert. This may be the case if the event manager is interested in undertaking some sort of economic evaluation of the event. Hiring a professional consultant requires less time for the event manager to evaluate the event and is generally easier for the organization. In addition, the event manager obtains the results from a neutral, external expert. This adds a degree of objectivity to the evaluation process which may be important where there are political issues surrounding the event. On the other hand, hiring an expert can be expensive and the external consultant should have a degree of familiarity with the event, which may reduce the pool of experts that the manager has to choose from.

The decision regarding which evaluation approach to use should be based on the purpose of the evaluation as well as what is being evaluated. If experts and standards exist, *professional judgment* might be best. If goals and measurable objectives exist for a program, evaluating by using those goals and objectives (*goal attainment*) as the foundation will be best. If one is interested in finding out what is happening without comparing to established goals, the *goal-free approach* may be superior. If the event manager is interested in evaluating one component of the event in relation to the inputs, throughputs, and outputs, then a systems approach such as the *CIPP model* will enable them to choose the elements to examine in relation to the broad purpose of the event. Regardless of the approach taken, event managers should also ensure that the evaluation is responsive to stakeholders. Evaluation reports are utilized for making decisions to improve the event, to continue, modify, or terminate the event or aspects of it and, in the process of doing so, help clients or participants evaluate themselves and their events.

Political, ethical, and moral decisions in event evaluation

There are many issues that arise during the course of conducting an evaluation, and event managers should be aware of political, legal, ethical, and/or moral issues that they could be confronted with when facilitating the event evaluation process. Given that multiple stakeholders are involved, all having differing views and/or agendas, evaluation, then, by its very nature is political. Henderson and Bialeschki (2002) make several suggestions that, if event managers adhere to them, should make the evaluation process less political. The first suggestion is to have a thorough understanding of the organization or event, including its history, development, evolution, who the key stakeholders are, who the decision makers are, and all facets of the operation of the event. Second, event managers should articulate a clear purpose to all stakeholders, and this purpose should drive the evaluation and be at the forefront during the evaluation process. Last, any conclusions or recommendations that event managers make as a result of the evaluation should be based on evidence: that is the data that were collected during the evaluation process. Subsequently, judgments regarding the value or worth of the event must be linked back to the purpose of the evaluation and be supported by data. In addition to these suggestions, Worthen et al. (1997) recommend knowing the answers to the following questions in order to have a thorough appreciation of any political issues surrounding the event:

Which individuals or groups have power, and who would have the most to gain/lose from the evaluation depending on the results? Have these parties endorsed the evaluation and agreed to cooperate?

How is the evaluator expected to relate to different stakeholders as an impartial outsider? Advocate? Consultant or subcontractor? Assistant?

From which stakeholders is cooperation essential? Have they agreed to cooperate and provide full access to the data?

Which stakeholders have a vested interest in the results of the evaluation?

Who will need to be informed during the evaluation about plans, procedures, progress, changes, and findings?

Ethical issues typically deal with what is right or wrong and how individuals responsible for facilitating the event evaluation should make thoughtful decisions based on principles. The Interagency Advisory Panel on Research Ethics (PRE) or the American Psychological Association (APA) have established ethical principles that event managers should use to guide event evaluations. Several of the more applicable principles involve a respect for: human dignity, free and informed consent, vulnerable persons, privacy and confidentiality, and being able to balance harms and benefits. *Respect for human dignity* aspires to protect the interests of individuals and forms the basis of the subsequent ethical obligations. *Respect for free and informed consent* requires that evaluators must acknowledge that individuals have the right to choose whether or not to participate in the evaluation and have the right to make free and informed decisions. *Respect for vulnerable persons* requires event managers to take extra precautions in order to protect the interests of individuals with a diminished competence and/or decision-making capacity, thus making them vulnerable. *Respect for privacy and confidentiality* means that the information collected during the evaluation process holds the expectation of privacy. Furthermore, information revealed by participants in the evaluation process should not have distinctive or recognizable features in order to maintain the anonymity of individuals. *Balancing harms and benefits* requires that event managers avoid, prevent, or minimize harm to individuals while maximizing the benefits of the evaluation. Overall, the foreseeable harms should not outweigh anticipated benefits of the evaluation project; otherwise it should not be undertaken.

In addition to political and ethical issues, event managers may also be confronted with a number of moral issues when facilitating the evaluation of an event. For example, Henderson and Bialeschki (2002) suggest a moral obligation to conduct the best evaluation one can. This is accomplished by being rigorous with their evaluation approach, sampling, and data collection strategies, and by reporting the results in a timely fashion so that they can be used to make improvements to the event. Further, being honest about what worked well and what didn't during the evaluation process is essential. Evaluators should not discount any results that may seem insignificant or fail to disclose negative results arising from the evaluation process.

Summary

This chapter focused on providing the event manager with the background knowledge to successfully facilitate the evaluation phase of event planning.

In doing so, evaluation was defined as the systematic collection and analysis of data in order to make judgments regarding the value or worth of a particular aspect of an event and distinctions were made between the terms evaluation, research and assessment. The chapter also explained why evaluation is necessary and identified several key evaluation questions. Five general steps when evaluating an event were detailed. Last, the chapter outlined a number of decisions required by the event manager in order to successfully facilitate the process of conducting event evaluations. This leads us to Chapter 8 and a presentation on the development of event evaluation tools and using knowledge from evaluations to inform the event renewal phase.

Chapter questions

1. Why is evaluation necessary in event management?
2. What questions does the event manager have to consider before evaluating an event?
3. What are the five key evaluation questions according to Rossi, Freeman, and Lipsey (1999)?
4. What are the five steps common to most evaluation projects?
5. List and describe six approaches to evaluating an event.

The event planning model: The event evaluation and renewal phase, Part II

Scott Forrester, Brock University

Common knowledge in event evaluation and renewal was discussed in Chapter 7 to provide the necessary background information required for a variety of decisions that an event manager will inevitably be faced with. Now it is time to move beyond this common knowledge to acquiring advanced knowledge regarding some specific evaluation tools in the context of event renewal. While it is beyond the scope of this chapter to cover all evaluation tools available to event managers, this section covers some of the more common tools including questionnaires, importance/performance (I/P) analysis, service-quality analysis, and evaluation of volunteer worth. There are also a number of methods available to evaluate the financial aspects of the event, including cost-effectiveness and cost efficiency, and measure its economic impact. However, this text will not be dealing with these strategies, as there are numerous textbooks that cover these methods in detail.

Developing questionnaires

Event managers can use questionnaires either as simple feedback forms targeting key stakeholders or event partners or as detailed visitor, participant, or spectator surveys (Allen, O'Toole, McDonnell, and Harris, 2002). The scope of the questionnaire will largely depend on the purpose of the evaluation, the level of detail needed in terms of the feedback required, as well as the criteria used to evaluate the event. Questionnaires can be used to obtain reliable quantitative (or qualitative) data regarding audience profiles and reactions and/or visitor patterns and expenditures (Allen et al., 2002). Regardless of what is being asked, event managers should generally use the following steps when developing a questionnaire to evaluate their event:

Step 1: Define the purpose of the evaluation.

Step 2: Determine the criteria to be used to evaluate the event.

Step 3: Develop the survey questions, structure and format.

Step 4: Determine sampling and administration strategies.

Information regarding steps 1 and 2 were presented in Chapter 6, so the remainder of the focus in this section will be on steps 3 and 4.

Developing the survey questions, structure and format

Henderson and Bialeschki (2002) noted that surveys can be used to ask a variety of questions regarding experience or behaviour, for example, what a person does or has done. What opinions, values, or attitudes, such as cognitive and interpretive processes, are held by the individual? We can ask how the person feels, and include questions on emotional responses from past or present events. Questions that elicit factual information from the respondent will provide knowledge information. Demographic information such as personal characteristics can also be obtained. Regardless of what is being asked, Salant and Dillman (1994) suggest that the following errors should be avoided when developing survey questions:

- *No double-barreled questions.* Questions must not group items if you want a response concerning each item separately. For example, if you were to ask patrons whether they thought the event staff was courteous, friendly, and responsive, you would not know which of the three (courteous, friendly, and responsive) they were referring to. If you intend to use these three as a global measure of quality service, then that is okay, but if you are interested in the three areas independently, then you need to separate them and ask three different questions.
- *Avoid loaded words.* Respondents tend to react more to a particular word or phrase than the question if strong feelings are aroused. Avoid words or phrases that stimulate strong positive or negative feelings.
- *Avoid loaded response categories.* The response categories should be balanced. For example, if you have two agree options such as agree and strongly agree, then the questionnaire should also have two disagree options such as disagree and strongly disagree.
- *Avoid loading the entire questionnaire.* The questionnaire as a whole should not reflect a bias. All questions must be open to the responder's opinion and not lead the respondent toward a particular bias.
- *Avoid leading questions.* Questions that have socially acceptable answers, that make obvious the viewpoint or position of the researchers, or that indicate an expected opinion or behaviour should be avoided.
- *Avoid vague words and phrases.* Ensure clarity in the wording used. For example, if the questionnaire asks for response options that involve words such as "sometimes" or "seldom," respondents may not be able to

differentiate between the categories. Instead, be more precise by quantifying the response, for example, "never have, less than 5, 6–10, and so forth."

■ *Avoid asking complex questions.* Break a complex question into several questions to aid understanding by the respondents.

■ *Avoid offensive or threatening questions.* For example, questions such as "What is your income?" may be too direct or personal for some respondents. If, however, you were to give them income ranges, they are more likely to respond.

■ *Avoid asking inappropriate questions.* Make sure that all questions on the survey relate to the purpose of the evaluation and are appropriate in nature.

In addition to avoiding those common errors when developing survey questions, event managers should also be aware of three of the basic response options or question structures that can be used: open-ended, closed-ended including unordered closed-ended and ordered forced choice, and partially closed-ended questions.

Open-ended questions are used when a variety of information is needed. The respondent provides an answer that produces qualitative data. For example, "Please indicate what you liked the most and the least about this event?" Instead of supplying respondents with answers that they could check off or circle, the respondents must write in their own responses. While responses to open-ended questions provide evaluators with more depth, they are often more time-consuming to code, input, and analyze.

Closed-ended questions obtain specific responses concerning options that are provided. For example, "Overall, how satisfied were you with the event?" (please circle one) very satisfied, satisfied, neutral, dissatisfied, or very dissatisfied.

The advantages to closed-ended questions are that they can be easily tallied and coded and are easy to administer and analyze. The disadvantages are that it is sometimes difficult to provide all the possible response options, and respondents are not given an opportunity to explain their answers. The event manager should also be aware that there are two types of closed-ended questions: unordered closed ended and ordered forced choice.

Unordered closed-ended questions include response options that have no particular value associated with them. For example, what events did you attend at the 2006 Winter Olympics in Turin, Italy? (circle all that apply) figure skating, downhill skiing, bobsled, ice hockey, and so on.

Ordered forced-choice questions rank responses using Likert scales, semantic differentials, rankings, and/or self-assessments. In the same example above, you could ask respondents to rank five events in terms of their liking. The least favourite receives a value of 1 while the most favourite would receive a value of 5.

Rankings involve questions that are designed to assess the relative meaning of things and generally ask respondents to rank in order a number of aspects of an event. For example, rank the following five Olympic sports from your favourite to least favourite to watch. Your favourite activity would receive a "1" and your least favourite activity would receive a "5": sailing, waterskiing, rowing, canoeing, and white water kayaking.

Likert scales typically offer 4–7 response options that include a range from positive to negative options. The question regarding respondents' overall satisfaction with the event above (under closed-ended questions) is an example of a Likert scale ranging from very satisfied to very dissatisfied. Some survey developers prefer to have a middle "neutral" or "no opinion" category, while others choose not to have one in order to force respondents to one side of the scale or the other.

Semantic differentials involve questions that use bipolar responses on opposite ends of the scale and ask respondents to circle a number that corresponds to their response. For example: "Please indicate how event staff responded to your needs during the event. Circle where you believe s/he falls on the scale." Responsive 6 5 4 3 2 1 Unresponsive.

Self-assessment questions ask respondents to describe where they fall on a scale. For example: "Based on a 1–10 scale with 1 being low and 10 being high, after reading this chapter, please rate your understanding of event evaluation."

Partially closed-ended questions offer some response options but also leave room for comments, typically through a last response option of "other." The goal should be to develop as many responses as possible in order to minimize "other" responses. For example, how did you hear about this event? Brochure, Television, Radio, Newspaper, Other _____ (please write your response in the space provided). Another example could be something like "Is this festival important to developing a sense of community pride among the residents of a Canadian city of your choice? _____ Yes _____ No. If no, why not? (Please write your response in the space provided).

There are a variety of different question types available to the event manager when evaluating an event. The event manager should consider their own information needs as well as the needs of stakeholders when determining which format is best. Once the question structure and format have been decided, event managers need to decide how they are going to administer the questionnaire. This requires decisions regarding both sample size and sampling strategies.

Determining sampling size and sampling administration strategies

The sample size and sampling strategy depend on the purpose of the evaluation project, design and data collection techniques, budget, time frame, and size of the population. Generally speaking, the more homogenous the population, the smaller the sample size needed. The closer the sample size is to the population, the smaller the sampling error will be. *Sampling error* refers to the difference between characteristics of a sample and the characteristics of the population. The smaller the error, the more reliable the data. *Non-sampling errors* are biases that exist due to who responds and how they answer a survey. The sources of bias could be due to question confusion, lack of knowledge of the respondent, concealment of the truth, or poorly constructed survey questions that failed to avoid the common errors alluded to earlier in the chapter.

Sample size

Since it is usually not feasible to survey everyone in attendance at an event (due to time, personnel, or financial restraints), event managers will have to decide what an appropriate sample size is. The sample size selected should take into account the purpose of the evaluation project, the design and data collection techniques, budget, time frame, and size of the population. When determining sample size, event managers should also be cognizant of the following: the desired level of sampling error, also referred to as the confidence interval, and the confidence level. The *confidence interval* or sampling error is the plus or minus number usually associated with the accuracy of political poll results or when reporting results from studies on the news. For example, if you use a confidence interval of 5 and 50% of your sample answers a question in a certain way, you can be certain that if you had asked the same question to your population, between 45% (50 − 5) and 55% (50 + 5) would have answered the same way. So the confidence interval really represents the range within the population that you could be sure would give the same result from the sample. The *confidence level* tells you how sure you can be and is expressed as a percentage. This number represents how often the actual percentage of the population would fall within the confidence interval when answering the same question. The 95% confidence level is most common in the social sciences and would be appropriate to use when evaluating events. This level indicates that you could be 95% certain that your results are accurate. Using this same example, when putting the two together, you could say that you are 95% sure (or confident) that the true percentage of the population is between 45 and 55%. Based on various population sizes and a 95% confidence level, the corresponding samples sizes for the 1, 5, and 10% confidence intervals obtained from the Sample Size Calculator The Survey System, http://www.surveysystem. com/sscale.htm, n.d. are presented in Figure 8.1.

The following example should illustrate how event managers can use this figure. Suppose you were charged with evaluating visitor satisfaction with a rowing regatta in your community and you knew the attendance was roughly 10,000 people. Based on a population size of 10,000, you can see from Figure 8.1 that you would need 4,899 respondents in your sample in order to be 99% confident that the actual response from the population would fall within $\pm 1\%$ of the proportion of respondents in the sample responding the same way. If you were looking for 95% confidence in the response to fall within $\pm 5\%$, you would need only 370 respondents. As you can see, there is a large difference in the required sample size depending on your desired confidence interval (or sampling error that you are willing to tolerate). Event managers will need to weigh the pros of using a small confidence interval, having small sampling error, with the cons associated with the corresponding large sample size, which is time-consuming and expensive.

Population size	Confidence intervals		
	1%	5%	10%
100	99	80	49
500	475	217	81
1,000	906	278	88
5,000	3,288	357	94
10,000	4,899	370	95
50,000	8,057	381	96
100,000	8,763	383	96
1,000,000	9,513	384	96
10,000,000	9,595	384	96

Figure 8.1 Sample sizes for various population sizes based on the 95% confidence level

Other observations event managers should make when using this table to determine appropriate sample sizes are that there is no specific proportion or percentage required in the sample based on the size of the population. There is an inverse relationship between the sample size and the confidence interval. This means the larger the sample size relative to the population size, the smaller the sampling error, and that for confidence intervals of 5% or greater; the required sample size does not increase dramatically for populations of 5,000 or more. As a general rule of thumb, event managers should maximize their sample size in order to decrease their sampling error.

Sampling approaches

Event managers typically have two options to choose from with respect to determining their sample: random probability sampling or non-random (non-probability) sampling. All members of the population, for example spectators at an event, have an equal chance of being selected in probability sampling, whereas all members do not have an equal chance of being selected in nonprobability sampling. Three common approaches to probability sampling include random, stratified random, and systematic sampling. Each member of the population has an equal chance of being selected when random sampling. This can be done through drawing names or assigning numbers to people, and then using a random numbers table. This approach typically results in the most reliable data and will best represent the population. If proportionate representation is sought, then event managers may want to use a stratified random sample by dividing the population into distinct subcategories called strata and then sampling from the separate strata (for example, lists, venues, times, or days). Another approach, systematic sampling, is a random sampling approach in which every "*n*th" person is selected (for example, if the population is 2,000, and you want a sample of 200, then you would select every 10th person).

Examples of nonprobability sampling approaches include purposive, convenience, quota, and snowball sampling. Purposive sampling occurs when certain individuals are chosen because you feel they represent the entire population. You may purposefully select people, venues, times, days, and so on from strata, but it is not random. For example, in evaluating visitor satisfaction with the 2006 Turin Olympic Games, you purposely sample visitors watching skiing-related events because you feel these individuals are representative of all spectators at the Olympics. The main caveat with this approach is that the group you feel may be representative of the entire population may not be so; thus, event managers should be cautious when generalizing the results beyond their purposive sample. However, if you were seeking to conduct interviews or focus groups, then purposive sampling would be quite appropriate, as the evaluator would be selecting individuals who would help them develop a better understanding of what is being evaluated and be in the best position to help the event manager answer the evaluation questions (Creswell, 2003).

Convenience sampling is another nonprobability sampling approach, whereby individuals are chosen because they are accessible. Typically, there are high error rates with this approach, as convenience samples are generally not representative of the entire population.

Quota sampling is another approach in which you are drawing a sample to fulfill a specific quota. For example, you may wish to survey the first 100 individuals to pass through the turnstiles, come to the counter, check in, or register. The main drawback to this approach is that once the quota is reached, no one else has a chance of being selected. Like other nonprobability sampling approaches, quota samples may not be representative of the entire population. Last, event managers may choose a snowball sampling approach in which they obtain a small initial group, sample, or list, and then get referrals from those individuals and so on until an adequate sample size has been reached. Again, like other nonprobability sampling approaches, quota samples may not be representative of the entire population, but they can be useful if individuals matching certain criteria are difficult to locate.

Survey administration strategies

Event managers should also be knowledgeable regarding the various ways that questionnaires can be administered when evaluating an event. Questionnaires can typically be administered by distributing them to a group, dropping them off and picking them up, via the Internet or by mail, or questionnaires can be administered through telephone, individual face-to-face or group interviews (Nardi, 2003). By administering questionnaires to a group, whether collecting them on the spot or dropping them off to be picked up later, the evaluator establishes personal contact with respondents, and they are given the opportunity to explain the questionnaire in person. This is a relatively low-cost approach and typically ensures higher response rates. However, if there are not many opportunities for event patrons to naturally be in a large captive group, then coordinating the logistics of getting people together will be a challenge. Internet questionnaires are becoming increasingly popular as a way to conduct research and to evaluate events. The event manager will have to decide whether to have computers with

Internet access on site or to give visitors something directing them to the website where the survey can be completed. There are a number of Internet-based companies that provide online survey development services. For more information, try checking out Survey Monkey (n.d.) on The World Wide Web.

If the type of event being evaluated is not necessarily conducive to administering questionnaires on site, then another option is to mail them once the event has concluded. In order to do this, event managers must have the mailing addresses of attendees as well as the money for printing, envelopes, and postage. While mailed questionnaires are relatively easy to administer and provide anonymity and confidentiality to respondents, they are also expensive and run the risk of low response rates, resulting in a nonresponse bias. In order to maximize response rates for mailed questionnaires, event managers should consider following the "Dillman process" (Salant and Dillman, 1994). This process involves mailing an advance letter of notice explaining the purpose of the study, followed by a cover letter and questionnaire shortly thereafter. A reminder postcard is then sent after 10 days, followed by a second follow-up letter after the due date with another cover letter/questionnaire. Last, a thank-you postcard is sent 10 days after the second letter is sent.

Questionnaires can also be administered via the telephone or through individual in-person or group interviews. These approaches generally have the advantages of giving the evaluator the opportunity to establish rapport with the respondents, and the ability to ask follow-up questions and to go into greater depth with certain responses. The opportunity to clarify questions is also provided. The drawback to these approaches is that they are both time and personnel intensive, which can lead to higher costs when evaluating the event (Henderson and Bialeschki, 2002).

Importance/performance analysis

The remainder of this chapter presents and explains several tools that event managers can use to evaluate the event. The I/P technique uses a measurement instrument (survey) to quantify the following two questions: how important are particular aspects of the event to respondents and how well did the event perform on those aspects. Essentially there are six steps in conducting an I/P analysis:

Step 1: Determine the attributes or aspects of the event to measure.

Step 2: Develop two sets of questions asking how important each aspect of the event is and also how the event performed on that aspect.

Suppose we developed a survey asking four importance questions using a 5-point Likert scale ranging from 1 = very unimportant to 5 = very important and four performance questions using a similar 5-point Likert scale ranging from1 = performed very poorly to 5 = performed very well (step 2). Let's assume we collected 200 surveys (step 3) and obtained the following importance and performance means for the four questions (step 4).

Importance questions mean/performance questions mean

a. Price of admission 4.25 a. Price of admission 4.50

b. Parking 3.40 b. Parking 4.10

c. Availability of restrooms 2.40 c. Availability of restrooms 1.75

d. Signage 1.90 d. Signage 3.95

Overall mean of importance questions Overall mean of performance questions

(4.25 + 3.40 + 2.40 + 1.90)/4 = 11.95/4 = 2.99 (4.50 + 4.10 + 1.75 + 3.95)/4 = 14.30/4 = 3.56

Figure 8.2 Example importance/performance analysis

Step 3: Administer the survey to collect the I/P data.

Step 4: Determine the means for each importance question and each performance question.

Step 5: Match the mean responses to the I/P questions for each aspect of the
event and plot the means on a grid where "importance" is on one axis and
"performance" is on the other axis.

Step 6: Determine the horizontal and vertical cross hairs and label the quadrants.

In the example in Figure 8.2, the goal is to graph the importance of each aspect of the event against the corresponding performance of that aspect of the event (step 5) to find out where we need to modify or recommend management efforts. The importance mean for the first aspect of the event (price of admission) is calculated by adding together the responses from the 200 surveys for this question and then dividing by 200 to obtain an importance mean value of 4.25. The same step can be followed to determine the performance mean for price of admission (which is 4.50). Continue calculating both the importance and performance means the same way for the other three aspects of the event (parking, availability of restrooms, and signage). Then plot the means for each of the four aspects of the event on the graph in Figure 8.3: Importance performance diagram. This has been done by taking the I/P means for the first aspect, price of admission (importance mean equals 4.25 and performance mean equals 4.5) and going up the vertical importance axis until you reach 4.25, and then traveling across 4.5 on the horizontal performance axis and plotting that attribute (a) at that point in the graph. Repeat this process until all of the remaining aspects of the event have been plotted on the graph. The next step is to determine the horizontal and vertical crosshairs (step 6). The grand means will be used to determine this and have been calculated above. The grand means are calculated by adding the means of the importance variables together and dividing by the number of those questions (in the example above, we have used four questions). For example, take the means of the four importance questions (4.25, 3.40, 2.40, 1.90), add them up (4.25 + 3.40 + 2.40 + 1.90 = 11.95), and then divide by the number of questions (4). So, 11.95/4 = 2.99. Then go up the importance axis to 2.99 and draw a line across the graph. This is the horizontal crosshair. This same procedure is repeated with the performance variables to determine the performance crosshair. Now, observe that the diagram has been divided into four sections or quadrants. The next step is to label the quadrants as shown in Figure 8.3.

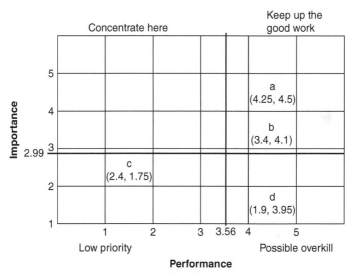

a = Price of admission
b = Parking
c = Availability of restrooms
d = Signage

Figure 8.3 Importance/performance diagram

The upper right quadrant, "Keep up the Good Work," indicates the aspects of the event that were of highest importance and highest performance, suggesting that the event performed well in these areas. The upper left section, "Concentrate Here," includes aspects of the event that are of high importance but were rated low in performance and represent areas requiring managerial attention. Less attention is needed for the lower sections, "Low Priority" and "Possible Overkill," because both are rated lower in importance. However, areas or aspects of the event falling into the "Possible Overkill" quadrant may suggest an overcommitment of resources, as these aspects of the event were rated low in importance but high in performance. I/P analysis can yield valuable information for event managers to assist in their justification for present and additional activities, staff, facilities, and funding or to justify resource allocation or reallocation to particular aspects of the event. The results of I/P analysis may also provide useful information for the design and implementation of various aspects of events.

Service-quality analysis

Another area that event managers may wish to evaluate is the quality of service provided by various services at the event. Service quality is defined as "the relationship between what customer's desire from a service and what they perceive that they received" (MacKay and Crompton, 1990, p. 47). Research conducted in the commercial sector studying a range of different services developed an approach for measuring service quality and concluded that service quality is comprised of five dimensions.

The five dimensions of service quality involve *reliability, responsiveness, assurance, empathy*, and *tangibles*. Reliability involves the ability to perform the promised service dependably and accurately. Responsiveness is a willingness to help customers and provide prompt service. Assurance involves employees' knowledge, courtesy, and ability to convey trust and confidence. Empathy and caring is characterized by individualized attention. And finally, tangibles involve appearance, physical facilities, equipment, personnel, and materials.

SERVQUAL (Parasuraman, Zeithaml, and Berry, 1988) is a measurement tool that event managers can use to determine how well they are meeting customers' service-quality expectations. The measurement is based on a comparison between customers' perceptions of actual service performance and their expectations for service performance. The survey consists of 22 statements related to respondents' expectations and 22 statements related to respondents' perceptions of the actual service they received. Service quality is then determined by taking the mean score for one perception statement and subtracting the mean score corresponding to the expectation statement (Service Quality = Perceptions − Expectations). A positive score in a particular statement shows that customer perceptions exceeded expectations. A negative score in that statement shows that customer expectations were not met. When conducting service-quality analyses, event managers also need to compute mean scores for all five dimensions for both the perception and expectation statements. This can be done by adding up the mean for the questions and measuring that dimension, and then dividing it by the number of questions used to measure that dimension. Service-quality analysis can then provide information about the gap between customers' expectations and perceptions of the service(s) provided by the event. This analysis can also aid in developing training programs for staff, justifying resource allocation or reallocation, making programming decisions about service successes and challenges, and providing comparisons between customers' perceptions and expectations over time. Overall service-quality analysis can be useful for event managers in all areas of event management where service quality is of concern.

Evaluating the value of volunteers

As volunteers are often crucial to the success of events, event managers should consider evaluating the contribution volunteers make to events. Evaluating volunteers and their worth requires creative thinking and the answers to three basic questions:

- How much are volunteers worth (if anything)?
- How can event managers demonstrate the worth of volunteers to an event?
- How can event managers demonstrate the worth or value of volunteers to the agency and the larger community? (Henderson, 1998).

Cost-effectiveness analysis provides event managers with one method to demonstrate the cost savings that volunteers can provide. Henderson (1998) suggests several steps when applying cost-effectiveness analysis to volunteers. First, itemize the direct costs such as salary savings, the cost of mileage payments, meals, printed materials and forms of recognition, along with office supplies needed and insurance. Second, establish the outputs, the activities completed by identifying the job and their tasks. For example, what is it that volunteers do, how many volunteers are doing these tasks, and what is the total number of volunteer hours contributed? Third, calculate the value of the volunteer hours contributed by determining what it would have cost to pay for the same services. Fourth, develop a ratio to show that for every dollar spent on volunteers, X amount of output is received. Henderson also notes that the value of the volunteer work is not the money saved but the actual worth/value of the contribution. She also suggests that other calculations can be done to assist event managers. The cost per volunteer, the cost per client, and the cost per service hour provided are all important contributors. A cost-effectiveness analysis can provide event managers with important information regarding the contribution of the services of volunteers. For more information, refer to the Knowledge Development Center's Volunteer Value Calculator (http://www.kdc-cdc.ca/weleng, n.d.). The Volunteer Value Calculator is designed to produce several different types of information on the economic value of volunteers such as human resource productivity measures, volunteer program efficiency measures, and community support measures that can all be assessed using this method. To find out more, event managers should also read the Knowledge Development Center's (n.d.) *Assigning economic value to volunteer activity: Eight tools for efficient program management.*

Using event evaluation to inform the event renewal

Earlier in this text, evaluation was defined as the systematic collection and analysis of data in order to make judgments regarding the value or worth of a particular aspect of an event. In this case, event managers are using the information gathered from the evaluation process to make judgments regarding the worth or improvement of the event. The final disposition or renewal of the event should be based on evidence gathered during the evaluation phase. When renewing the event, Rossman and Schlatter (2003) outline three choices for event managers: (a) operate the event again with no changes, (b) modify the event, or (c) terminate the event.

If the event manager chooses to operate the event again without any changes, then the results of the evaluation should explain why the event was so successful in order to justify this decision. However, earlier in this textbook, contingency and complexity theory suggested that even if the event was extremely successful, it is likely that it will still need to be changed or modified because of the contextual factors within the environment in which it would operate in the future. Factors such as location, future competing events, and changes in staffing or available resources to deliver the event are likely to require some degree of change for future events. In addition, when renewing the event, event managers may decide to modify the event. These modifications should be supported by data gathered during the evaluation process. How difficult it will be for an event manager to implement change to the event will likely depend on two factors: the degree of change and the amount and type of information available about the advisability of change. If the event is at the end of its life cycle, event managers may decide to terminate the event altogether.

Rossman and Schlatter (2003) warn that there are three primary forces that work against eliminating programs: staff, patrons, and organizational politics. Staff typically feel a sense of ownership in an event and are reluctant to change. Event managers need to make the staff realize that change is normal and is part of event management. At times, patrons, usually a core group of participants, may lobby against any decision concerning cutting "their" event. These individuals may be small in numbers but can exhibit intense emotional responses to a discussion for discontinuance. Also, organizational politics can often interfere when trying to eliminate events. For example, board members or higher-ranking administrators often advocate for groups lobbying for event continuation. These forces working against changes to, or elimination of, events only reaffirm the importance of the evaluation and renewal phase of the event planning model. According to Rossman and Schlatter, careful evaluation can help overcome these obstacles to eliminating events. For example, as part of the evaluation process, clear criteria could be established at the outset for terminating the event. These criteria would be agreed upon by various stakeholding groups. Clear goals and objectives could be established for the event and then the event evaluated based on them. Decisions about termination could also be made from an objective economic standpoint in terms of whether or not the event was profitable or produced the intended economic impact on the local community.

If the results from evaluating the event indicate that elimination of the event is inevitable, there are three strategies available to event managers: event retrenchment, staged elimination, and sudden elimination (Rossman and Schlatter, 2003). Event retrenchment involves continuing an event with reduced expenses. Since the retrenched event is not the same as originally offered with higher levels of previous funding, attendance and appeal will decline, leading to a gradual and natural elimination of the event. Staged elimination involves reducing aspects of the event in stages phased in over time so that attendees can find alternative events to meet their needs. Sudden elimination is just as it sounds and is likely to cause the greatest public outcry. However, it avoids running a subpar event in future years.

When making judgments about the value or worth of the event during the evaluation and renewal phase, event managers are often faced with having to make recommendations to the various event stakeholder groups. Recommendations are "specific tactical proposals for action that eliminate, replace, or augment current actions to steer a program, personnel, policy, place, or participant into preferred directions" (Riddick and Russell, 1999, p. 329). These recommendations are also proposed courses of action to be followed, based on the conclusions arrived at during this last phase of the event planning model. Recommendations answer the question, "What needs to be done/could be done based on findings?" Recommendations also suggest how the evidence from this phase might be applied in practice. For example, recommendations might suggest a reallocation of resources, advocate offering the same services to others, and propose reordered priorities or changes in policy, programs, services, activities, or events. The recommendations put forward might also rank event strengths and weaknesses according to their importance or performance. Results from the evaluation and renewal phase might also allow event managers to make recommendations regarding how to solve service-delivery problems, reach new target markets, operate more equitably or efficiently, and increase fiscal resources. Event managers may make recommendations with respect to future evaluations based on the findings regarding sampling and data collection/analysis approaches. Recommendations might also include what to evaluate or a need for additional information in a particular area. Regardless of the recommendation being made, Riddick and Russell suggest that event managers choose recommendations for implementation based on several factors including:

Importance: the need to prioritize recommendations that are most central to the organization's mission/goals;

Practicality: the need to be practical given the organization's budgetary constraints, staff, and other resources;

Time: the stakeholders are often more interested in supporting recommendations that can be executed in the immediate future; and

Compatibility: recommendations that are compatible with one another and the mission/vision of the event are also more likely to be implemented.

When making recommendations to event stakeholders, Riddick and Russell (1999) describe three typical audiences: fully invested people, interested people, and slightly interested people. Fully invested people mostly consist of event directors, advisory/governing board members, stockholders, city councilors, other senior event staff and personnel, or those outside of the event with a vested interest in the event. When making recommendations to fully invested people, Riddick and Russell suggest that event managers provide copies of the written evaluation report, call a staff meeting to discuss the recommendations, meet with the organization's policy makers, and develop a "program" of recommendations to be implemented. There is a need to build a positive organizational climate about the process of evaluation and also to plan carefully for dealing with negative recommendations. When making recommendations to interested people, such as event and potential event sponsors, Riddick and Russell suggest conducting an "in response" campaign. Some strategies involved in this process might be to write and submit a trade magazine article, prepare a popularized version of the report, or give a presentation at a professional conference. Slightly interested people require less direct dissemination of the results from the evaluation process, so issuing a press release or providing coverage in local newspapers might be sufficient for these groups.

Conclusion

This chapter, built on the previous common knowledge developed in Chapter 7, focused on moving the event manager toward acquiring advanced knowledge in the form of developing and using tools to evaluate the event. How to use knowledge from event evaluations to inform the renewal of the event was also discussed. In doing so, questionnaires, I/P analysis, service-quality analysis, and evaluating volunteer worth were all described as tools available to the event manager. Common errors to avoid were also covered when developing survey questions, survey question formats, distribution methods, and sampling issues regarding sample size and sampling strategies. The chapter also outlined a number of issues surrounding the disposition or renewal of the event. The three decisions event managers can make regarding event renewal and forces working against the elimination of events and how to overcome them were pointed out. The term recommendation was defined in the context of event evaluation. Different types of recommendations that event managers can make when renewing the event were highlighted. Four suggestions were offered to help the event manager decide what recommendations to make. Three typical audiences and their characteristics and needs were described which would influence the recommendations made to stakeholders. Event evaluation, the fourth and final step in the event planning model, is necessary in order to make data-driven, informed decisions regarding the renewal of the event.

Event managers that develop the skill to evaluate events are valuable in the industry. Those with excellent event evaluation skills can stand out from other employees and provide value added to the event and to the event-management industry.

Chapter questions

1. List the general steps that managers should follow when developing a questionnaire to evaluate an event.
2. What errors should be avoided when developing survey questions?
3. Define and give an example of sampling and nonsampling error.
4. Define confidence interval and confidence level.
5. What is importance/performance and service-quality analysis?

Event bidding

Cheryl Mallen, Brock University

Photograph by Shawn Whiteley

This chapter discusses the process of bidding to procure a sport, recreation or tourism event. The chapter defines the key elements that are typically contained in the bid process. These include a feasibility study, an outline of timelines and mandatory requirements for the bid, sometimes referred to as a candidature document, a bid questionnaire, a bid submission or dossier, and a bid tour. Reviewing a number of candidature documents and bid questionnaires is encouraged to develop your common knowledge about the requirements of bidding. This chapter often references the processes and documents utilized by the International Olympic Committee (IOC) in its selection of host cities for the Olympic Summer or Winter Games. This is one of the most formalized and high-profile bidding efforts in the world and is particularly relevant to the sport, recreation and tourism sectors, as the Olympic Games include elements of all three in the staging of this biennial event. An emphasis is then placed on the critical factors for successful bids as outlined in the literature. This is followed by a presentation and discussion on the proposition that there is one key redundant factor necessary in successful event bidding.

What is a feasibility study, candidature document, bid questionnaire, and bid dossier?

There are four primary documents used in the IOC's event bidding process in order to capture the detailed information necessary for it to compare bids and select a host city. While not all bid processes utilize this terminology to describe the mandatory elements required for an eligible bid, they do represent the kinds of information necessary for a successful bid. These documents include *a feasibility study, candidature document, bid questionnaire*, and a *bid dossier*.

First, a feasibility study is an assessment that presents an expert opinion on the capability of a group to stage or host the particular event. An ability to host involves a determination as to the availability of the necessary resources required to host the event. Resources such as competent and experienced human resources, facilities and equipment, financial resources, and technical resources are elements that need to be assessed. A feasibility study outlines whether pursuing an event bid is a practical and reasonable initiative and determines the plausibility of meeting the bid requirements with the resources available.

Second, a candidature document outlines the critical path of deadlines and processes that must be followed for a bid submission to be eligible for consideration. Third, a bid questionnaire must be completed. The bid questionnaire is often contained in the candidature document is a list of questions that must be answered in order for a bid to be considered complete by the governing body or organization that is awarding the rights to host the event. The fourth key document in event bidding is a bid submission or bid dossier. This document provides the overall plan and strategy and resources as well as outlines supplementary details, plans, and testimonials of support to set the bid apart from the other competitors. The bid submission or dossier will provide answers to the list of questions posed in the bid questionnaire. Each question must be answered, and every answer in the bid dossier must be recorded in the same order and correspond directly to the number assigned in the bid questionnaire. The bid questionnaire provides the format and frames the context for a bid dossier and must be followed precisely.

One of the best examples of a candidature document and bid questionnaire is provided by the IOC and is available for viewing on its website. To access the document go to http://www.olympic.org. One document to access from this site is the 2014 *Candidature Procedure and Questionnaire.* This 265-page document outlines the candidature procedures for the 2014 Olympic Winter Games, including the deadline dates, signatures required, the schedule of payments, guarantees required, the bid questionnaire, presentation layout, and requirements along with an outline for the visit by the evaluation commission and the selection decision process. An Olympic bid questionnaire is subdivided into the 17 Themes outlined in Figure 9.1. Each theme is further subdivided into a series of questions that must be answered in the bid dossier.

To advance your common knowledge on the process of bidding, it is suggested that you select at least three events that are of interest to you and review their event candidature documents and bid questionnaires. Many of these documents can be located on the World Wide Web. Another example is the European Football Championship Final Tournament. The bid documents for this event can also be found at http://www.uefa.com. You will find a number of bid documents on this site, such as the 2012 bid regulations and a 2005 report on five bid dossiers for Euro 2012. Yet another example is the Fédération Internationale du Sport Universitaire (FISU) or the International University Sports Federation at http://www.fisu.net/site/page_950.php. This site has an area that you can access called: Bidding procedure 2013 Universiades. Be sure to review the critical path of deadlines required for bids as the FISU deadline for submitting a bid for the 2013 Universiade is March 15, 2008. Also, you may want to approach festivals, conferences, and conventions in your area to obtain their bid documents.

Theme	Sample bid questionnaire topic areas to be answered in a bid dossier
Theme 1: Olympic Games concept and legacy	The event vision, impact, legacy, motivation, and plans for sustainable development
Theme 2: Political and economic climate and structure	Guarantees provided, government structure, stability, per capita income, inflation rate, referendum results, and opinions concerning support
Theme 3: Legal aspects	Stipulation of authority, event exclusivity, trademark protection, official languages
Theme 4: Customs and immigration formalities	Visa regulations, guarantee of entrance for those with Games accreditation, health and vaccination requirements, restrictions on media broadcasts, regulations on imported print media, guide dogs, and equipment
Theme 5: Environment and meteorology	Construction agreements and guarantees, protocols to protect the environment, geographical features, environmentally and culturally protected areas, collaborate efforts, plans and systems to manage the environment, the environmental impact, temperatures, humidity, precipitation, wind directions, and strength
Theme 6: Finance	Budget template outlining the financial details, including capital investment, cash flow, sponsorship and contributions, ticket sales, licensing, lotteries, disposal of assets, subsidies, and other hosting costs
Theme 7: Marketing	Guarantees of a marketing program, domestic sponsorship, ticketing, advertising, and advertising controls
Theme 8: Sports and venues	Venue descriptions, competition schedules, technical manuals for meeting competition standards, venue responsibilities and the tendering process and agreements, reporting, monitoring and management plans, workforce, and sport experience
Theme 9: Paralympic Games	Plans for financial, security, accommodations, transportation, sport venues, opening and closing ceremonies, finances, and accessibility and so on for hosting the Paralympic Games
Theme 10: Olympic village	Concept, location, venue design and construction, financing, including guarantees for construction, types of accommodation, distance from competition venues, control of commercial rights, accessibility, and post-event use

Figure 9.1 Themes and topic areas requiring answers in the International Olympic Committee bid questionnaire

Theme	Sample bid questionnaire topic areas to be answered in a bid dossier
Theme 11: Medical services and doping control	Plans for meeting the world anti-doping code and the IOC anti-doping rules, guarantees of investment in anti-doping, medical service facilities, public health authorities, epidemiological issue in the region and systems for managing Games medical expenses, including serving visiting foreign nationals
Theme 12: Security	Safety and peaceful hosting guarantees, international, national, regional and local government security involvement, analysis of risks concerning fire, crime, traffic, terrorism, security organizations and intelligence services to be involved and financial planning for security
Theme 13: Accommodation	Hotel room capacity, guarantees on room availability and room rate and other pricing controls, construction guarantees, work timelines and finances, binding contracts, accommodation tables with maps outlining sites and distances
Theme 14: Transportation	Traffic management guarantees, including public and private transport, control centres, distances, airport capability, parking and additional transport infrastructure, training and testing, timelines, and authorities
Theme 15: Technology	Guarantees of competent bodies offering communication services, systems and broadcast capabilities for print, radio, television and internet, network support
Theme 16: Media operations	Provision of broadcast centres for print, radio, television, and internet outlets, construction, timelines, financing, media transport, and accommodation
Theme 17: Olympism and culture	Protocols, plans for ceremonies including opening, closing and awards ceremonies, provision of intent, location, seating capacity, financing and facilities

Figure 9.1 (Continued)

What is a bid tour?

A bid tour involves hosting the members of a bid evaluation commission that will make the selection of the winning bid. The opportunity to stage a bid tour generally means that the bid submission has been placed on the short list of potential groups that are eligible to host the event. The tour offers an opportunity to present the information outlined in the bid dossier, to tour and highlight facilities and ceremonies planned, to demonstrate local community and business support for the bid, and to promote why your bid should win the competition to host.

A bid tour involves arranging for the needs of the bid evaluation commission members from the moment of their arrival until their departure. To meet this requirement, an event manager facilitates the adaptation of the event planning model phases specifically for a bid tour.

To begin, a bid tour follows the phases in the event planning model and the development phase. This involves the facilitation of elements such as the organizational structure for governance of the tour, the policies and volunteer practices, along with the determination of how corporate social responsibility can be incorporated within the tour. See Chapters 3 and 4 for a discussion of these topics. Next, the event operational phase for a bid tour involves the facilitation of the written operational plan for the bid tour itself. The operational plan involves arranging for components such as transportation, accommodation, entertainment, tours of the facilities, and a presentation of the bid to the commission members. In order to complete the plan for the bid tour, an event manager must cultivate the operational planning network, and facilitate the creation of operational plans that are logical, sequential, detailed, and integrated along with the inclusion of contingency plans and a plan refining process. See Chapter 5 for further details on the event operational phase. Further, a bid tour involves implementing the operational plans. See Chapter 6, the Event Implementation, Monitoring and Management Phase for elements to consider while instituting details within this phase. Finally, bid evaluation criteria must be specifically tailored for the bid tour. Review Chapters 7 and 8 for further details on this phase. In addition, the bid evaluation must take into account the priorities of the bid commission members, as they will ultimately make the decision on the winning bid.

To understand the evaluation criteria used by bid evaluation committee members, a review of the literature has identified several factors that appear to be critical in winning at the bid process. These critical factors are outlined below.

What are the critical factors in a successful bid?

The literature outlines several factors for successful event bidding; however, different studies describe an assortment of elements that lead you in many directions. We will review the key factors for success offered by researchers such as Emery (2002), Westerbeek, Turner, and Ingerson (2002), and Persson (2000).

This text forwards the proposition that there is one particular element that is vital to successful bidding.

To begin, Emery (2002) suggested five essential factors for event bid success. These factors include:

Possessing relevant professional credibility

Fully understanding the brief and formal/informal decision-making process

Not assuming decision-makers are experts, or that they use rational criteria for selection

Customizing professional (in)tangible products/services and exceeding expectations

Knowing your strengths and weaknesses relative to the competition (p. 323).

Emery (2002) purported that: "credibility and capacity to deliver are fundamental to any application, but not normally the discriminating factor between success and failure" (p. 323). Emery emphasized bid success was "dependent upon in-depth knowledge of networks, processes and people – in other words external political support at the very highest levels of government and the commercial sector" (p. 329). Therefore, the organizing team itself is actually an element that could make a difference in the pursuit of a winning bid. Emery suggested that an organizing team should be made up of members that have considerable experience with successful events. The need to develop experience in event management is also the theme of Chapter 11: An Integral Approach to Experiential Learning: A Foundation for Event Management and Personal Development.

Emery (2000) also stated that "the information process and protocol must never be underestimated" (p. 329). Some of the bid organizing teams must have experience in the political aspects of bidding, as this area is an important element in the bid process. According to Emery, this means that a bid needs to be politically positioned for success. In addition, Emery suggested that an assumption concerning the use of rational and consistent criteria to select the winning bid may not be correct. An interpretation of this view is that the key factors for winning a bid may actually change depending on the members on the bid commission that are evaluating a bid submission. Each member's personal perspective on the priorities for the bid must be somehow ascertained and then met. Thus, trying to anticipate the receptivity of a bid commission with several different members is a complex task that is underscored with uncertainty, but it is a necessary part of a successful bid process.

Another researcher, Persson (2000) suggested that a success factor for an Olympic Games bid involved "the fit between the bidder's and the IOC members' perceptions of the bid offers" (p. 27). This implies that the bid committee members must anticipate what the IOC will perceive as important in a bid. The IOC bid commission has several members, and the priorities of a bid are therefore subject to personal bias or agenda. Thus, Persson and Emery (2002) assert that a key component to achieve success in a bid is gaining understandings of the priorities of the bid commission members and meeting those priorities through political positioning of the bid.

Persson (2000) further offered that infrastructure was important to the success of a bid. Infrastructure, according to Persson, involved the capacity for the provision of appropriate accommodation, transportation, venues, finances, telecommunications, and technology as well as a top-notch media centre.

Ingerson and Westerbeek (2000) indicated that experience in event hosting was a key element for success along with the scope of knowledge of the members on the bid team. This is based on the contention that the more experience a member has, the greater the opportunity they have previously had to develop relationships that may drive the success of the current bid and ultimately the event itself. As Westerbeek, Turner and Ingerson (2002) have stated: "The ability to organize an event is evidenced by having a solid track record in organizing similar events" (p. 318). Thus, another theme arising from the literature is that experience hosting previous events is a key factor for future success in bidding.

There is a general consensus by Emery (2002), Persson (2000), and Ingerson and Westerbeek (2000) that the political aspects of a bid are vitally important to bid success. However, other researchers continue to promote additional success factors.

Westerbeek et al. (2002) promoted stability as a key factor for bid success. Stability was defined as involving politics, but from a different perspective than politically being positioned for advantage with the bid commission. The political reference in this instance meant the stability of the country and municipal politics of the city, along with the stability of the financial support for an event.

Westerbeek et al. (2002) outlined eight factors that were important in the process of bidding. Although these researchers emphasized sport event bidding, these factors are also very applicable to recreation and tourism events. The eight factors outlined by Westerbeek et al. included:

Ability to organize events: This element involves multiple items such as the intraorganizational network established to manage an event, the technical expertise within the network, the equipment, and the overall financial support for the bid.

Political support: This element involves the support from the government for the event bid. This support is used to assist in gaining access to financial and human resources, as well as access to facilities.

Infrastructure: This element involves providing convincing proof of the availability of excellent facilities and an ability to meet event component requirements to deliver the transportation, accommodation, and so on to produce an event.

Existing facilities: This element involves the current status of the major event facilities at the time of the bid submission.

Communication and exposure: This element involves the host city's reputation as a destination and the available support system to handle the technological communication system requirements for hosting and promoting the event.

Accountability: This element involves proof of the event's reputation, presence, and support in the event market, previous success in hosting events, and excellent venues.

Bid team composition: This element involves the talent mixture of the members involved in the development of the bid as important for increasing the perception of the bid to evaluators. The bid team members should be able to provide a high level of profile, build relationships, have the skill to manage the complexity of a bid, and provide credibility concerning expertise to host.

Relationship marketing: This element involves the ability to gain access to the members of a bid evaluation team and to influence these members to promote a bid through the development of "friendship."

The eight factors for success in bidding outlined by Westerbeek et al. (2002) above are listed in order of priority. This suggests that the most important factor in bidding is proof of one's ability to organize the network of personnel and the finances for an event.

Management effectiveness as indicated by Kerzner (1995) was dependent upon an ability to balance a number of items such as time constraints, cost and performance with the pressures of the environment, including political pressures. While Kerzner discussed project management, the link between the fields of project management and event management is apparent and represents one of the focal points in this text.

A relatively new element is gaining prominence in the literature and is promoted in this text as an important factor in event bid success. Over the last

10 years, environmentalism has moved onto the agenda. The environmental resources of the world, including forests, fisheries, water, soil, and air, are at risk and have created a social and environmental challenge (Hart, 1997). According to Al Gore (2006), this challenge includes "an unprecedented and massive collision between our civilization and the Earth" (p. 214).

In an attempt to meet this worldwide environmental challenge, an event bid should outline how protecting the environment will be considered and managed during the event. For example, the Fédération Internationale de Football Association (FIFA) released a legacy report on the environmental practices from the Germany World Cup (FIFA, 2006). This report illustrated efforts made by the event organizers to promote sustainable environmental practices. The International Federation of Motorcycling (IFM, 2006) produced a code for protecting the environment to be followed when producing events. This is now instituted for all races. In addition, in 1999 the IOC established Agenda 21, a document designed to bring its members into a program that supports the environment (IOC, 2007). This Agenda was promoted on the IOC website as "putting sport at the service of humanity." In 2006 the IOC released an athlete code of conduct which stated athletes were environmental role models (IOC, 2006). The IOC code of conduct presented six key principles that included avoid wasting water, avoid wasting energy, travel as efficiently as possible, consume responsibly, dispose of waste properly, and support environmental conservation and education. The IOC expects event organizers and athletes to protect and promote sustainability of the environment. As major events and games can be a driver for tourism, the IOC code of conduct can also be extended to tourists.

Sport, recreation and tourism bid submissions or dossiers should indicate how the event and its participants will protect this worldwide concern for our environment. Events are a critical component in managing the environment, and the bid dossier should illustrate the importance of conserving the environment.

Overall, the literature suggests a number of critical factors for bid evaluation success. The suggestions are multidirectional, which increases the complexity and the uncertainty of bidding. The complexity stems from an environment where multiple groups must come together to create a cohesive event bid.

To further enhance your common knowledge on factors for success in bidding, a bid committee member from a world hockey championship has provided the key factors in the bidding process. See Figure 9.2: Key bid factors from an industry perspective by Jim Rooney. These factors present additional areas of importance when constructing a bid dossier.

The multiple areas of emphasis contained in a bid may create a complexity that could strain the cohesiveness of any given committee and thereby

Maximize bid confidentiality: Once the bid committee has been selected and briefed, it is important that all members sign confidentiality, exclusivity, and noncompetitive clause agreements to ensure that the strategies and documentation prepared remain the privy of the bid group. In addition, it is important to keep all bid documents confidential and privileged until the presentation time period.

Clearly define bid committee member roles: It is incumbent on the event manager to set out the roles clearly, as each member must know and support the responsibilities and contributions of the whole bid effort. Clarification of each member's role is critical to the success of the bid.

Communicate, communicate, and communicate: Providing bid committee members with contemporary technology for communication is a key to success. The technology will further allow for maximum connection between the core committee members. In addition, a critical path must clearly define the communication strategy and processes.

Test areas of concern: In every bid there are elements that are not readily accepted by all members and therefore cause concern or the rise of a red flag. Each of these areas must be tested to ensure they pass at least three "testings" of the ideas before they are added to the bid dossier.

Use an external examiner: It is essential that the operational plan in its entirety be reviewed by an external examiner that will offer suggestions and alternatives to any issue. An external examiner can also provide an interpretation of what else is necessary to meet the requirements in a bid questionnaire.

Be environmental-friendly: It is incumbent on the bid committee to meet the expected standard for energy use and environmental policies. An environmental-friendly strategy must be adopted for all aspects of the bid, with waste management being essential.

Figure 9.2 Key bid factors from an industry perspective by Jim Rooney

compromise the potential for success. In addition, there is political complexity. This means the guiding documents outline the bid requirements, though intangibles, such as underlying political requirements, are not explicitly stated in a bid questionnaire. This political agenda may be important in the final decision-making in event bidding. This means uncertainty is inherent in the bidding process. In the end, only one group is awarded the prize in a bid competition. The rest have to bear the cost of competing in the process without receiving anything in the end.

To assist in working through the complexity and uncertainty of the bid process, the question is posed: Is there one critical factor that can be used to enhance the opportunity for a successful bid? This textbook promotes that there is *one* critical factor in event bidding.

What is the one critical factor for bid success?

This text forwards the proposition that *communication* has been underplayed in the literature and should be positioned as *the one critical factor* in event bidding.

In Chapter 3, communication was defined by Greenberg (2002) as "the process through which people send information to others and receive information from them" (p. 217). An application of this definition means a bidding process "constitutes a communication process between the actors involved" (Persson, 2000, p. 139). Thus, event bidding is conducted within a social context. This places the communication element as the key factor to win an event bid.

Communication in event bidding is discussed in the literature, although the support is not emphatic that communication is the key factor in successful bidding. The literature indicates that: "Event bidding is about communication to a degree, initially you have got to have communication, and you've got to be a really, really sharp communicator" (Horte and Persson, 2000, p. 67). Westerbeek et al. (2002) included communication as one of the eight key factors in bidding; however, they indicated it was in a group of elements that were "more likely to be supporting rather than vital factors" (p. 317). Westerbeek et al. (2002) and Jim Rooney stated communication as important in event bidding; however, they discussed communication from the perspective of providing contemporary technology for use in facilitating communication during the event.

This text positions communication as the one key factor in successful bidding because the event context is teeming with opportunities to advance the success of a bid with the use of written, verbal, and visual communication. An ability to communicate underlies every task in the bid process and can therefore be a deciding factor in the success of a bid dossier, a bid tour, and all other components in the bid process.

Communication is critical in a bid dossier. A dossier must clearly and succinctly express the intention to host and provide answers to a bid questionnaire. This document communicates the proposed plan for hosting an event. The level of planning detail communicated (Level 1, 2, or 3) in the document can hinder or enhance the success of the articulated plans and can influence the interpretations concerning bid activities made by the bid commission members in their assessment. Depending on the event, a bid dossier may also require written communication in more than one language. An ability to clearly express the bid details and the subtle nuances of the bid in multiple languages is an opportunity to position the bid for success.

Communication is a critical factor in conducting a bid tour. A written operational plan for a bid tour explicates the activities to be conducted. In addition, verbal communication is used to aid the network members implementing the bid tour plans to clearly understand the tasks. Poor communication can impact the success of a bid tour, illustrating that communication is a critical factor.

Formal and informal verbal communication is a critical factor in a successful bid. Examples of formal verbal communication opportunities include structured meetings with the bid commission members to present the highlights of the bid, meetings with key stakeholders such as the key sponsors or venue managers and meetings used to build relationships with the grassroot supporters such as volunteers, small businesses and organizations. Examples of informal verbal communication include casual conversations with the bid commission members evaluating the bid or with grassroot supporters of a bid. Each formal and informal communication opportunity can facilitate the transfer of knowledge concerning the bid or bid tour to all members in the bid network and to the bid commission members. Poor formal and informal communication can, from this viewpoint, profoundly impact the success of an event.

Visual communication is also a critical factor in bid success. The inclusion of visual elements in presentations, such as the use of diagrams in the bid dossier, video presentations, or fireworks in the bid tour, can enhance either the understandings of the bid detail or the enthusiasm for a bid. Visually communicating the bidder's message can have a significant impact on the success of a bid.

Communication technology is a critical factor in bid success. The use of the latest technology that allows for excellent verbal, written and visual communication can clearly demonstrate the host's ability to maximize the use of technology in the conduct of the event.

Communication is also an underlying critical factor in the majority of bid activities that go beyond the topics covered in this text. For example, the financial component of a bid relies on an ability to communicate facts and figures that will attest to the host's financial capacity to successfully host the event with no negative long-term impact on the community following the event. Marketing and sponsorship in event bidding rely heavily on the ability to enticingly convey the opportunity to be a partner in the event as well as what marketing and sponsorship opportunities might be secured. Written, verbal, and visual communication along with the communication technology are all critical factors in the success of marketing and sponsorship proposals.

The bid process involves communicating to groups such as the network members, the potential sponsors, and the bid commission members. Communication is the critical factor in event bidding and must be facilitated in a manner that enhances the overall bid effort. Facilitation was discussed in Chapter 3 as a means to create a synergistic energy for effective communication (Vidal, 2004). Your facilitation skills will be tested throughout the bid process. A focus on enhancing communication at all levels when facilitating an event bid is a critical factor for success.

Conclusion

Overall, this chapter defined a feasibility study, candidature document, bid questionnaire, bid dossier, and bid tour. The viewing of a number of candidature documents, bid submissions, and bid questionnaires was encouraged to develop your common knowledge about the requirements of bidding. Critical factors for success from the literature were outlined, and the author presented the concept that communication is the most critical factor for success in event bidding.

Chapter questions

1. Describe a feasibility study, a candidature document, a bid questionnaire, and a bid dossier.
2. List at least five key elements of successful bidding that were outlined in the literature.
3. Do you feel that concern for the environment should be part of the bid process?
4. Do you agree with the author's assertion that communication is the one key factor in successful event bidding? If not, why? If yes, explain how you see how communication is utilized in the process of facilitating an event bid.
5. Based on the information offered on key elements for successful bidding in this chapter, what should the members of the bid team be able to bring to any bid initiative?

Facilitating quality in event management

Craig Hyatt, Brock University

Photograph by Shawn Whiteley

Every event manager wants to produce a *quality* event. While this seems a fairly simple and straightforward concept, you must remember that most events have at least four different sets of stakeholders: the participant performers or athletes, the staff and volunteers, the sponsors, and the spectators or tourists. Each set of stakeholders will emphasize different criteria when analyzing the quality of the event. For example, the performers may indicate quality is based on the equipment, staging, and the amenities in the locker room. To the volunteers, a quality event may involve obtaining experience that advances their personal skills and provides them with event clothing. The sponsors may indicate that quality involves having unlimited product sampling opportunities or being able to mingle with clients in a hospitality area. The spectators may want short lines for quick access into the venue, for food and beverages and excellent sight lines from their seats. Can an event manager meet all of these quality requirements? Within each of the four stakeholder groups, quality is a relative concept. Each person involved in an event will have a personally determined idea as to what quality means. This fact challenges event managers.

In this chapter, we will examine how various theorists have defined quality over the past three decades. The theoretical concepts of quality will then be applied to the role of the event manager facilitating the staging of an event. The challenge to define quality for the role of the event manager will be discussed, and quality statements to guide an event manager will be developed.

What is quality?

For years, both academic theorists and industry practitioners have attempted to define quality. During the first half of the twentieth century, the service industry was not as prevalent as it is today (especially in the sport, recreation and tourism industries), and the manufacturing and purchasing of durable goods was a much more prominent concern. Quality was thought of in terms of ruggedness and longevity and was often expressed in terms of meeting measurable specifications for the size and strength of manufactured parts. Quality was the business of the quality control department. This department was responsible for the inspection of the goods before they left the factory. This quality process enabled mistakes to be caught and fixed without the consumers ever knowing they once existed.

During the second half of the last century, there was a gradual shift in our economy's focus from manufacturing to services. The rise of the service industry meant a change in how quality was conceptualized. Unlike manufactured goods, services are simultaneously produced and consumed, making it very difficult to

Quality is conformance to specifications	Product conforms to a design or specification (Gilmore, 1974, cited in Garvin, 1988) Conformance to requirements (Crosby, 1979)
Quality is excellence	Achieving or reaching for the highest standard (Tuchman, 1980, cited in Reeves and Bednar, 1994)
Quality is meeting and/or exceeding customer's expectations	Extent of discrepancy between customers' expectations/desires and their perceptions (Zeithaml, Parasuraman and Berry, 1990)
Quality is value	The dynamic process of value creation (Saad and Siha, 2000) How well an enterprise performs relative to consumer's cost (Watkins, 2006)

Figure 10.1 A synopsis of definitions of quality within Reeves and Bednar's four categories of quality

catch and fix service mistakes without the customer's knowledge. In this environment, services often require the knowledgeable input of the consumer to ensure a quality outcome. This meant quality was no longer expressed just in terms of physical specifications; it is now conceived in terms of meeting the expectations of the customer.

Quality of service with respect to the customer was introduced in Chapter 8 in a discussion on creating event evaluation questionnaires. Quality of service was stated as being based on *reliability, responsiveness, assurance, empathy,* and *tangibles*. However, there are other definitions of quality in the literature that will now be discussed.

Reeves and Bednar (1994), in their study on the evolution of the meaning of quality, concluded that the essence of all the various definitions of quality resulted in only four basic categories: *quality is conformance to specifications; quality is excellence; quality is value;* and *quality is meeting and/or exceeding customers' expectations*. The classification scheme of quality is now presented and outlined in Figure 10.1 A synopsis of definitions of quality within Reeves and Bednar's four categories of quality.

Quality is conformance to specifications

Defining quality as conformance to specifications provides the product or service providers and the consumers with a standard that can be agreed upon, prior to making a transaction in the marketplace. If the product's quality is called into question, the specifications are examined. This means that: "Quality is the degree to which a specific product conforms to a design or specification" (Gilmore, 1974, cited in Garvin, 1988, p. 41). If the product meets the specifications, it is of quality. If it does not meet the specifications, it is not.

In 1979, this definition of quality was expanded by corporate executive Philip Crosby when he presented a broader definition applicable when one is just concerned with a product. He defined quality as "conformance to requirements" (1979, p. 17). Crosby explained that whatever it is that we are examining for quality, including "quality of life," must be broken down into its component parts so each component part can be specifically defined in such a way as to make it measurable. If each component part is compared to a predetermined acceptable measure and meets that specification, the entire entity is considered of quality. As he stated:

> Those who want to talk about quality of life must define that life in specific terms, such as desirable income, health, pollution control, political programs, and other items that can each be measured. When all criteria are defined and explained, then the measurement of quality of life is possible and practical. (p. 17)

Thus, the concept of quality as conformance to specifications has expanded to apply not only to products, but also to services.

Quality is excellence

Quality conceived as excellence requires something to be as good as it can be. If an alternative is found to be better, yours is no longer thought to be of quality. When Henry Ford introduced his Model T Ford as a "universal car," he said it must have certain attributes (Ford and Crowther, 1922). The first attribute concerned the quality of the materials used:

> Quality in material to give service in use. Vanadium steel is the strongest, toughest, and most lasting of steels. It forms the foundation and superstructure of the cars. It is the highest quality steel in this respect in the world, regardless of price. (p. 68)

While Ford did not define quality, it is obvious from his description that excellence was the determinant factor of quality. Ford indicated quality steel was the best steel available at any price.

Tuchman's (1980) definition also indicates that quality is excellence. Tuchman indicated that quality

> *means investment of the best skill and effort possible to produce the finest and most admirable results possible ... quality is achieving or reaching for the highest standard as against being satisfied with the sloppy or fraudulent ... it does not allow compromise with the second-rate (cited in Reeves and Bednar, 1994, p. 420).*

Quality as excellence means being distinguished as exceptional for a product or service.

Quality is value

Quality conceived as value implies consumers of less-than-perfect products or services can still perceive them as quality if they are positioned financially as providing value. In other words, if you "get what you pay for," then quality transactions involve providing value instead of absolute excellence.

Saad and Siha (2000) emphasized quality as more than just an end result; it is an ongoing "dynamic process of value creation" (p. 1152). An interpretation of this definition of quality was offered by corporate executive Dave Watkins (2006). He indicated: "Quality defines how well an enterprise satisfies the performance element in the value equation" (p. 23). He clarified the concept by indicating that "the customer defines value (performance relative to cost)" (p. 23). Both definitions acknowledge that quality is relative to the price consumers pay for the product or service. Those who pay more want more in return.

Quality is meeting and/or exceeding customers' expectations

Quality has been conceived as meeting and/or exceeding customers' expectations. However, when it comes to defining expectations for a service, varied opinions prevail.

Zeithaml, Parasuraman, and Berry (1990) noted that "service quality, as perceived by customers, can be defined as the extent of discrepancy between customers' expectations or desires and their perceptions" (p. 19). This definition is of some use when considering the expectations of event attendees. It acknowledges that each patron is unique and may have unique needs or wants that they wish to fulfill by attending your event. It also notes that the onus is on the attendee to decide if their expectations were fulfilled.

Current definitions of quality and the lack of guidance for event managers

Do the current definitions of quality fall short when it comes to event management? This author believes, yes, this is the case. Let's briefly reexamine all four basic definitions of quality to examine their shortcomings when they are applied to the role of an event manager.

To begin, the definition of quality as conformance can be applied to event management. This definition applies when there are predetermined specifications in a contract for the stage and lighting or for equipment. However, there are no predetermined, agreed-upon specifications for service. Can you imagine getting everyone involved in an event to agree on what specifically constitutes, for example, an "entertaining" event? What about how long lines should be if an event involves tens of thousands of people? Should service still be able to be provided within a minute or two as some may expect? The specifications are not perceived in the same manner by all stakeholders, as they are not predetermined in writing. There is the opportunity for stakeholders to apply their personal idea of specifications. Even if all of the stakeholders could agree on specifications for many elements in an event, the event manager does not have control over all elements, such as the entertainment outcomes.

When quality is defined as excellence, there are factors that hinder an event manager from meeting this standard. For instance, the budget or resources may not be available to make every component of the event the best it can be. Compromises must be made if the budget is restrictive. Does this mean that any event that is forced to compromise due to budgetary restrictions should not be staged as it is will not be a quality event? If it is staged, can an event manager ever meet the standard of quality?

When quality is defined as value, the notion is that the consumer incurred a cost for attending the event. In many cases, events are free to spectators and tourists. Even if a spectator pays nothing to watch an event, that person still needs to know that it is worth the time it takes to attend.

The notion of providing quality as value is applicable to event admission charges. Let us imagine a spectator paying 100 Euro for a ticket to an outdoor music festival that includes a prime vantage point near the stage, an exclusive food court, reserved seats, and a souvenir T-shirt. Now consider another spectator paying 15 Euro for a general admission ticket to the same event that includes only a small section of lawn overlooking the distant stage. Both have a quality experience if they think their money was well spent. When there is no fee and when a fee is charged, what constitutes quality? Can an event manager ever meet the quality expectations if value is established individually by every member of every stakeholder group?

When quality is defined as meeting and/or exceeding customers' expectations, not all customer expectations can be expected to be realistic. The old adage, "you can't please all of the people all of the time" is something event managers should never forget. For instance, if an event manager facilitates easy parking and venue access, food, restrooms, excellent sight lines, and performers but the consumer wanted free child care then the evaluation of the event as meeting expectations is based on different categories. Also, not every person who wants an autograph from a performer may get one. Can a food and beverage service offer enough international cuisine to meet the tastes of all stakeholders? Not every credit card will be accepted at the box office. If the expectations for an event are personally established, is it realistic to believe an event manager can meet and/or exceed all of the expectations? It is our contention that some expectations may be unreasonably high. Can an event manager realistically meet the expectations of every stakeholder (all performers, every volunteer, the sponsors, and each spectator or tourist)? If an event manager used the definition of quality as meeting and/or exceeding expectations to guide their work, could they ever be successful? Would there not always be some of the many stakeholders unhappy as they would be defining the expectations personally? What if one or more operational network members involved in staging an event were unhappy because they were not given a T-shirt? Does this mean the event manager did not produce a quality event? Determining a definition of quality that guides an event manager to complete their facilitation role is a challenge.

While the definitions of quality in the literature offer good points, none are truly applicable to all types of events. This certainly does not mean that quality should be disregarded by the event manager. It simply means that every event manager needs to create a unique quality statement that can guide their work.

Creating a guiding quality statement for event management is a difficult task. There are many issues that arise as an event manager attempts to define quality specifically for their role and their tasks. Examples of these issues are discussed below.

Issues in defining quality in event management

One of the parameters concerning quality statements is to concentrate on all the items the event manager can control. Your event cannot promise a level of excellence if management literally cannot deliver at that level due to circumstances beyond their control. What follows is a list of issues that can directly affect whether or not stakeholders can have their reasonable expectations met. As you will see, many of them involve circumstances over which the manager has little control.

Conflicting stakeholder expectations influence quality perceptions

What happens when one stakeholder group has expectations that are in direct conflict with the expectations of another stakeholder group? Consider the potential tension between event performers and sponsors. The title sponsor may have a hospitality area near the action where they entertain existing or potential clients or host employees that are being rewarded for achieving excellence. As part of a great experience for their guests, they may wish performers to be available for autographs, photos, and chatting with the guests. The performers, on the other hand, might want to focus on their tasks and may consider time in a hospitality area to be a distraction. As such, they may expect to have no obligation to interact with sponsors or their guests. Even when contracted to do so, they may provide only a minimal level of service. An event manager is expected to facilitate a positive outcome from these two contradictory expectations. By promising the elements she or he can control and making it clear that they cannot deliver certain elements that are outside their control, an event manager can potentially modify a stakeholder's reasonable expectations and facilitate a satisfactory outcome for all parties.

Limited control over inputs influences quality

An event needs inputs. The event manager will need to order supplies from the venue and from outside suppliers. Depending on the nature of the event, you may have to order all of the items for a media conference to be held just prior to the event. For instance, the order may include a platform and tables to seat the members to talk to the media, along with tablecloths, microphones, chairs for the media, and so on. A technical check is held just prior to the media conference, and all is determined to be working well. However, during the media conference, one microphone has technical problems. Does this constitute an event that does not provide quality, or does the manner in which you handle the issue mean the event is of quality? If you have a technician on hand to manage the issue or have preplanned the use of an extra microphone for such a case, is the event a quality event? The answer is obvious. As has been mentioned before, contingency planning is of paramount concern for an event manager.

Financial constraints influence quality

Most event managers must deal with some financial constraints due to issues concerning cash flow. If cash flows become unexpectedly tight, you might not be able to afford the inputs necessary to meet the reasonable expectations of some of your stakeholders. For example, many of your spectators may wish to purchase high-end items at your souvenir stand, such as embroidered sweatshirts. However, the cost to you to order these items is high, and given the time it takes for the garment supplier to fill a large custom order, you must place the order weeks in advance and give them a delivery date a few weeks before the actual event as insurance in case of delays on the part of the supplier. This might mean that you are paying for these sweatshirts before you have the large cash flows that you expect to generate during the actual event (same-day ticket sales, sales at the concession stand, sales at the souvenir stand, etc.). Ideally, the event manager will be financially savvy enough to have sponsors pay part of their sponsorship fees well in advance of the event, to encourage spectators to buy their tickets or passes well in advance, etc., and to have a budget that takes these advanced cash flows into account. This will help ensure that there is sufficient cash flow long before the day the event opens in order to buy all the quality inputs required. If, however, in the weeks leading up to the event the actual revenues from sponsorship and advanced ticket sales fall short of the projected numbers forecast in the budget, there may not be funds needed to purchase high-end items like embroidered sweatshirts when the time comes to place the order. This is not good. The event manager may be forced to buy cheaper items (such as silk-screened T-shirts made of a cotton-polyester blend) to stock the souvenir stand. When the spectators finally attend the event, many will not find the items that they are looking for and will leave the event without having their reasonable expectations met. Chances are they will tell their friends that they had an experience that failed to meet their expectations and add that what they perceived as a lack of quality will keep them from returning. If many other attendees do the same, your event may enter a downward spiral from which it will never recover.

How can the event manager avoid this type of negative perception? There are no easy answers. Issues of finance and cash flow plague many businesses and organizations. If financial survival depends on selling sponsorships and tickets in advance, then you, the event manager, must educate the sales staff that sales success in the months and weeks before the event is crucial. As for the bigger picture, all students interested in event management may want to consider learning all they can about the sales process; the quality of your future event may depend on your ability to sell.

Contingency plans influence quality

No event manager needs to be told that things can go wrong with the event. Managers need to plan ahead to hopefully identify every potential bump in the road in order to develop contingency plans. For example, an experienced event manager can anticipate that the food wholesaler may not deliver the exact product that was ordered. In such a case, a contingency plan may empower the director of concessions to call an alternative wholesaler to arrange the delivery of the necessary product. This is fairly straightforward and ensures a quality product.

However, not all contingency plans can be implemented in such a straightforward manner. Consider an outdoor event that cannot be held in inclement weather, such as a fireworks show. A simple contingency plan for a fireworks show is to advertise both the specific date (weather permitting) on which the event will be held and the rain date should the show be cancelled due to bad weather. The problem lies in the unpredictability of bad weather. Imagine your fireworks show is slated to take place at 21:00 on a Saturday, with the following day listed as the rain date. Starting on the Wednesday before, the weather forecasts call for evening thunderstorms on Saturday. You can be sure that the phone will start ringing that Wednesday with worried potential attendees asking if the event will be postponed. Maybe the folks who are calling live a few hours away and plan on leaving home mid-afternoon on Saturday to do some shopping and enjoy dinner before the fireworks. They do not want to spend many hours in the car and not see fireworks. While you understand their situation, you also know that even if the weather forecast is true, an evening thunderstorm could mean rain from 17:30 until 18:30, leaving plenty of time for things to dry out enough for the 21:00 show. Or it could mean rain starting at 23:00, long after the event is over. You also know that for every attendee who could easily attend the event on the rain date, there is one who cannot. Maybe hundreds of tourists have planned a weekend getaway around your event and have hotels booked for Saturday night only, having to return to their hometowns during the day on Sunday. If you postpone the fireworks a day or two in advance and it turns out that things are dry enough at 21:00 on Saturday that you could have had the show, the out-of-town tourists will probably conclude that their reasonable expectations were not met.

If you wait until the night of the show and decide to postpone, the folks who drove in that day who just as easily could have rescheduled their day trip until the following day will probably conclude that their reasonable expectations were not met. As the event manager, what can you do?

Unfortunately, the nature of weather forecasting often means the event manager must rely on his or her gut instincts leading up to the event. If in the hours leading up to the event it still looks like there is a reasonable chance that the event can go ahead as scheduled, the event manager may elect to proceed until the skies open just minutes before the start time. If, however, the noon weather forecast clearly shows a massive slow-moving weather system heading your way that meteorologist state will bring six straight hours of heavy rain starting at 19:00, the event manager may announce the postponement of the event at 13:00. In most cases involving inclement weather, the telephones at the event's headquarters may ring nonstop before, during, and after the event with folks wanting to know if the event is still a go, wanting to know when the decision to cancel (or not) will be made, wanting to know why the decision to postpone the event was not made sooner, wanting to complain that their weekend plans were ruined by the poor decisions of the event staff, etc. The best an event manager can do is to train the staffers handling the phones on what to say to the callers and how to say it. If all the staffers are briefed on the reasons why decisions to proceed or to postpone are made, they have the opportunity to educate the callers. This education may actually enlighten the caller to the point where they conclude that their expectations for the event management might not have been as reasonable as they thought. In such a situation, the caller (who questioned the quality of the event when the phone call was first made) will not have that opinion by the time the phone call is over.

Although there are difficulties, an event manager is expected to be able to produce work that is of quality. Therefore, they must be able to define a quality statement to guide their work.

Creating a quality statement to guide event managers

Every event manager who wishes to provide a quality product or service should address the issue in a written statement. Each quality statement should address both the specific definition of quality and how the quality will be delivered.

There is no standard way to create a quality statement. A quick internet search reveals a large number of organizations attempting to create quality statements. The quality statements can be as short as two sentences and as long as multiple pages. If a statement is too short, there is the chance that it will be so vague as to be meaningless. If it is too long, it might not be memorable enough to serve as a useful guide.

At this time, think of an event that you see yourself managing someday. Take some time right now to create a quality statement for this event. Consider what the literature offers when defining quality and what elements you can utilize from this literature. Consider also that the event may currently have a mission statement, vision statement, and a statement of values. Your quality statement should be congruent with these other event statements. The difference is that the quality statement you are developing must guide your work as a facilitator and be available as a realistic platform to evaluate your work throughout and at the end of an event.

Your quality statement needs to seamlessly integrate the facilitation activities that you are personally responsible for as an event manager. Go back to Figure 10.1: An event planning model to review the main categories of responsibility.

A sample quality statement

Imagine a 3-on-3 basketball tournament that is held annually in a small city. It is organized and managed by a local youth basketball organization, who has named it "Rally in the Valley." The tournament is meant to both be a celebration of the game of basketball, and a fund-raiser for the organization. Temporary outdoor courts are set-up throughout a park located in a residential neighbourhood just off of the city's downtown. Dozens of teams, grouped according to age, sex, and skill level, will play games all weekend until winners in each division are determined late on Sunday afternoon. What could a quality statement for Rally in the Valley look like?

Quality statement for rally in the valley

Rally in the Valley is committed to meeting or exceeding the reasonable expectations of all the event's stakeholders, including the players, spectators, sponsors, volunteers, and city government. Rally in the Valley management will actively encourage the input of all stakeholder groups for the purpose of mutually determining what constitutes "reasonable expectations." This process will be ongoing, as "reasonable expectations" may change from year to year as the event evolves. A thorough training process to educate the volunteers will be implemented before the event that will empower them to handle routine stakeholder concerns during the event, so that reasonable expectations can be met in a timely manner. Rally in the Valley management will be in constant radio contact with volunteers, should non-routine stakeholder concerns arise during the event. In such cases, management will meet with any concerned stakeholder as soon as possible to rectify the concern. After the event's completion, Rally in the Valley management will make themselves available to meet with concerned stakeholders to rectify any issues regarding meeting their reasonable expectations.

While it is debatable whether or not this quality statement has too much or too little detail, it seems to meet the basic requirements of a quality statement: to define quality and to indicate how quality will be delivered.

To provide further input to guide you in developing a personal quality statement, here are some comments about quality from members in the event management industry.

> With only one chance at a first impression, it is crucial to carefully plan for all possible situations. Planning well thought-out contingencies for situations are often times the difference between a successful event and an event that will no longer be continued.
>
> (Andrew Pittam, Operations Manager, Event Properties
> International Management Group [IMG] Canada)

> Whatever happens on the field or court will take care of itself. We want the visiting team to be impressed by the way we treat them; beginning from the moment they arrive until their departure from our campus. That is our philosophy that guides the quality in our game operations.
>
> (Tom Calder, Director of Athletics and Recreation, Johns
> Hopkins University, Division 1 Men's Lacrosse National Collegiate
> Athletic Association [NCAA] Champions, 2007)

> A well managed event in a clean, modern facility with superior customer service and a product that exceeds expectations will create satisfied customers and ambassadors for your event. A poorly managed event, on the other hand, can negate the effects of all the money you've spent and work you've put into attracting patrons to your event. A poorly managed event that detracts from the fan experience will cost you patrons in the future and limit the ability of your event to grow and flourish.
>
> (John Pesetski, Director of Advertising and
> Promotions, National Hot Rod Association)

You achieve excellence when your staff has high standards for everyone, performers and guests alike that enter your event facility. Each employee must give their utmost attention to detail to ensure a positive experience. When you achieve this, your day is successful and the quality which you try so hard to attain is recognized by a wide variety of people.

(Rob Staverman, Director of Event Operations,
United Center, Chicago, Illinois, USA)

Quality is critical in providing an outstanding experience for our 30,000 participants and enhancing our brand. Collectively we develop a plan which helps us stay focused and on track. Our ultimate goal is for participants to have a positive experience and return to our event year after year.

(Lindsay Crosby, Manager, Run for the Cure, Canadian
Breast Cancer Foundation, Toronto, Ontario, Canada)

There are many guiding quality statements. Each event manager needs a personally crafted statement of quality to guide their work.

Conclusion

No event manager wants to put in countless hours dedicating their energy to stage an event that lacks quality. All of the careful planning leading up to the event must be done with quality in mind. Because of the unique components of each event, managers must define quality in a way that makes sense for their particular situation. To better ensure that their conceptualization of quality is met, they must also institute policies in a quality statement that are meaningful and easy to implement. Managers should also be mindful that other issues, such as conflicting stakeholder expectations, limited control over inputs, financial constraints, and contingency planning, can create challenges for anyone wishing to facilitate a quality event. Event management is a complex and challenging field, and a personally established statement of quality to guide the facilitation of an event is a key element in succeeding in this industry.

Chapter questions

1. Describe how the four basic categories of quality (conformance to specifications, excellence, value, and meeting or exceeding customers' expectations) can create problems for an event manager.

2. Discuss how stakeholder perceptions, limited control, financial constraints, and contingency plans affect an event manager striving for quality.
3. Describe a guiding quality statement for use if you were an event manager.
4. What issues arise as you attempt to create a definitive guiding quality statement?
5. Why is quality an elusive concept in event management?

An Integral approach to experiential learning: A foundation for event management and personal development

Beth Jowdy, Southern New Hampshire University

Mark McDonald, University of Massachusetts, Amherst

Kirsty Spence, Brock University

Photograph by Mike Cheliak

To be successful as an event manager, one must have an in-depth understanding of the various areas outlined in this text. Understanding and obtaining knowledge in these areas, however, is only the beginning of your development as an event manager. Your capacity to advance your knowledge as an event manager will be enhanced by taking an Integral approach to the experience of managing a "real world" event.

With this outcome in mind, this chapter is organized into four sections: first, you will learn about an Integral approach to experiential learning; second, you will read about how the Integral approach is applied to experiential event management courses; third, you will learn more about maximizing your personal development in event management; and fourth, you will recapitulate the key concluding points that we have covered in this chapter.

By the time you complete this chapter, you will understand how to learn and develop from the experience of managing an event. In other words, you will have a framework that can be used to understand your event management experiences in and out of the classroom and how such a framework contributes to your personal development.

Integral approach to experiential learning

Defining experiential learning

Based on personal experience, you are no doubt familiar with the traditional approaches to learning within the context of a classroom environment. These traditional approaches to classroom learning usually include a standard lecture and discussion format, where the teacher disseminates information and you receive and then demonstrate your understanding of course content through various forms of evaluation such as tests, written papers, and presentations.

Using this approach, the course content that you learn about is explicitly outlined in a course syllabus, and classes are framed by both course textbooks and academic readings. In contrast, within the context of experiential learning, you as a student are expected to be an active participant in your own learning through involvement in determining the learning subjects and subsequent outcomes.

Experiential learning theory dates back to the 1930s with Dewey's (1938) *theory of experience and education*. Dewey believes that by learning from experience, theory, and practice can be united. Further, every experience allows for students' personal development according to their physical, intellectual, and moral growth, which could and should prepare them for later experiences of a deeper and more

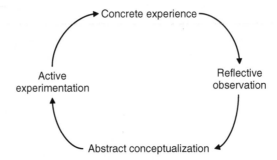

Source: Adapted from *Experiential learning: Experience as the source of learning and development* (p. 33) by D.A. Kolb, 1984, Englewood Cliffs, NJ: Prentice Hall. Copyright 1984 by Prentice-Hall Inc.

Figure 11.1   Kolb's experiential learning model

expansive quality. Aligned with Dewey's philosophy, Kolb (1984) believes that reflection and observation transform concrete experiences into more purposeful actions of students.

Kolb (1984) defines *experiential learning* as "the process whereby knowledge is created through the transformation of experience" (p. 38). According to Kolb, learning occurs when individuals encounter an experience, deal with the experience through observation and reflection, ask questions and form generalizations, and seek to answer the questions or solve problems. From this, Kolb developed a model (see Figure 11.1) as a practical way of understanding how the individual learns from experience through four elements: concrete experience, reflective observation, abstract conceptualization, and experimentation.

In addition to Dewey (1938) and Kolb (1984), a number of theories and approaches to experiential learning have emerged in higher education. These theories and approaches represent two major theoretical streams. The first theoretical stream includes Dewey and Kolb and other pivotal theorists (Boud and Walker, 1991; Lewin, 1951; Mezirow, 1991; Piaget, 1951; Schön, 1983). This stream focuses on learning and meaning as it is derived from an experience by the *individual* and his or her creation or construction of personal knowledge, independent of others in the classroom or shared experience.

The second theoretical stream is representative of perspectives which focus on *collective* inquiry (Argyris, 1991; Argyris and Schön, 1996; Fenwick, 2000, 2001; Holman, Pavlica, and Thorpe, 1997; Kayes, 2002; Taylor, 1998; Vince, 1998; Yorks and Kasl, 2002). According to these theorists, learning does not take place independently of cultural, historical, and social relationships; learning occurs through an understanding of the shared meanings based on students' encounters with others (social knowledge).

Wilber's Integral approach

The pivotal theories that make up these two theoretical streams can be viewed within an even more expansive *Integral approach*. Wilber's All Quadrant, All Level (AQAL) Integral model (Wilber, 1995, 2000a, 2000b) can be applied to the potential learning and personal development available to you when involved in event management experiences (see Figure 11.2: Wilber's AQAL Integral approach). The AQAL model offers a more holistic approach when integrating both individual and collective perspectives and can be applied to experiential learning within the event management realm.

By applying an integral approach, we can more holistically understand our experiences and our personal development through four central perspectives, which acknowledge the individual and collective and the interior and exterior of experiences. Such an application can create a full view of the problems that event managers face and identify various solutions to remedy such problems. Within this chapter, you will be able to identify ways in which these perspectives, known as the four quadrants, can help you learn from event management experiences.

Upper Left (UL)	Upper Right (UR)
Interior individual	Exterior individual
Representative of a student's subjective feelings, experience, and intentions within an event management experience.	Representative of the objective, empirical, and measurable aspects of the student, including his or her physical actions and physiological changes.
Lower Left (LL)	Lower Right (LR)
Interior collective	Exterior collective
Representative of the shared meanings held by the collective group of students, which are given meaning by being embedded within the context of an event management experience.	Representative of all objective, empirical, and measurable organizational aspects (such as systems, structures, and processes) and how these functionally fit together to create an effective and successful event.

Source: Adapted from Ingersoll (2005) and Wilber (1995, 2000a, 2000b, 2006).

Figure 11.2 Wilber's AQAL Integral approach

Through the AQAL model, we can view our reality (such as what we experience) through *upper and lower halves*, which provide us with individual and collective perspectives respectively. Perspectives associated with the upper half relate to the development of the individual aspects of reality, whereas perspectives associated with the lower half relate to the development of the collective aspects of reality.

Our reality can also be viewed through *left- and right-hand paths*, where the left-hand path relates to both an individual's and the collective group's subjective interpretation of reality, whereas the right-hand path relates to both an individual's and the collective group's empirical study of the exterior perspectives of reality. The upper and lower halves and the left- and right-hand paths come together in an integral way to represent *four quadrants*. A description of each quadrant is discussed below.

> *Upper Left (UL)*: Central to the UL quadrant is the interior and subjective *development of a person's intention, consciousness, experience, and motivation*. When developing, the person becomes increasingly aware of his or her experiences, immediate thoughts, and feelings. Through self-reflection, dialogue, and creation of symbolic imagery, the person is able to interpret and derive meaning from an awareness of the experiences he or she encounters and the thoughts associated with these experiences.
>
> *Lower Left (LL)*: Central to the LL quadrant is the interior and inter-subjective *development of the collective culture, characterized by shared worldviews, values, feelings, and language*. From the perspective of this quadrant, the collective culture develops around communication of shared meaning and interpretation, which is always sensitive to the context in which the collective culture is embedded. When considering the intersection between the UL and the LL quadrants, a person always interprets their thoughts based on how they fit with those representative of the collective group embedded within a specific context.
>
> *Upper Right (UR)*: Central to the UR quadrant is *the objective, exterior, and observable form of any person, thing, or event*. When applied to observable things in a work setting, the UR quadrant is characterized by job descriptions, wage levels, and individual tasks. When applied to people, the UR quadrant is characterized by objective observations of others' behaviour, such as their physical actions (such as when people smile, grimace, or cry) and physiological changes (for example, when we track others' brainwaves or hormonal levels).

185

Lower Right (LR): Central to the LR quadrant is *the objective, exterior, and observable form of the various collective groups that comprise the total functioning organizational system.* Within a work setting, the LR perspective relates to all technologies, forces of production, and institutional systems, structures, and processes that interconnect to form an effective and workable system.

Wilber (2006) states, "the quadrants are simply the inside and the outside of the individual and the collective, and the point is that all four quadrants need to be included if we want to be as integral as possible" (p. 23). This means that no half (upper or lower), path (left-hand or right-hand), or quadrant (UL, LL, UR, LR) is supreme or more valuable than any other. All perspectives are honoured as equally significant to your learning and personal development and are interconnected as important perspectives when explaining organizational behaviour and in generating creative and cogent solutions to the problems we face within event management settings. So, what does this mean in the context of event management and your course?

Applying the integral approach to event management

Perhaps, your primary objective in taking this course is to learn about the various aspects of event management. If so, you may be interested in understanding course content through the lens of the LR quadrant. For example, you would pay particular attention to the legal, administrative, communication, and other organizational systems that influence how efficiently and effectively an event functions. Or, if provided the opportunity to execute a "real-world" event as part of the course, you may be interested in and want to learn about the required skills, personal traits, and characteristics that are necessary for an individual or a collective group to be successful. If so, you would pay particular attention to your own and others' behaviours (UR) and your interpretations of your feelings (UL) when intense pressures become a focal point.

You may also engage in an event management course because of the sense of camaraderie and teamwork inherent in the profession. If so, you would pay particular attention to learning about the shared values and culture among event management groups (LL). Of course, you may be interested in all of these perspectives offered in an event management course, in which case you would pay attention to all four quadrants of the AQAL Integral model. Paying attention to any one or all four of the quadrants will influence how you view and subsequently work on event management tasks.

While each of your learning interests represents a legitimate and anticipated outcome of participation in an event management course, taken separately and without proper integration, your learning experience will not be maximized. The purpose of an event management course must include and go beyond knowledge and skills to include your personal development. Knowing "how to" organize and manage an event does not necessarily mean that you are an effective manager or that you have the competencies necessary to work with others in an emotionally charged environment such as event management. Applying Wilber's Integral approach to an experiential event management course that provides the opportunity to execute a real-world event exposes you to the depth of learning and personal development that is available through this and all future personal and professional experiences.

One other way to understand the application of the Integral model is to relate the four quadrants to the components necessary for meaningful experiential learning (Andresen, Boud, and Cohen, 2000; Boud, 1993; Boud and Walker, 1990). When you first register into an experiential event management course or are first employed within an event management organization, you do not operate in isolation of others, nor do you operate in isolation of the environment in which you study or work.

All internal and external stakeholders are necessary and critical to your development and the event's success. The experiential learning components of *personal foundation, intent,* and *learning milieu* are crucial to understanding the relationship between the individual, the collective, and the environment. When applied to the four quadrants, the relationship between these elements and your experience is clarified.

Individual

One's *personal foundation* is seen to exist in the individual, interior subjective "reality" characteristic of the UL quadrant. It is comprised of one's interpretations of his or her previous experiences, history in learning situations, assumptions, values, and conceptual frameworks (Boud, 1993; Boud and Walker, 1990). These previous experiences, assumptions, and values can affect what "I" do, how "I" do it, and my confidence and ability to act when working with others (Boud and Walker, p. 63). How "I" think, what "I" believe to be true about my abilities and about others directly impacts my ability to learn and engage in new experiences. For example, your prior experience with your performance as a member of a team serves as a foundation in forming your perspectives, abilities, and confidence levels, impacting your future as a valuable and contributing member of an event management team.

Similarly, *intent* also exists in the subjective reality characteristic of the UL quadrant and is defined as the rationale for which the learner chooses to engage in a particular course or experience. Intent may be linked to core values, ideals, or a desire to learn about a particular career firsthand (Boud and Walker, 1990). Within an experiential setting, it is the intent that prompts and affects how much effort "I" make toward achieving my learning goals and exploring interactions and observations within the framework of my event management experience.

For example, an individual who aspires to be the General Manager of a professional soccer franchise might be strongly motivated to work on the operational aspects of a grassroots soccer tournament. Additionally, intent can exist in the individual exterior "reality," characteristic of the UR quadrant of any experience. From this UR perspective, intent would be revealed through the objective and observable aspects of an individual's behaviour. For example, a student consistently showing up at 7:45 a.m., prepared with all required management tasks, for weekly 8:00 a.m., marketing department meetings might suggest a strong positive intent.

In essence, as the student self-observes behaviours and physiological responses during a particular experience, insight into their intent is heightened. If one's actions and behaviours do not fit with those necessary to meet a particular learning or event management goal or to accomplish a particular task, then the intent (desire) may be lacking. As individuals, our personal foundation and our intent influence the intellectual and emotional content we derive from experiences. Thus, it is important that we are aware of their presence and influence while involved in an experiential event management course.

Collective

As a student with a personal foundation and intent, you constantly interact with the experiential *learning milieu* or environment (Boud & Walker, 1990). Thus, your experience also exists within the interior and exterior collective realities of Wilber's model. Specifically, the environment includes the culture, rituals, norms, and values associated with an experiential event management course and are characteristic of the LL quadrant. The environment also includes the formal requirements, practices, procedures, and standards associated with an event management course and are characteristic of the LR quadrant.

For example, within an event management course or organization, some values may include teamwork, professionalism, and dedication, while some norms may be taking initiative, taking responsibility, and accepting constructive criticism. Your experience will be affected by your understanding of the purpose and appropriateness of these shared values and norms in relation to your own values and expectations. Furthermore, a lack of mutual understanding of the values and norms by group members may impact both productivity and individual learning.

Correspondingly, it is important to recognize the role and the effects of various organizational systems (for example, financial systems, human resource systems), structures (such as an organizational chart), and processes (for example, communication) as they interact among and between individuals, departments, and the organization. Various organizational systems, structures, and processes are characteristics of the LR quadrant and make functioning possible, both for individual members and for groups within the event management course. For example, event management classes are often broken into various departments where each department has its particular set of tasks, processes, and procedures. To effectively and successfully execute an event, however, there are systems and processes in place that interconnect these departments. Therefore, the individual must observe and understand how one department's functioning and productivity have an impact on other departments. In addition, event managers need to understand how departmental processes and procedures fit into the larger organizational system.

Maximizing personal development in experiential event management settings

In preparing for your event management experiences, whether in an academic course setting or when working as a professional in the field, you should recognize that you play an active role in the learning process. More specifically, it is likely that you will experience a sense of deeper learning and personal development that is available to you when you become proactive, take risks, and engage in an Integral approach to learning from experience.

An important process that contributes to deeper learning through the Integral approach is reflection. Reflection is characteristic of the UL quadrant in all forms of experiential learning and may result in numerous positive outcomes for students. For example, reflection increases a student's aptitude for change, flexibility, productivity, and innovation (Langer, 1989). Additionally, Boud, Keogh, and Walker (1985) note that the reflective process contributes to new perspectives on one's experience as well as changes in one's behaviour, feelings, attitudes, and values. Rogers (2001) believes that the ultimate intention of reflection "is to integrate

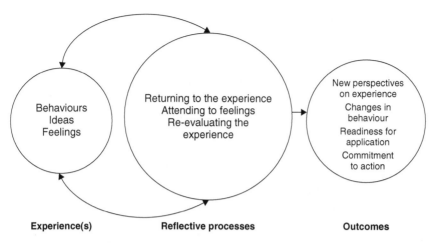

Source: Adapted from *Reflection: Turning experience into learning* (p. 36), by D. Boud, R. Keogh and D. Walker, 1985, London: Kogan Page. Copyright 1985 by David Boud, Rosemary Keogh, David Walker and contributors.

Figure 11.3 Components of reflection

the understanding gained into one's experience in order to enable better choices or actions in the future as well to enhance one's overall effectiveness" (p. 41).

While there are multiple theories and approaches related to reflection, common characteristics of *reflective processes* include: identifying a problem and making a deliberate decision to seek a solution; collecting additional information regarding the problem prior to taking further action; and taking action, testing, or experimenting with new understandings based on the reflective process (Rogers, 2001). Boud et al.'s (1985) model (see Figure 11.3) is presented as a way for students to envision and understand the process of reflection.

Their model includes two main components: the *experience* and the *reflective process*. First, the experience can be any situation or event (such as working under a strict deadline to create a promotional flyer) arising from some kind of discomfort. The totality of an experience, inclusive of reflective objects (for example, behaviours, ideas, and feelings of which students become aware), serves as a starting point in the process. Once an experience is complete, the individual can initiate a reflective process to recapture and evaluate the experience. The reflective process is comprised of three major elements: first, *returning to the experience*; second, *attending to feelings*; and third, *reevaluating the experience*.

The first element of the reflective process requires returning to the experience to recapture or replay observations of events as they happened, what occurred, and your reactions to the experience. As you recapture an event, describing your feelings and behavioural responses is important to reveal new insights and perspectives and to clarify your personal perceptions.

The second element, attending to feelings, requires you to utilize positive feelings and remove obstructive feelings. Utilizing positive feelings can provide you with motivation to face challenging tasks in learning and can help you understand an event more clearly. Moreover, obstructive feelings can block your learning process and, if they are not removed, can form a barrier for your future reflection and awareness.

The third element, *reevaluating the experience*, is comprised of the four aspects of association, integration, validation, and appropriation. *Association* is the reflective connection one makes between ideas and feelings that occur as part of the experience. As new information from the reflective process is linked with existing knowledge and feelings, learners may discover that inconsistencies between old attitudes and new feelings require reassessment. Upon making links and addressing inconsistencies, *integration* allows the student to identify relationships, discriminate, and draw conclusions with new information, ideas, and attitudes when seeking insight into particular issues.

During *validation*, the student determines the authenticity of new ideas and feelings that result during integration and then tests new approaches and perspectives in new situations. For any new knowledge to be fully integrated into the type of learning most valuable within reflection, a final element, called *appropriation*, is necessary (Boud et al., 1985). The reflective process at the appropriation stage refers to a unity of feeling and intellect. The knowledge you gain through appropriation becomes part of your value system and "is less amenable to change than other knowledge which we accept and work with but do not make our own to the same degree" (p. 34).

Environmental conditions are also necessary for promoting and enabling active reflection. These conditions include autonomy, feedback, access, and connection to others, stimulation by others, and significant performance demands (Rogers, 2001; Seibert and Daudelin, 1999). In addition, the facilitator plays an important role in promoting reflection (Loughran, 1996; Schön, 1987; Seibert and Daudelin, 1999).

The facilitator's role includes assisting the student in evaluating incidents within the event management experience, identifying and being aware of feelings, and effectively taking appropriate action within the experience. When promoting reflection, the facilitator must provide the student with support and encouragement by actively listening to his or her reflections and by acting as a sounding board during discussions. This can be accomplished by providing access to resources that assist reflection and by putting the student's needs and interests first.

Boud et al. (1985) point out that the stages and elements of reflection are not independent of each other, nor do they occur in a linear fashion. Reflection is a process that involves a continual cycling back and forth between the elements and a possible exclusion of some stages, depending on the situation. Therefore, reflection is not a step-by-step process that leads to a definitive end. Instead, understanding the elements of the reflection process that lead to outcomes of personal development is important when related to your event management experiences and to your future career.

Activities for reflection

There are a number of techniques used to facilitate reflection. Most often, reflective activities come in the form of structured exercises that "provide a framework for guiding individuals in broadening and deepening their analysis and synthesis of challenging situations and integrating these challenges effectively to enhance their professional effectiveness" (Rogers, 2001, p. 47). Examples of several such activities include the use of guided questions to initiate reflection on specific developmental experiences (Seibert and Daudelin, 1999) and seminar group discussions focused on reflective topics (Loughran, 1996).

As well, students can utilize critical incidents to analyze experiences (Brookfield, 1990) as well as learning partners to exchange ideas and explore personal interests (Boud and Knights, 1996; Robinson, Saberston, and Griffin, 1985). Planned debriefing exercises based on simulated experiences (Lederman, 1992) can also be utilized as part of the reflective process. Of course, students can use reflective journals (Cameron and Mitchell, 1993; Davies, 1995; Heinrich, 1992; Loughran, 1996; Pierson, 1998) or written portfolios (Boud et al., 1985) to help guide the reflective process.

Reflective journal writing is the technique we recommend to you to initiate self-reflection in event management. A primary purpose of reflective journal writing is to support the kind of reflective thinking that will help you achieve deeper levels of learning from your event management experiences (Boud, 2001; Moon, 1999a, 1999b). Journal entries may be representative of whatever creative format you feel comfortable using (for example, streams of consciousness, images, sketches, and poems) to explore what you bring (strengths and weaknesses) to an experience or what you desire from your involvement in an experience. Students may also use journals to uncover meanings embedded in actions and to facilitate the incorporation of feelings and responses to ideas related to working with others (Davies, 1995; Patterson, 1995; Ray, 1994; Rittman, 1995).

A list of initial guiding questions and examples of potential topics for reflection is provided in Figure 11.4: Reflective journal writing in event management.

Questions to initiate and guide reflective writing.	How do you see yourself upon entering the class?
	How do you envision yourself at the end of the semester?
	What desires, needs, and expectations do you have for yourself, the course facilitator(s) and class/group members?
	What concerns (what-if questions) do you have regarding your role within the class and department and your abilities to contribute?
	What do you want to be (character) and to do (contributions and achievements) by the time you finish?
	Within what areas do you think you should focus your improvement and development efforts?
Issues and topics to explore throughout the semester.	Challenges that you face when working with others/ groups.
	Analyze reactions and behaviours during interactions with others, the classroom environment and the facilitator.
	Describe an experience (such as an encounter or situation) in detail and analyze what you might change or not change if encountering a similar situation in the future. Describe what you learned about yourself and others through the experience.
	Outline concerns, issues, satisfactions, dissatisfactions, positive and negative feelings. Explain why and how these might be important for learning.
	Question all implicit and explicit assumptions (such as your own, the facilitator's, those inherent in event management and sport, recreation and tourism management theory and practice).
	Explore previous experiences (such as sport, recreation or tourism management, academic work, other) that do or do not help your personal performance in the event management experience.
	Describe the social environment (such as specific "norms" and values) of the class and how it has shaped your behaviour and the behaviours of your classmates.

Figure 11.4   Reflective journal writing in event management

Application of four quadrants to personal development

Individual reflection is representative of the UL quadrant and is a significant part of the learning process. You may recall, however, that personal development should not be reduced to one quadrant; rather, each quadrant is equally significant and directly correlated with all of the others in relation to your development as an event manager. Therefore, individual reflection (UL), individual observation (UR), collective shared meanings (LL), and collective observed processes, procedures, and systems (LR) together form an Integral approach and make available to you a depth of learning and development through event management experiences.

Therefore, maximizing your personal development requires an active exploration and application of the themes representative of all four quadrants to your experiences in event management. To guide you and your course facilitator through the application process, a set of recommended learning activities associated with the AQAL model is provided in Figure 11.5: Application of the four quadrants to personal development in event management. This list is a starting point and should by no means limit how you explore and apply the quadrants. As you become more familiar with the associated learning themes of each quadrant, you may find additional activities that help you explore and make connections between your experiences and the Integral approach. What is most important is that you take an Integral approach to your personal development when involved in event management experiences.

Conclusion

Unlike traditional approaches, the experiential approach to event management requires you to actively participate in the process to learn and create knowledge. Through active participation in event management, you are exposed to a unique opportunity that can contribute significantly to your development as an event manager, as a member of a working organization, and as a human being. Individuals, however, do not learn or develop in isolation of others or of the environment in which the event management experience occurs. Therefore, to maximize personal development, the authors recommend that students take an Integral approach to their experience.

Wilber's AQAL model offers an Integral approach to learning in that both the individual and collective perspectives are honoured. Specifically, the Integral approach allows for the examination of your event management experience through four quadrants, each with its own perspective. The UL quadrant is characteristic of reality from the individual interior perspective, while the UR quadrant is characteristic of reality from the exterior individual perspective.

Furthermore, the LL quadrant is characteristic of reality from the interior collective perspective, and the LR quadrant is characteristic of reality from the

Recommendation	Quadrant(s)	Learning activity example(s)
Reflective and observational activities taking place prior to, during and at the conclusion of the event.	Upper Left (UL) Individual reflection and dialogue. How "I" come to interpret the experience. Deeper self-understanding. Transformation of personal value.	Student writes a journal entry after each class/staff meeting to explore and interpret their feelings and observations with respect to their role in the meeting, how this affects their perception of their work and future actions.
	Upper Right (UR) Objective observations. Individual analyzes reactions physically "seen." Determine how one's behaviour fits or does not fit the situation.	Course facilitator presents students with a challenge facing an event organization. For example, one issue could be the need to increase the level of self-leadership (Neck and Manz, 2006) among the members. The student is to observe and then during and after the event reflect on their personal understanding of why the problem exists and how they would interpret and potentially address the problem (Argyris, 1991).
Students share and communicate with the event course facilitator what they wish to get out of the experience regarding personal development.	Upper Left (UL) Individual reflection and dialogue. How "I" come to know and interpret the experience. Deeper self-understanding. Transformation of personal values.	Student creates a personal vision statement describing their needs, desires/expectations (of themselves, class facilitator and/or event organization) and concerns related to the event management course (Sweitzer and King, 1999). The student will also convey an understanding of their role within the organization, the role of the course facilitator, and the meaning of the event. This vision statement should be shared with the class facilitator prior to commencing the event management course. Student revisits the vision and writes a follow-up statement at the conclusion of the event to explore if and how the vision was or was not fulfilled, including any personal feelings/self-understandings, problems experienced, or change in values.

Figure 11.5 Application of the four quadrants to personal development in event management

Recommendation	Quadrant(s)	Learning activity example(s)
Activities focused on reporting/recording what particular behaviours, issues (such as power, leadership, communication) are observed and how and if behaviours practiced by individuals and groups match/fit with the formal systems adopted within the organization.	Lower Right (LR) Objective observations of interlocking systems. Functional fit of structures and processes. How systems influence actions and behaviours.	Student records examples of when observed behaviours did not match the desired behaviour of the system. In doing so, the student describes the observed behaviour and any positive or negative outcomes/consequences of that behaviour. Course facilitator provides a list of guided questions that helps student address whether or not what was observed is good or better practice than the formal organizational system "theory" (Cuneen and Sidwell, 1994). Is the behaviour/practice a better fit in terms of organization effectiveness than the system/theory? What does this mean?
Increase the student's awareness of their individual behaviour and their behavioural responses/reactions to others in the event organization.	Upper Right (UR) Objective observations. Individual analyzes reactions physically "seen." Determine how one's behaviour fits or does not fit situation.	Course facilitator observes the "behaviour" of the student in a certain setting (such as under tight deadlines, working on a new initiative). The facilitator informs the student of the particular behaviour and students are asked to describe their behaviour and observe the reactions of those involved. The student repeats this a couple of times and concludes by responding to questions: What did you learn about yourself from observing the reactions of others toward your behaviour; and, How or would you change your behaviour/actions to elicit different responses?
Challenge students to verbally articulate their feelings during the experience as a vehicle for communicating their understanding of unspoken/ written practices, organizational goals and shared values, ethics/morals within the organization and how it relates to their personal development.	Upper Left (UL) Individual reflection and dialogue. How "I" come to know and interpret the experience. Deeper self-understanding. Transformation of personal values.	Student and course facilitator meet monthly to discuss what the student has learned and observed regarding unspoken practices/shared value within the organization. The student uses this meeting as a vehicle to ask questions and seek more insight regarding their interpretation and understanding of the unspoken practices and shared values (for example staff members provide only constructive criticism after presentations of the organization).

Figure 11.5 (Continued)

Recommendation	Quadrant(s)	Learning activity example(s)
	Lower Left (LL) Collective inquiry. Mutual understandings that exist in a culture. One's values in relation to those shared with the organization.	Student makes a brief presentation to course facilitator describing the differences between theory learned in coursework and practice as well as new understandings regarding unspoken practices within the organization that helped or hindered their personal development.
Course facilitators take an active role in helping students recognize and make sense of the self-development and knowledge that can result from an event management experience.	Upper Left (UL) Individual reflection and dialogue. Deeper self-understanding.	Facilitator engages in regular communication with the student and is accessible throughout the course to answer questions and help the student "help themselves" to sort out feelings of anxiety and confusion that arise.
	Upper Right (UR) Individual analyzes reactions to behaviours physically "seen". How one's behaviour fits or does not fit situations. Lower Left (LL) Mutual understandings that exist in a culture. One's values related to those shared with the organization. Lower Right (LR) Functional fit of structures and processes. How systems influence actions and behaviours.	Provide a list of guided questions throughout the experience that encourage students to take note of and interpret relationships between theory and practice while encouraging students to seek to understand new theories and meanings derived from their encounters with the course facilitator, colleagues and the organizational system.

Source: Adapted from "An Integral Approach to Sport Management Internships" by
E. Jowdy, M. McDonald, and K. Spence, 2004, *European Sport Management Quarterly, 4*,
227–229. Copyright 2004 by Meyer and Meyer Sport.

Figure 11.5 (Continued)

exterior collective perspective. When applying the associated learning themes representative of the four quadrants, students can more deeply understand their own and others' experiences throughout the event management process and all future personal and professional experiences.

In this chapter, you are provided with a list of recommended activities, representative of the four quadrants, which you can engage in to understand your experiences from an Integral approach. In addition to these activities, you should be aware that you bring a personal foundation and intent to each experience that influences what you derive and how you develop from your experiences.

As a result, an important first step in your personal development is to examine each (personal foundation and intent) through reflection (UL) and observation of your behaviours (UR). Correspondingly, as a member of an event management organization, you constantly interact with the experiential learning milieu. Upon entering the course, then, you should also make efforts to understand the culture, rituals, norms, and values (LL) and recognize the role of various systems (LR) relevant to the efficient functioning of the event organization.

The steps and activities mentioned above are only the beginning. Whether you are a student in a classroom or an executive working for an agency, all events are experiential in nature, and everything you experience as an event manager has UL, UR, LL, and LR perspectives and, thus, learning themes. Everything you encounter has the potential to deepen your learning and provide new insights that can be applied to future work experiences. More important, if Integrally approached, your experiences contribute to a greater purpose: your development as a person beyond the field of event management.

Chapter questions

1. The authors discuss two major theoretical streams within experiential learning. List and explain these two streams.
2. Explain how the two experiential learning streams come together in Wilber's Integral approach.
3. Define the following perspectives associated with Wilber's AQAL model including (a) upper and lower halves, (b) right- and left-hand paths, (c) upper-left, lower-left quadrants, and (d) upper-right, lower-right quadrants.
4. Describe how the four quadrants relate to the components necessary for meaningful experiential learning.
5. What are the components of reflection and why is the relationship between reflection, experiential learning, and personal development important?

Conclusions

Lorne J. Adams, Brock University

Photograph by Mike Cheliak

Event Management – It sounds finite. It sounds like a discrete point in time. Indeed, it has a beginning and an end point, but event management is certainly not static. It is best to view events as dynamic, complex, and ever-changing entities. No two events are the same; what worked in one situation may not necessarily work in a different but similar situation. That is why this text does not provide you with a series of prescribed checklists that you can simply mark off as you go along. While checklists are helpful, they are static and do not, cannot, take into account the contingency that you will have to deal with. We have spent some time introducing you to some theories that support the notions of change, contingency, and complexity. We suggest that you do further reading in that area. A sound theoretical framework will provide you with an anticipatory set that will help you deal with deviation and the inevitable unforeseen issues. In fact, a message that we have delivered is the need for anticipation in the short term and in the long term. As a critical element in the dynamic system of event management you should now understand that anything you do has the potential to affect many other things. Some of those outcomes will be positive; others will create unforeseen outcomes.

We have also stressed the importance of setting goals and writing them with clarity. Goals need to be communicated clearly to everyone involved. The less clarity, the greater the chance for misinterpretation, and we want everyone to be on the same page and heading in the same direction. You will note throughout the text how often the need for clear goals is expressed both directly and indirectly.

We also have spent a good deal of time talking about planning and committing that planning to paper. You should also be aware that planning exists on a continuum with overplanning and underplanning as polar opposites. The more uncertain we are, the greater the tendency to overplan. The concrete act of planning can become a trap; it can become an end in itself. Immersing yourself in the process feels good; it feels like you are actively involved in problem solving and it produces a highly detailed, visible product – the plan of the event. The more certain we are about an event, perhaps by having done it a number of times, the greater the tendency to underplan. You know what to do because you've been there before or "this is the way it has always been done." Unfortunately, this approach leads to many assumptions about, for instance, who is responsible for what, or what needs to be done. Because the plan is unstated, the chance for oversight or misinterpretation increases dramatically.

Somewhere between these polar extremes is the amount of planning that is right, not only for the event but also for the people involved. Where is that magic place that is not too much and not too little? Unfortunately, there is no way of prescribing where that might be. It is, as we have referred to, in those indeterminant zones (Schön, 1983) that go beyond simply what you have been taught. Experience will help you find that place. As an emerging professional, take the opportunity to volunteer at different events and do as many different jobs as you can. As you begin to see events from different perspectives, you will see how written plans affect your particular function. You will then be developing "event sense" in the same way experiences in the lived world help you develop common sense. You will learn that there are very few absolutes either in life or in event management. There are lots of "sometimes," "in many cases," "in general," "based on my experience." You will also see the need for establishing priorities but will also come to understand that priorities too can change. You have probably already experienced that as part of your academic journey. Ask yourself if your priorities are the same now as when you first entered university. In fact, you could look at getting a degree as personal event management. Goals, plans, priorities are all important but subject to change and deviation. Many things can cause change, and they all can provide different effects. You have had to manage all those things in the pursuit of your degree and probably have been fairly successful thus far.

We have also pointed out the need to analyze events. It is essential to analyze errors, where they might have come from, what processes were in place that set the stage for their occurrence, and so forth. At some point in time you will accept your own fallibility that sometimes errors are a direct result of our own action or inaction, and that we tend to court disaster in our own unique ways through prior experience, bias, or ability. Error, however, is only a small part of the overarching need for evaluation. Once again though, evaluation needs to be placed in context. For what purpose, to what end is evaluation being conducted? What is or should be evaluated? These questions have been posed in previous pages, and we have tried to give you a reasonable starting point to answer them.

Many different authors have tried to bring to bear their experience and to condense a vast amount of knowledge into manageable and useful sketches that will help you develop the tools to be a successful event manager. None of the chapters is intended to be conclusive. We have recommended throughout the text that you continue to read in the several areas – to develop common knowledge that will help you develop advanced knowledge. Some of the chapters will seem like they are speaking directly to you; they will resonate with your experience, skills, and present abilities. You will struggle with some of the chapters, as they will take you outside the comfort zone of your present skills and abilities. This is the place you want to be; it is where the most development will take place. Spend time with them until you are comfortable, and then seek out the next place of discomfort. We have mentioned in several places that events will grow and evolve – so will you. If the previous pages have been or can be an agent in that evolution, we have done our job.

Appendix A: Example of an operational plan for the National Collegiate Athletic Association (NCAA) Men's Basketball Championship, Round 2, San Jose, California: The hospitality component

Lauren Thompson

The following chart offers an example of an event operational plan. This particular plan outlines examples of the operational details for the hospitality functions for an elite National Collegiate Athletic Association (NCAA) Men's Basketball Championship, Round 2 held in San Jose, California. The event included a 4-day schedule, Wednesday to Saturday. A total of three games were held during the 4 days (two games on Thursday and one on Saturday). Four teams participated with two being eliminated after Thursday's games. Wednesday and Friday were practice days. At the end of the 4 days, the winning team moved to the next stage of the tournament to be held at a different facility. An American university served as the host for this event, using a professional sport-level facility as the venue.

As the hospitality coordinator for this event, I have created an operational planning chart to provide you with an example of the types of responsibilities that are included when preparing to stage hospitality areas and coordinating all elements using volunteer assistance. The general duties of the overall hospitality committee included, but were not limited to, creating and fulfilling all catering contracts for the event for athletes, coaches, official evaluators, officials, staff, volunteers, and the basketball committee representatives for lunches, dinners, beverages, and snacks. This required hospitality plans to be staged at the event venue and the host hotel.

As you review the chart below, position yourself as the individual responsible for implementing each detail listed. Record any arising questions as you consider how you are to implement the plan. Develop additional level 3 detail for the plan. How would you advance and adapt this plan if you were responsible? Also, how would you adapt your personal operational plan to ensure you have prepared all items in advance?

Time frame	Task	Responsibility
3 months prior	*Budget development* Obtain the budget for the hospitality committee from the host university – develop a budget overview chart to personally keep track of your hospitality spending – continuously develop the budget details to have a realistic picture of the budget at all times	Facilitated by the event hospitality coordinator
	Hospitality preparation Create an overview of all of the hospitality areas to be set up in the competition venue, the potential capacity, constituents to cater to, food/beverage requirements for patrons and volunteers, and equipment requirements – include: staff/media buffet, locker rooms, officials' rooms, official evaluators' room,	Event hospitality coordinator

Time frame	Task	Responsibility
	basketball committee room, black room/press conference area, media refreshment area and breakfast/evening hospitality room at the host hotel – include: constituent to cater to athletes, coaches, officials, official evaluators, media, host university staff, volunteers and basketball committee	
	Competition venue facility manager meeting Meet the host venue's facility manager and event coordinators with host university staff – go on a site visit and become familiar with the venue – determine: the hospitality food and beverage areas, all set-up details, storage areas available, including size and access process – obtain diagrams of the facility and create a specific site-map of all event hospitality areas – develop a written timeline and list of hospitality preparation or set-up details	Event hospitality coordinator and competition venue facility manager
	Confirmations Confirm set-up areas with the host university staff by: – communicating with the facility manager the site-map timeline and details	Event hospitality coordinator
	Competition venue food services meeting Arrange meeting with the facility's food services manager – prepare for meeting by creating an outline of the different areas for hospitality services, the number of people to cater to, and the type of food/beverage to be served for discussion – obtain the already existent sponsorship contacts and the list of products that will be provided that apply to the hospitality component of the event	Event hospitality coordinator and competition venue food services manager

Time frame	Task	Responsibility
	– attend meeting and discuss the catering options based on the event budget and the type and number of people for catering service – also discuss event beverage sponsors who will provide certain products to be served – determine the appropriate area and time for product dropoff – develop potential catering contracts (determine approval process for approving and signing contracts) – confirm catering contracts at venue with the host university staff – communicate with the facility's food services manager the final food/beverage requirements for the venue catering contracts. Notify them that the delivery times will be communicated at a later date once game and practice times are established	
	Host hotel meeting Arrange meeting with host hotel to discuss hotel hospitality area and menu options/ contracts for the daily media breakfast and evening drinks and snacks – attend meeting with the host hotel and determine the area for media hospitality and the hours of operation, and establish the food and beverage contracts. These should be served in a buffet-style format. During the evening hospitality time, a server will be required to serve alcoholic beverages. All of the details should be agreed upon based on the hospitality committee's budget – confirm hotel catering contracts with the host university staff	Event hospitality coordinator and host hotel food services representative

Time frame	Task	Responsibility
	– communicate with the host hotel the final food/beverage requirements for the catering contracts	
	Coordinate sponsor hospitality details – work with the sponsor committee to communicate to event sponsors the details for hospitality product time and dropoff at the venue and host hotel	Event hospitality coordinator and the sponsor committee
2 months prior	*Hospitality volunteer development* Obtain the tentative schedule for event game and practice times from the host university – determine the hospitality areas where volunteer staff will be needed – determine the number of volunteer staff required to fulfill the duties of the hospitality areas – determine the potential shift times for the volunteer positions based on the tentative schedule for game and practice times – communicate the staffing requirements to the staffing coordinator. Ensure to include extra bodies to help cover positions in case of dropouts or no shows. The staffing coordinator will be responsible for volunteer recruitment and assignment	Hospitality coordinator and staffing coordinator
	Hospitality signage Determine all signage needs for the hospitality areas – provide diagram of all signage placement in the venue and host hotel – communicate to the host university the signage required and its placement (including date and time requirements)	Hospitality coordinator and signage committee
1 month prior	*Volunteer assignment* Obtain the list of contacts who will be volunteering for the hospitality component from the staffing coordinator	

Time frame	Task	Responsibility
	– determine the appropriate hospitality volunteer shifts for each of 4 days of the tournament – assign the volunteers in the contact list to daily hospitality shifts – prepare a daily schedule of events, individual schedules, and list of responsibilities and duties to be included in the volunteer training packages for the hospitality committee to distribute at volunteer training. Also include the venue site map of the hospitality areas – submit the hospitality committee documents for the volunteer training packages to the staffing coordinator and determine the volunteer training dates. The staffing coordinator will make all of the training packages and call each volunteer to inform them of their training times – create volunteer training agenda for the volunteer training night. Following the main presentation, volunteers will be broken up into committees for 30 minutes for specialized training and a venue walk-through	
2 weeks prior	*Volunteer hospitality training* – attend volunteer training sessions – conduct a specific training session to communicate all of the hospitality committee details to the assigned volunteers – conduct a walk-through of the venue and point out where all of the hospitality areas are as well as the beverage storage area to be used if beverages are running low before new delivery times – show the volunteers where the proper entrances and exits are and where radios (if necessary) and credentials can be picked up	Hospitality coordinator and staffing coordinator

Time frame	Task	Responsibility
	– ensure time is allocated for a question-answer period – for those hospitality volunteers unable to attend the training, ensure that arrangements are made for them to pick up their training package and uniform and communicate any essential information from the training session	
	Credentials or accreditation – arrange for the creation of credentials or accreditation for the hospitality coordinator and all of the hospitality volunteers for the competition venue and host hotel. The credentials indicate the name and access areas the person is allowed to enter – arrange for the distribution of credentials for the hospitality coordinator and hospitality volunteers – distribute information to all volunteers concerning their access, entrance areas for the competition venue and host hotel, and their credential access allowance – understand the system for replacing credentials should anyone lose or forget their credentials	Hospitality coordinator and credentialing coordinator
	Confirmations – confirm all game and practice times with the host university – confirm and adjust the catering and staffing details, if needed – contact the sponsor committee and ensure food/beverage event sponsors' product and delivery times are confirmed and exact delivery site and contact names are provided. Ensure all deliveries will take place the day before the event begins. Keep an overview of contact names and numbers to call should deliveries be delayed	Hospitality coordinator

Time frame	Task	Responsibility
	− confirm with facility manager the set-up areas and where signage is to be hung (and how it is to be fastened) − confirm signage has arrived at facility from the Signage Committee to the venue and delivered to the facility manager − confirm with the food services manager at host hotel: the catering contracts, all menu items, including breakfast and evening catering requirements, delivery times, clean-up times, sponsor product use and placement, the signage to be placed at the hotel directing patrons to the hospitality area and the signage in the hospitality area to be hung by the event volunteers − receive a copy of all finalized contracts from the venue and host hotel and review details again	
	Event daily review meetings − arrange a meeting time and location with the host university venue and host hotel facility managers for each morning of the event to ensure all hospitality details are reviewed and are correct	Hospitality coordinator, competition venue facility manager, and the host hotel facility manager
Day before the event	*Final preparations* − arrive at venue and conduct a venue walk-through to oversee that all hospitality areas are in the proper spots and are set up correctly, and that all of the necessary signage is present − ensure all sponsor product has been delivered and stored at the proper location − check into the hotel − conduct a walk-through of the host hotel hospitality areas and ensure all are correctly set and signage is up	Hospitality coordinator

Time frame	Task	Responsibility
Day 1: Practice day	*Event day activities*	
6:30 am	– arrive at host hotel hospitality area be sure to have credentials on hand – ensure that all breakfast setups are complete, and that the proper food is out for the buffet and signage is out properly – speak with the hotel representative in charge and retrieve an extension number to call if any food/beverage is running low	Hospitality coordinator and volunteer A
7:00 am–10:00 am	– greet all media guests into the breakfast room – check for proper credentials upon each person's entry	Volunteer A
8:00 am	– go to the competition venue and be sure to have credentials on hand – conduct walk-through of the competition venue hospitality areas to ensure all areas are set up correctly – conduct a final volunteer briefing session	Hospitality coordinator
8:30 am	– meet with the competition venue food services manager to confirm all daily catering details	Hospitality coordinator and competition venue food services manager
8:45 am	– report to media refreshment area and go through your checklist to ensure that all food, beverage, and supplies (cups, napkins, bowls, tablecloths, cloths to wipe up spills, and so on) have been delivered to the media refreshment area – ensure tables are set – one for beverage distribution and the other for snacks to be distributed	Volunteers B, C, D and hospitality coordinator

Time frame	Task	Responsibility
8:30 am–5:00 pm	– main duty is to be a floater and conduct regular checks on every hospitality area to ensure its smooth functioning as well as to fulfill any special requests and manage volunteers	Hospitality coordinator
9:00 am	– work areas and courtside areas open to the media	Competition venue facility manager
9:00 am–5:00 pm	– work in the media refreshment area – drinks should be poured for the media by the volunteers in order to save product – ensure that the area is kept tidy at all times – the food services staff will be doing regular deliveries; however, if product is running low, communicate to either the coordinator or one of the food services staff. If necessary, use stock from the storage area – the janitorial staff to complete regular cleanup as scheduled; however, if their services are required at other times, communicate to either the coordinator or one of the janitorial staff directly – volunteers at the media refreshment area will take turns eating lunch and take breaks as scheduled, ensuring that the area is never unattended	Volunteers B, C, D
10:00 am	– arrive at venue and be sure credentials are on hand – gather beverages from storage areas and fill two coolers in each locker room with drinks and ice (one water and one a sponsored replenishment drink). Ensure different flavours of the replenishment drink are present. The coolers and buckets of ice will already be placed in the locker rooms by the food services staff	Volunteer E

Time frame	Task	Responsibility
10:00 am–4:30 pm	– conduct regularly scheduled check of the locker rooms to ensure coolers remain stocked with fresh ice throughout the duration of the day. *Note*: do not enter the locker rooms if they are occupied by the teams	Volunteer E
10:30 am	– team entrance opens	Competition venue facility manager
10:30 am	– ensure that the basketball committee room is set up and that their meals, beverages, and snacks are all in place	Volunteer F
11:00 am–2:00 pm	– ensure that the basketball committee room stays tidy and meal food stays hot and fresh – the food services staff will be doing regular deliveries; however, if product is running low, communicate to either the coordinator or one of the food services staff	Volunteer F
11:00 am–4:30 pm	– ensure that the basketball committee room stays tidy and snacks and beverages stay stocked – the food services staff will be doing regular deliveries; however, if product is running low, communicate to either the coordinator or one of the food services staff. If necessary, use stock from the storage area	Volunteer F
11:00 am	– facility opens to the public	
11:00 am	– arrive at venue and obtain credential – ensure that the media/staff buffet area is set up and that the correct food, beverages, and supplies are in place according to the catering contracts – put up the "staff only" buffet sign in the staff/media buffet area	Volunteer G

Time frame	Task	Responsibility
11:30 am– 12:30 pm	– check the buffet area to ensure it is ready and then communicate over the radio that the staff buffet is ready and for all coordinators to send their volunteers when they are able to get away for their meal – staff buffet takes place – ensure the area remains tidy and stocked and that no bottles leave the area. All drinks must be poured into cups – the food services staff will be doing regular deliveries; however, if product is running low, communicate to either the coordinator or one of the food services staff – the janitorial staff will be doing regular cleanup; however, if their services are required communicate to either the coordinator or one of the janitorial staff	Hospitality coordinator and volunteer G
12:00 noon–12:50 pm	Team #1 practice	
12:30 pm– 2:00 pm	– ensure the "media buffet" sign is up in the staff/media buffet area – welcome the media personnel into the buffet area – check for proper credentials at the door – watch for and keep any person without proper media credentials out of the area – ensure the area remains tidy and stocked and that no bottles leave the area. All drinks must be poured into cups	Volunteer G
12:30 pm	– ensure the delivery and proper set up of Team #1's box lunches into their locker room is made on time	Volunteer E
12:30 pm	– ensure that the area for the press conferences is set up and the beverages and supplies are stocked	Volunteer F
1:00 pm-1:50 pm	Team #2 practice	

Time frame	Task	Responsibility
1:00 pm–3:30 pm	– press conferences take place – ensure the area remains tidy and stocked	Volunteer F
1:30 pm	– ensure the delivery and proper set up of Team #2's box lunches into their locker room is made on time	Volunteer E
2:10 pm–3:00 pm	Team 3 practice	
2:40 pm	– ensure the delivery and proper set up of Team #3's box lunches into their locker room is made on time	Volunteer E
3:10 pm–4:00 pm	Team 4 practice	
3:40 pm	– ensure the delivery and proper set up of Team #4's box lunches into their locker room	Volunteer E
4:30 pm	– arrive at hotel hospitality area and ensure that the proper snacks and beverages are set up and a server is present for the cash bar	Volunteer A
5:00 pm–8:00 pm	– greet all media guests into the hospitality room – check for proper credentials upon each person's entry	Volunteer A
5:30 pm	– ensure all hospitality areas are tidy and any necessary products or supplies are put away – confirm all shift times for the following day	All volunteers and hospitality coordinator
Day 2: Game day		
6:30 am	– arrive at hotel hospitality area – ensure that all breakfast set ups are complete and the proper food is out for the buffet	Volunteer A
7:00 am–10:00 am	– greet all media guests into the breakfast room – check for proper credentials upon each person's entry	Volunteer A

Appendix A

Time frame	Task	Responsibility
8:00 am	– arrive at venue – conduct walk-through of the venue to ensure all hospitality areas are set up correctly	Hospitality coordinator
8:15 am	– meet with the food services manager to confirm all daily catering details	Hospitality coordinator
8:30 am–11:00 pm	– the main duty is to be a floater and conduct regular checks on every hospitality area to ensure its smooth functioning as well as to fulfill any special requests	Hospitality coordinator
8:30 am	– arrive at venue – gather beverages from storage areas and fill two coolers in each locker room with drinks and ice. The coolers and buckets of ice will already be placed in the locker rooms by the food services staff	Volunteer E
8:30 am–9:30 pm	– ensure the locker room coolers remain stocked with fresh ice throughout the duration of the day. Ensure regular checks are made of the coolers; however, do not enter the locker rooms if they are occupied by the teams	Volunteer E
9:00 am	– team entrance opens	
9:30 am	– arrive at venue – ensure that all food, beverages, and supplies (cups, napkins, bowls, tablecloths, and so on) have been delivered to the media refreshment area – set up both tables neatly. One table should be used for beverages and the other for snacks	Volunteers B, C, D
10:00 am–11 pm	– work the media refreshment area. Drinks should be poured for the media by the volunteers in order to save product	Volunteers B, C, D

Time frame	Task	Responsibility
	− ensure the area is kept tidy at all times − the food services staff will be doing regular deliveries; however, if product is running low, communicate to either the coordinator or one of the food services staff. If necessary use stock from the storages area − the janitorial staff will be doing regular cleanup; however, if their services are required communicate to either the coordinator or one of the janitorial staff − volunteers at the media refreshment area will take turns eating lunch and dinner and taking breaks, ensuring that the area never remains unattended	
10:00 am	− backstage work areas open to the media	
10:00 am– 1:50 pm	− closed practices (Team #1, #2, #3, #4)	
10:30 am	− arrive at venue − ensure that the basketball committee room is set up and that their meals, beverages, and snacks are all in place	Volunteer F
11:00 am– 2:00 pm	− ensure the basketball committee room remains tidy and meals stay hot and fresh − the food services staff will be doing regular deliveries; however, if product is running low, communicate to either the coordinator or one of the food services staff	Volunteer F
11:00 am– 7:00 am	− ensure the basketball committee room remains tidy and snacks and beverages stay stocked − the food services staff will be doing regular deliveries; however, if product is running low, communicate to either the coordinator or one of the food services staff	Volunteer F

Time frame	Task	Responsibility
12:00 noon	– arrive at competition venue – ensure that the media/staff buffet is set up and that the correct food, beverages, and supplies are in place according to the contracts – put up the "staff only" buffet sign – confirm with the facility manager the proper spot for delivery of pizza at 5:00 pm – obtain a credit card from the host university staff to order pizza for the volunteers – call a local pizza restaurant and preorder 50 large pizzas of various kinds to be delivered to the venue for 5:00 pm. Ensure to communicate the location for dropoff and the credit card information for payment – communicate the details of the pizza delivery to the volunteer running the staff/media buffet area, as this will be the area used for dinner – communicate the details of the pizza dinner to the food services staff. Beverages will be required in the staff/media buffet area by 4:30 pm	Volunteer G Hospitality coordinator
12:30 pm–1:30 pm	– check the buffet area to ensure it is ready and then communicate over the radio that the staff buffet is ready and for all coordinators to send their volunteers when possible – staff buffet takes place – ensure the area remains tidy and stocked and that no bottles leave the area. All drinks must be poured into cups – the food services staff will be doing regular deliveries; however, if product is running low, communicate to either the coordinator or one of the food service staff	Hospitality coordinator Volunteer G

Time frame	Task	Responsibility
	– the janitorial staff will be doing regular cleanup; however, if their services are required communicate to either the coordinator or one of the janitorial staff	
1:30 pm–4:00 pm	– welcome the media personnel into the buffet area – check for proper credentials and turn away any person who does not have the proper media credential – ensure the area stays tidy and stocked and that no one leaves the area with bottles. All drinks must go into cups	Volunteer G
2:30 pm	– ensure that the official evaluators' room is set up and the accurate snacks and beverages are present – ensure that the officials' room is set up and the accurate snacks and beverages are present – ensure that the cheerleading warm-up area is stocked with snacks and beverages	Volunteer F
3:00 pm–10:00 pm	– ensure the official evaluators' room stays tidy and stocked with snacks and beverages – ensure the officials' room stays tidy and stocked with snacks and beverages – ensure the cheerleading warm-up area remains tidy and stocked with snacks and beverages – the food services staff will be doing regular deliveries; however, if product is running low in the cheerleading warm-up area, communicate to either the coordinator or one of the food services staff. If necessary use stock from the storage area	Volunteer F
3:00 pm	The doors open to the public	

Time frame	Task	Responsibility
4:00 pm	– call the pizza restaurant to confirm delivery of 50 large pizzas at 5:00 pm – gather three hospitality volunteers to meet at the delivery location to help bring in the pizzas	Hospitality coordinator
4:30 am	Game #1	
5:00 pm	– report to the pizza delivery location – bring the pizzas into the staff/media buffet area and set them up buffet style, separating the different kinds – ensure the beverages have been set up in the staff/media area – hang up the "staff-only" sign in the staff/media buffet area	Hospitality coordinator and three hospitality volunteers Volunteer G
5:15 pm	– communicate over the radio that the pizza is ready and for all coordinators to send their volunteers when possible	Hospitality coordinator
5:30 pm	– ensure the box lunches have been delivered into the official evaluators' room – ensure the box lunches have been delivered into the official's room	Volunteer F
6:00 pm	– ensure the box lunches have been delivered to the game #1 team locker rooms – ensure the holding area for the press conferences is set up and the beverages and supplies are stocked	Volunteer E
6:30 pm–10:30 pm	– press conferences take place – ensure the holding area remains tidy and stocked with beverages	Volunteer F
7:00 pm	Game #2	
7:30 pm	– pizza dinner ends – put any leftover pizzas into the volunteer room	Volunteer G

Time frame	Task	Responsibility
9:00 pm	– arrive at hotel hospitality area and ensure the proper snacks and beverages are set up and a server is present for the cash bar	Volunteer A
9:30 pm–12:00 noon	– greet all media guests into the hospitality room – check for proper credentials upon each person's entry	Volunteer A
9:30 pm	– ensure the box lunches have been delivered to the game #2 team locker rooms	Volunteer E
11:00 pm	– ensure all hospitality areas are tidy and any necessary products are put away – confirm shift times for the following day	All volunteers and coordinator
Day 3: Practice day	Follow the same logical steps as were used on day 1 based on the following daily schedule: 10:30 am – Backstage work areas open to the media 12:00 noon – Team entrance opens 1:00 pm–2:30 pm – Team #1 closed practice 3:00 pm–4:30 pm – Team #2 closed practice 1:30 pm–4:30 pm – Press conferences/ interviews	
Day 4: Game day	Follow the same steps used on day 2 based on the following daily schedule: 10:00 am – Team entrance opens 11:00 am – Backstage work areas open to the media 11:00 am–11:50 am – Team #1 closed practice 12:00 noon–12:50 pm – Team #2 closed practice 4:00 pm – Game 6:00 pm–8:00 pm – Press conferences/ interviews	

– During any downtime in their assigned areas, the hospitality volunteers were asked to help cover other hospitality areas. On occasion during their downtime, the volunteers had permission to watch the basketball games/practices.

Appendix B: Facilitation issues and suggestions for the implementation, monitoring, and management phase of the planning model

Scott McRoberts

A key challenge when staging an event involves the facilitation of the operational network members during the implementation, monitoring, and management phase of the planning model. Communication between the network operational members is essential for success. In addition, it is important to facilitate the management of some common implementation issues such as communication, motivation and direction, credentialing issues, and personnel issues. Each issue is outlined below, and suggestions for event managers to facilitate their management are offered.

Facilitating communication

The facilitation of an effective communication processes is crucial for an event to run properly. Experience indicates that the majority of communication issues arise in the first hours of the opening of an event. This can often cause mass confusion over the communication lines (such as radios, walkie talkies, or clear com's) established for an event. From my experience at a National Collegiate Athletic Association (NCAA) Men's Basketball Championship and the San Francisco International Children's Games, where over 400 volunteers and 100 staff were involved in each event, at least one-third of the operational network members need to be connected to the communication system radios. Therefore, an event manager must facilitate the proper use of the communication system as a key element in helping to resolve situations in a fast and timely manner. In addition, the proper use of the communication system aids to keep the airways clear in case of an emergency.

The following are a few strategies for proper communication or radio protocol:

Departmentalize the operational network members into different channels on the system (such as transportation on a different radio channel than food and beverage). Be sure to provide a list of channels to all network members on the communication system to make it easy to contact each event component.

Facilitate with a calm voice and slow delivery of your message (speaking fast indicates panic and lack of comfort with the situation as well as the likelihood of having to repeat your message to be understood).

Facilitate the use of the communication system by making sure all users state their name first followed by the person's name they are attempting to contact (such as: "John to Jane, come in"). This eliminates the use of the communication system to ask who they are trying to contact.

Facilitate the use of the finishing word "over" to aid others on the system to know when a person has completed their statement(s).

Facilitate the use of the communication system by training members to not interrupt conversations until they have been completed, unless it is an emergency. Facilitate the use of the term "clear" to indicate when a conversation is over so that the next person waiting for air time can proceed.

Facilitate a stated protocol for when and how the communication system battery packs are to be recharged, if applicable. Also, preprogrammed times for changing the battery packs to ensure all communication system devices are working at all times must be facilitated. No casual chatter should be allowed on the system, as it wastes the battery charge.

Facilitate the ability to speak to individuals privately should the need arise. It is important that a private line is available for such circumstances.

Facilitating motivation and direction

Sport, recreation and tourism events that are staged for longer than one day in length require an event manager to facilitate a high level of morale and energy throughout the members of the operational network, and this can be a challenge. You may be aware of the phrase "it's all about the first impression." However, in event management it is also the reverse; the last impression of the event is also vitally important to participants, spectators, sponsors, and all partners. It is important for the event manager to consistently facilitate the interactions with network members staging the event to maintain the professionalism from the first to the last day of the event.

One way to facilitate a high level of motivation is to constantly show a presence. The event manager must be available and responsive to network members' issues. This involves facilitating the care and concern of each member for a fair and effective process for providing breaks or rotating positions. It is also the event manager's role to provide a sense of appreciation throughout the event. A simple comment such as "good job" can mean a lot to a member.

Facilitating appropriate direction to operational network members during the staging of an event is also an important role for an event manager. The following are a few strategies for facilitating direction with a process for continuous dialogue to aid production.

> After an initial briefing meeting prior to the start of an event, a daily production meeting can be held. This meeting can be offered at the end of the event day or held in the early morning hours each morning of the event. It is important that this meeting be facilitated to stay on the agenda topics and conducted in a short time period (such as in one hour's time).
>
> Another process can be a debriefing page posted for members to review. This provides members with an overview of changes and can confirm activities as well as can be presented in an inspirational and upbeat message to aid morale.

Whatever process is used, it is important that an event manager facilitates event changes with the operational network members and eliminates the occurrence of repeated problems. An event is conducted in an environment of change and interpretations that can lead to issues or problems. It is important that a process for continuous dialogue is established and facilitated to allow key personnel the opportunity to collectively provide input on the current state of the implementation, monitoring, and management of an event and to provide positive suggestions for moving the event forward.

Facilitating through credentialing issues

A key challenge in event management involves the credentialing or accreditation process at an event. This can be a large issue if an event anticipates a significant media presence. The following are suggestions for alleviating credentialing issues:

- Facilitate a process to develop an understanding of the number of individuals that may attend but have not registered for a credential or accreditation pass and a system for managing these individuals upon arrival. It is important to have a plan in place as well as personnel to deal with this issue. It is also important to monitor the process and to adapt to be able to provide additional personnel should they be needed or to reassign members should there be only a few unregistered individuals arriving.
- There will be credentials that have misspelled names or provide the wrong access within the event venue. Having a credential machine on site with a dedicated and qualified person to operate the machine will help resolve these issues in a timely manner.
- Subdivide all credentials alphabetically and spread out the distribution sites of each group of alphabetical credentials to make the process efficient without a lot of congestion.

Facilitating personality issues

It is important for an event manager to facilitate the management of common situations that arise due to the personalities of the members within the operational network. There are three common issues that every event manager should be cognizant of and be prepared to manage: the fan versus the worker scenario, personality conflicts, and the need to rotate members to other positions for the purpose of advancing their experience.

The fan versus worker scenario is common in the majority of events. Volunteers apply for a role in an event because they have an interest in the product. This situation can produce one of two potential outcomes. The first outcome is a great operational network member who, because of their interest in the event, maintains professionalism and attention to their position or duties. The second outcome is a network member who becomes a spectator and is looking for access to participants, autographs, and perks that mean they do not pay attention to their position or duties. It is important for an event manager to establish, communicate, and facilitate the rules for participation at the outset and create a zero tolerance policy for infractions. These infractions are witnessed in all types of events and can have an adverse effect on the motivation, direction, and professionalism of others involved in the event.

Personality conflicts abound in event management. It is important for an event manager to position members within their strengths and to manage personality conflicts as they arise. Long hours at an event can lead to short fuses or those who are impatient with others they are working with. Other conflicts arise from individuals who think tasks should be completed in a particular manner that differs from what is in the operational plan. Facility managers must be cognizant of these types of situations and facilitate the efficient and effective management of the conflicts in a timely manner. One way to establish a process that aids to alleviate such conflicts is to rotate members within a series of positions.

Facilitating a rotation of members between a series of event positions is a good way to meet the needs of members that ask to expand their experiences and develop their skills, to help keep members alert during events that are staged over many days as well as to alleviate personality conflicts. A process that does not impede the outcome of a successful event must be developed to offer the opportunity to "shuffle" event operational members to a new post or a series of new posts. While doing this it is important that event mangers be cautious, as they must first provide the training to cover the new duties and must involve the members in the production meetings that update the members. In addition, the member must be flexible and competent to manage a changing environment of tasks.

Learning the strengths of the members is difficult, especially when there are potentially hundreds of members involved in staging an event. In some situations there may be members that are better suited to positions that require continued interaction with people, whether it involves celebrities, event members, or consumers. Having an upbeat and positive member that can think on their feet will only reflect positively on the event as a whole. Furthermore, you may be able to determine if an individual is better suited to one specific task, one which may not involve decision making. Therefore, rotating members is a difficult activity to facilitate and, once begun, it requires constant monitoring and management. If facilitated effectively, a rotating process can leave event members happier and more experienced in the end.

Conclusion

The role of the event manager is very complex. The environment is forever changing. It is important that the event manager facilitates the event implementation, monitoring, and management activities to ensure the vision of the event is accomplished. Therefore, the vision must be conveyed to all event operational members, and they must be reminded of the vision throughout the staging of the event, especially as common implementation issues are being managed.

Remember, an important person in the entire process is the event manager. This means you must facilitate your own process to maintain control of your emotions, remain calm, be positive, and present a positive perspective while managing all implementation issues. This includes presenting an attitude that situations can be solved positively, in a timely manner, with demonstrated professionalism and confidence. The manner in which an event manager conducts themselves highly influences the operational network members and ultimately the outcome of the event.

An important element for an event manager is to enjoy the facilitation process and see the fruition of well-prepared tasks or activities happen over many tireless nights. Relaxation techniques aid an event manger to worry about only the elements they can control and to have an overall perspective of the event to be able to determine which elements these involve.

References

Chapter 1 Traditional and niche sport, recreation and tourism events

Bell, D. (1973). *The coming of post-industrial society*. New York: Basic Books.

Choo, W. and Bontis, N. (Eds). (2002). *The strategic management of intellectual capital and organizational knowledge*. New York Oxford University Press.

Cobb, P., Confrey, J., diSess, A., Lehrer, R. and Schauble, L. (2003). Design experiments in educational research. *Educational Researcher, 32*(1), 9–13.

Hall, H. (2001). Input-friendliness: Motivating knowledge sharing across intranets. *Journal of Information Science, 27*(3), 139–146.

Hirschhorn, L. (1984). *Beyond mechanization: Work and technology in a post-industrial age*. Cambridge, MA: MIT Press.

Homer-Dixon, T. (2001). *The ingenuity gap: Can we solve the problems of the future?* Toronto, ON: Vintage Canada.

Jensen, R. (1999). *The dream society: How the coming shift from information to imagination will transform your business*. New York: McGraw-Hill.

Kouzes, J. and Posner, B. (2003). *Credibility: How leaders gain and lose it, why people demand it*. San Francisco: Jossey-Bass.

Kozlowski, S., Brown, K., Weissbein, D., Cannon-Bowers, J. and Salas, E. (2000). A multilevel approach to training effectiveness: Enhancing horizontal and vertical transfer. In K.J. Klein and S.W.J. Kozlowski (Eds), *Multilevel theory, research and methods in organizations* (pp. 157–210). San Francisco: Jossey-Bass.

Limerick, D., Cunnington, B. and Crowther, F. (1998). *Managing the new organization: Collaboration and sustainability in the post-corporate world* (2nd ed.). Sydney: Business and Professional Publishing.

Sproull, L. and Kiesler, S. (1991). *Connections: New ways of working the networked organization*. Cambridge: MIT Press.

Zuboff, S. (1988). *In the age of the smart machine: The future of work and power*. New York: Basic Books.

Chapter 2 The concept of knowledge in event management

Beeth, M. (1995, April). *Conceptual change instruction: Some theoretical and pedagogical issues*. Paper presented at the Annual Meeting of the National Association for Research in Science Teaching, San Francisco, CA.

Bell, D. (1973). *The coming of post-industrial society: A venture in social forecasting.* New York: Basic Books.

Blackler, F. (1995). Knowledge, knowledge work and organizations: An overview and interpretation. *Organization Studies, 16*(6), 1021–1046.

Boisot, M. (2002). The creation and sharing of knowledge. In W.C. Choo and N. Bontis (Eds), *The strategic management of intellectual capital and organizational knowledge* (pp. 65–77). New York: Oxford University Press.

Brown, J. and Duguid, P. (1991). Organizational learning and communities-of-practice: Toward a unified view of working, learning and innovation. *Organization Science, 2,* 40–57.

Castells, M. (2000). *The information age: Economy, society and culture* (2nd ed.). Oxford: Blackwell.

Carney, M. (2001). The development of a model to manage change: Reflection on a critical incident in a focus group setting – An innovative approach. *Journal of Nursing Management, 8*(5), 3–9.

Collins, H. (1993). The structure of knowledge. *Social Research, 60,* 95–116.

Conner, K. and Prahalad, C.K. (2002). A resource-based theory of the firm: Knowledge versus opportunism. In W.C. Choo and N. Bontis (Eds), *The strategic management of intellectual capital and organizational knowledge* (pp. 103–131). New York: Oxford University Press.

Drucker, P. (1994). The age of social transformation. *Atlantic Monthly, 275*(5), 53–80.

Edvinsson, L. and Malone, T. (1997). *Intellectual capital.* New York: Harper-Business.

English, M. and Baker, W. (2006). *Winning the knowledge transfer race.* New York: McGraw-Hill.

Fullan, M., (2001). *Leading in a culture of change.* Etobicoke, ON: John Wiley.

Grant, R. (1996). Prospering in dynamically competitive environments: Organizational capability as knowledge integration. *Organization Science, 7,* 375–387.

Gupta, A. and MacDaniel, J. (2002). Creating competitive advantage by effectively managing knowledge: A framework for knowledge management. *Journal of Knowledge Management Practice, 3*(2), 40–49.

Harris, L., Coles, A. and Dickson, K. (2000). Building innovation networks: Issues of strategy and expertise. *Technology Analysis and Strategic Management, 12*(2), 229–241.

Homer-Dixon, T. (2001). *The ingenuity gap: Can we solve the problems of the future?* Toronto, ON: Vintage Canada.

Kogut, B. and Zander, U. (1992). Knowledge of the firm, combinative capabilities, and the replication of technology. *Organization Science, 3*(3), 383–397.

Leonard, D. and Sensiper, S. (2002). The role of tacit knowledge in group innovation. In W.C. Choo and N. Bontis (Eds), *The strategic management of intellectual capital and organizational knowledge* (pp. 485–499). New York: Oxford University Press.

Nelson, R. and Winter, S. (1982). *An evolutionary theory of economic change.* Cambridge, MA: Belknap.

Nonaka, I. and Takeuchi, H. (1995). *The knowledge-creating company: How Japanese companies create the dynamics of innovation.* New York: Oxford University Press.

Nonaka, I., Toyama, R. and Konno, N. (2000). SECI, Ba and Leadership: A unified model of dynamic knowledge creation. *Long Range Planning, 33,* 5–35.

Polanyi, M. (1966). *The tacit dimension.* New York: Anchor Day.

Ritchie, S. (1998). *Accessing science teachers' personal practical theories.* Paper presented at the Australasian Science Education Research Association Conference, Darwin, Australia. Retrieved March 3, 2004 from: http://www.fed.qut.edu.au/projects/asera/PAPERS/Ritchie.html.

Schorr, L. (1997). *Common purpose: Strengthening families and neighbourhoods to rebuild America.* New York: Doubleday, Anchor Books.

Spender, J. (1996). Making knowledge the basis of a dynamic theory of the firm. *Strategic Management Journal, 17*(S2), 445–462.

Spender, J. (2002). Knowledge management, uncertainty, and the emergent theory of the firm. In C. Choo and N. Bontis (Eds), *The strategic management of intellectual capital and organizational knowledge* (pp. 149–162). New York: Oxford University Press.

Stehr, N. (1992). *Practical knowledge: Applying the social sciences.* London: Sage.

von Krogh, G. and Grand, S. (2002). From economic theory toward a knowledge-based theory of the firm. In C. Choo and N. Bontis (Eds), *The strategic management of intellectual capital and organizational knowledge* (pp. 163–184). New York: Oxford University Press.

von Krogh, G., Ichijo, K. and Nonaka, I. (2000). *Enabling knowledge creation: How to unlock the mystery of tacit knowledge and release the power of innovation.* New York: Oxford University Press.

Winter, S. (1987). Knowledge and competence as strategic assets. In D. Teece (Ed.), *The competitive challenge: Strategies of industrial innovations and renewal* (pp. 159–184). Cambridge, MA: Ballin.

Zack, M. (1999). Developing a knowledge strategy. *California Management Review, 41*(3), 125–145.

Chapter 3   The event planning model: The event development phase, Part I

Imprint – Event manager as a facilitator

Bens, I. (2000). *Facilitating with ease!: A step-by-step guidebook*. San Francisco: Jossey-Bass.

Drucker, P. (1946). *Concept of the corporation*. New York: John Day.

Greenberg, J. (2002). *Managing behaviour in organizations*. New Jersey, NY: Prentice Hall.

Laird, D. (1985). *Approaches to training and development*. Reading, Mass: Addison-Wesley.

Lambert, V. and Glacken, M. (2005). Clinical education facilitators: A literature review. *Journal of Clinical Nursing, 14*, 664–673.

Nonaka, I., Toyama, R. and Konno, N. (2000). SECI, Ba and Leadership: A unified model of dynamic knowledge creation. *Long Range Planning, 33*, 5–35.

Peel, D. (2000). The teacher and town planner as facilitator. *Innovations in Education and Training International, 37*(4), 372–380.

Rogers, C. and Friedberg, H.J. (1994). *Freedom to learn*. New York: Merril, Macmillan College Publishing.

Sawyer, K.R. (2006). Group creativity: Musical performance and collaboration. *Psychology of Music, 34*(2), 148–165.

Thomas, G. (2004). A typology of approaches to facilitator education. *Journal of Experiential Education, 27*(2), 123–140.

Vidal, R. (2004). The vision conference: Facilitating creative processes. *Systemic Practice and Action Research, 17*(5), 385–405.

Imprint – Facilitating event structure for governance

Vancouver, 2010 (2007). *Organizing committee*. Retrieved May 25, 2007 from: http://www.vancouver2010.com/en/OrganizingCommittee

Kilmann, R., Pondy, L. and Slavin, D. (1976). The management of organization design: Strategies and Implementation, New York: North-Holland, Vol. I, (Eds).

Kuro5hin (2005). *Niche sport of the day–slalom skateboarding.* Retrieved June 10, 2007 from: http://www.kuro5hin.org/story/2005/9/13/74129/0483

Slack, T. and Parent, M. (2006). *Understanding sport organizations: The application of organization theory* (2nd Ed.). Champaign, IL: Human Kinetics.

Imprint – Facilitating event management using a network perspective

Andersson, P. (1992). Analyzing distribution channel dynamics: Loose and tight couplings in distribution networks. *European Journal of Marketing, 26*(2), 47–68.

Badaracco, J.L. (1991). *The knowledge link: How firms compete through strategic alliances.* Boston, MA: Harvard Business School Press.

Brass, D.J. and Burkhardt, M.E. (1992). Centrality and power in organizations. In N. Nohria and R.G. Eccles (Eds), *Networks and organizations: Structure, form and action* (pp. 191–215). Boston, MA: Harvard Business School Press.

Contractor, F. and Lorange, P. (1988). Competition vs. cooperation: A benefit/ cost framework for choosing between fully-owned investments and cooperative relationships. *Management International Review, 30*(1), 31–54.

DiMaggio, P. and Powell, W.W. (1983). The iron cage revisited. Institutional isomorphism and collective rationality in organizational fields. *American Sociology Review, 48*, 147–160.

Doz, Y. and Hamel, G. (1998). *Alliance advantage: The art of creating value through partnering.* Boston, MA: Harvard Business School Press.

Granovetter, M. (1985). Economic action and social structure: The problem of embeddedness. *American Journal of Sociology, 91*(3), 481–510.

Kearins, K. and Pavlovich, K. (2002). The role of stakeholders in Sydney's green games. *Corporate Social Responsibility and Environmental Management, 9*, 157–169.

Krackhardt, D. (1992). The strength of strong ties: The importance of *philos* in organizations. In N. Nohria and R. Eccles (Eds), *Networks and organizations: Structure, form, and action.* Boston: Harvard Business School.

Lang, J.C. (2004). Social context and social capital as enablers of knowledge integration. *Journal of Knowledge Management, 8*(3), 89–103.

Parent, M.M. and Seguin, B. (2007). Factors that led to the drowning of a world championship organizing committee: A stake holder approach. *European Sport Management Quarterly, 7*(2), 187–212.

Parent, M.M. and Seguin, B. (forthcoming). Developing a framework of evolution and issue patterns for large-scale sporting event organizing committees and their stakeholders. *Journal of Sport Management.*

Porac, J.F., Thomas, H. and Baden-Fuller, C. (1989). Competitive groups as cognitive communities: The case of Scottish knitwear manufacturers. *Journal of Management Studies, 26*(4), 397–416.

Salancik, G. and Pfeffer, J. (1978). A social information processing approach to job attitudes and task design. *Administrative Science Quarterly, 23,* 224–253.

Scott, W.R., Ruef, M. and Mendel, P.J. (2000). *Institutional change and healthcare organizations: From professional dominance to managed care.* Chicago, IL: University of Chicago Press.

Stotlar, D. (2000). Vertical integration. *Journal of Sport Management, 14*(1), 1–7.

Weick, K. (1976). Educational organizations as loosley-coupled systems. *Administrative Science Quarterly, 21*(1), 1–19.

Weick, K.E. (1982). Management of organizational change among loosely coupled elements. In P. D. Goodman and Associates (Eds), *Change in organizations* (pp. 375–408). San Francisco: Jossey-Bass.

Chapter 4   The event planning model: The development phase, Part II

Imprint – Facilitating volunteer management practices

Bussell, H. and Forbes, D. (2002). Understanding the volunteer market: The what, where, who and why of volunteering. *International Journal of Nonprofit and Voluntary Sector Marketing, 7*(3), 244–257.

Bussell, H. and Forbes, D. (2007). Volunteer management in arts organizations: A case study of managerial implications. *International Journal of Arts Management, 9*(2), 14–28.

Brudney, J. and Nezhina, T. (2005). What is old is new again: Achieving effectiveness with volunteer programs in Kazakhstan. *Voluntas: International Journal of Voluntary and Nonprofit Organizations, 16*(3), 293–308.

Downward, P. and Ralston, R. (2007). The sport development potential of sport event volunteering: Insights from the XVII Manchester Commonwealth games. *European Sport Management Quarterly, 6*(4), 333–351.

Fairley, S., Kellett, P. and Green, B. (2007). Volunteering abroad: Motives for travel to volunteer at the Athens Olympic Games. *Journal of Sport Management, 21,* 41–57.

Farrell, J., Johnston, M. and Twynam, D. (1998). Volunteer motivation, satisfaction and management at an elite sporting competition. *Journal of Sport Management, 12,* 288–300.

Getz, D. (1991). *Festivals, special events and tourism.* New York: Van Nostran Reinhold.

Gordon, L. and Erkut, E. (2004). Improving volunteer scheduling for the Edmonton Folk Festival. *Interfaces, 34*(5), 367–376.

Karkatsoulis, P., Michalopoulos, N. and Moustakatou, V. (2005). The national identity as a motivational factor for better performance in the public sector. *International Journal of Productivity and Performance, 54*(7), 579–594.

Kaufman, R., Mirsky, J. and Avgar, A. (2004). A brigade model for the management of service volunteers. *International Journal of Nonprofit and Voluntary Sector Marketing, 9*(1), 57–68.

Kemp, S. (2002). The hidden workforce: Volunteers learning in the Olympics. *Journal of European Industrial Training, 26*(2–4), 109–116.

Kim, M., Chelladurai, P. and Trail, G. (2007). A model of volunteer retention in youth sport. *Journal of Sport Management, 21,* 151–171.

Manchester 2002. (2002). Final report. Retrieved from http://www.gameslegacy.com/cgi-bin/index.cgi/10 [electronic version].

Marunchak, K. (2006). *Capacity and transformational development within the 2005 Canada Summer Games Host Society.* St. Catharines, ON: Masters thesis, Brock University.

Murk, P. and Stephan, J. (1991). Volunteers: How to get them, train them, and keep them. *Economic Development Review, 9*(3), 73–75.

Ralston, R., Lumsdon, L. and Downward, P. (2005). The third force in events tourism: Volunteers at the XVII Manchester Commonwealth Games. *Journal of Sustainable Tourism, 13*(5), 504–513.

Rodsutti, M.C. (2005). How HR can help in the aftermath of disaster. *Human Resource Management International Digest, 13*(6), 18–20.

Shin, S. and Kleiner, B. (2003). How to manage unpaid volunteers in organizations. *Management Research News, 26*(204), 63–71.

Stevens, J. and Anderson, D. (2007). Canada Games volunteer management proposal, building capacity with volunteers: Part 1 – Guiding Principles.

Taylor, T., Darcy, S., Hoye, R. and Cuskelly, G. (2006). Using psychological contract theory to explore issues in volunteer management. *European Sport Management Quarterly*, 6(2), 123–147.

Volunteer Canada (2001). *The volunteer management audit: The Canadian code for volunteer involvement.* Ottawa: Ontario. [electronic version].

Wilson, A. and Pimm, G. (1996). The tyranny of the volunteer: The care and feeding of voluntary workforces. *Management Decision, 34*(4), 24–40.

Imprint – Facilitating event policy development

Bain, L. (1990). Critical analysis of the hidden curriculum in physical education. In D. Kirk and R. Tinning (Eds), *Physical Education, Curriculum and Culture: Critical issues in a contemporary crisis.* London: Falmer Press.

Craig, T. (1997). *Disrupting the disembodied status quo: Communicology in chronic disabling conditions.* Ph.D. dissertation, Southern Illinois, University at Carbondale.

Craig, T. (2000, October). *A funny thing happened on the way up to renown: On the concrete essence of chronic illness and the intercorporeal weight of human suffering.* Paper presented at the Society for Phenomenology and the Human Sciences, State College, Pennsylvania State University.

Eco, U. (1976). *A theory of semiotics.* Bloomington: Indiana University Press.

Freire, P. (1987). Letter to the North American teacher. In Ira Shor (Ed.), *Freire for the classroom: A sourcebook for liberatory practice* (pp. 211–214). Portsmouth, NH: Boynton-Cook.

Graff, L. (1997). Excerpted from *By definition: Policies for volunteer management.* Graff and Associates.

Lanigan, R. (1988). *Phenomenology of communication.* Pittsburgh: Duquesne Press.

Merleau-Ponty, M. (1962). *Phenomenology of perception, [Translation by Colin Smith, translation corrections by Forrest Williams and David Guerruere].* New Jersey: Routledge & Kegan Paul.

Schön, D. (1983). *The reflective practitioner: How professionals think in action.* New York: Basic Books.

Schön, D. (1987). *Educating the reflective practitioner.* San Francisco: Jossey-Bass.

The human science of communicology: A phenomenology of discourse in Foucault and Merleau-Ponty, (1992). Pittsburh, PA: Duquesne University Press.

Webster's New Collegiate Dictionary. (1985). Markham, ON: Thomas Allen and Sons.

Wendall, S. (1996). *The rejected body.* New York: Routledge.

Imprint – Facilitating corporate social responsibility

Alsop, R.J. (2006). Business ethics education in business schools: A commentary. *Journal of Management Education, 30*(1), 11–14.

Carroll, A. (1994). Social issues in management research. *Business and Society, 33*(1), 5–25.

de Jongh, D. and Prinsloo, P. (2005). Why teach corporate citizenship differently? *The Journal of Corporate Citizenship, 18,* 113–122.

Frederick, W. (2006). *Corporation be good! The story of corporate social responsibility.* Indianapolis, IN: Dog Ear Publishing.

Gardberg, N. and Fombrun, G. (2006). Corporate citizenship: Creating intangible assets across institutional environments. *Academy of Management Review, 31*(2), 329–346.

Garriga, E. and Melé, D. (2004). Corporate social responsibility theories: Mapping the territory. *Journal of Business Ethics, 53,* 51–71.

Kotler, D. and Lee, N. (2005). *Corporate social responsibility: Doing the most goodyou're your company and your cause.* Hoboken, NJ: Wiley.

Matten, D. and Moon, J. (2004). Corporate social responsibility education in Europe. *Journal of Business Ethics, 54,* 323–337.

Ramasamy, B. and Woan Ting, H. (2004). A comparative analysis of corporate social responsibility. *The Journal of Corporate Citizenship, 13,* 109–123.

Votaw, D. (1972). Genius became rare: A comment on the doctrine of social responsibility Pt I. *California Management Review, 15*(2), 25–31.

Chapter 5 The event planning model: The event operational planning phase

Bowen, H. (2006, February). *The Salt Lake organizing committee: 2002 Olympics.* Boston: Harvard Business School Publishing.

Doherty, N. and Delener, N. (2001). Chaos theory: Marketing & management implications. *Journal of Marketing Theory and Practice, 9*(4), 66–75.

Galbraith, C. (1990). Transferring core manufacturing technologies in high technology firms. *California Management Review, 32*(4), 56–70.

Grant, R. (1996). Prospering in dynamically competitive environments: Organizational capability as knowledge integration. *Organization Science, 7,* 365–387.

Grant, R. (2001). The knowledge-based view of the firm. In C. Choo and N. Bontis (Eds), *The strategic management of intellectual capital and organizational knowledge* (pp. 133–148). New York: Oxford University Press.

Keirsey, D. (2003). *Existence itself: Towards the phenomenology of massive dissipative/replicative structures.* Retreived May, 27, 2003 from http://users.viawest.net/~keirsey/pofdisstruct.html

Kogut, B. and Zander, U. (1992). Knowledge of the firm, combinative capabilities, and the replication of technology. *Organization Science, 3*(3), 383–397.

LaDuke, B. (January–February 2004). Knowledge creation: The quest for questions. *The Futurist,* 66–68.

Mallen, C. and Adams, L. (2006). Inspiring student insights for change. *Academic Exchange Quarterly, 10*(3), 214–218.

Malone, T. and Crowston, K. (1994). The interdisciplinary study of coordination. *Computing Surveys, 26*(1), 87–119.

Matusik, S. (2002). Managing public and private firm knowledge within the context of flexible Firm boundaries. In C. Choo and N. Bontis (Eds), *The strategic management of intellectual capital and organizational knowledge.* New York: Oxford University Press.

Owen, R.G. (2001). *Organizational behavior in education.* Boston: Allyn and Bacon.

Rose-Rioux, M. (2007). *Organizational capacity and knowledge transfer: A qualitative case study of the 2007 Canada Winter Games host society.* Unpublished Masters thesis, Brock University, St. Catharines, ON.

Stacey, R. (1996). *Complexity and creativity in organization.* San Francisco: Berrett-Koehler.

Symes, C. and McIntyre, J. (2000). Working knowledge: An introduction to the new business of learning. In C. Symes and J. McIntyre (Eds), *Working knowledge: The new vocationalism and higher education* (pp. 123–134). Buckingham: SRHE & Open University Press.

Wijngaard, J. and deVries, J. (2006). Performers and performance: How to investigate the contribution of the operational network to operational performance. *International Journal of Operations & Production Management, 26*, 394–411.

Chapter 6   The event planning model: The event implementation, monitoring, and management phase

Bowen, L. (2006). A brief history of decision making. *Harvard Business Review*, 1–7.

Dörner, D. (1996). In R. Kimber and R. Kimber (Eds), *The logic of failure: Recognizing and avoiding error in complex situations.* Cambridge, MA: Perseus Books. Trans.

Garvin, D. and Roberto, M. (2001). What you don't know about making decisions. *Harvard Business Review*, 1–8.

Githell, J. (2000). Paradox of coordination and control. *California Management Review, 42*(3), 101–116.

Hammond, J., Keeny, R. and Raiffer, H. (2006). The hidden traps of decision making. *Harvard Business Review*, 109.

How to stay the course: Sensing and responding to deviations from plan. (2006). *Harvard Business School Press*, 1–19.

Konijnendijk, P. (1994). Coordinating marketing and manufacturing in ETO companies. *International Journal of Production Economics, 37*, 19–26.

Mallen, C. (2006). *Rethinking pedagogy for the times: A change infusion pedagogy.* Unpublished Ed.D. dissertation. Toowoomba: University of Southern Queensland.

Mintzberg, H., Raisinhani, D. and Thêorét, A. (1976). The structure of 'unstructured' decision processes. *Administrative Science Quarterly, 21*(2), 246–275.

Noble, C. (1999). Building the strategy implementation network. *Business Horizons*, 19–28.

Monitoring performance: Looking for what's going wrong and right. (2006). *Harvard Business School Press*, 1–11.

Schön, D. (1983). *The reflective practitioner: How professionals think in action.* London: Temple Smith.

Keeping on Track: Monitoring Control. (2006). Harvard Business Review.

Wijngaard, J. and deVries, J. (2006). Performers and performance: How to investigate the contribution of the operational network to operational performance. *International Journal of Operations & Production Management, 26,* 394–411.

Chapter 7 The event planning model: The event evaluation and renewal phase, Part I

Chelimsky, E. (1997). The coming transformations in evaluation. In E. Chelimsky and W.R. Shadish (Eds), *Evaluation for the 21st century: A handbook* (pp. 1–26). Thousand Oaks, CA: Sage.

Creswell, J. (1994). *Research design: Qualitative and quantitative approaches.* Thousand Oaks, CA: Sage.

Erwin, T.D. (1993). Outcomes assessment. In M.J. Barr and Associates (Eds), *The handbook of student affairs administration.* San Francisco, CA: Jossey-Bass.

Fetterman, D.M., Kaftarian, S.J. and Wandersman, A. (Eds), (1996). *Empowerment evaluation: Knowledge and tools for self-assessment & accountability.* Thousand Oaks, CA: Sage.

Getz, D. (1997). *Event management and event tourism.* Elmsford, NY: Cognizant Communication Corporation.

Henderson, K.A. and Bialeschki, M.D. (2002). *Evaluating leisure services: Making enlightened decisions.* State College, PA: Venture Publishing.

Isaac, S. and Michael, W. (1981). *Handbook in research and evaluation.* San Diego, CA: Edits.

Jones, G., George, J. and Langton, N. (2005). *Essentials of contemporary management, (1st Canadian ed.).* Toronto, ON: McGraw Hill.

McDavid, J.C. and Hawthorn, L. (2006). *Program evaluation and performance measurement: An introduction to practice.* Thousand Oaks, CA: Sage.

Merriam-Websters Dictionary. (n.d.). *Evaluation.* Retrieved May 10, 2007 from http://www.m-w.com/

Riddick, C.C. and Russell, R.V. (1999). *Evaluative research in recreation, park, and sport settings: Searching for useful information.* Champaign, IL: Sagamore.

Rossi, P., Freeman, H. and Lipsey, M. (1999). *Evaluation: A systematic approach* (6th ed.). Thousand Oaks, CA: Sage.

Rossman, J. and Schlatter, B. (2003). *Recreation programming: Designing leisure experiences* (4th ed.). Champaign, IL: Sagamore.

Schuh, J. and Upcraft, M.L. (November–December 1998). Facts and myths about assessment in student affairs. *About Campus*, 2–8.

Scriven, M. (1972). Pros and cons about goal-free evaluation. *Evaluation Comment*, *3*, 1–7.

Stake, R.E. (1975). *Evaluating the arts in education: A responsive approach*. Columbus, OH: Merrill.

Stufflebeam, D.L. (1971). The relevance of the CIPP evaluation model for educational accountability. *Journal of Research and Development in Education*, *5*, 19–25.

Webster's on-line dictionary. (n.d.). *Evaluation*. Retrieved May 21, 2007 from http://www.websters-online-dictionary.org

Worthen, B.R., Sanders, J.R. and Fitzpatrick, J.L. (1997). *Program evaluation: Alternative approaches and practical guidelines* (2nd ed.). White Plains, NY: Longman.

Chapter 8   The event planning model: The event evaluation and renewal phase, Part II

Allen, J., O'Toole, W., McDonnell, I. and Harris, R. (2002). *Festival and special event management* (2nd ed.). Brisbane, AU: John Wiley.

Creswell, J. (2003). *Research design: Qualitative, quantitative, and mixed methods approaches* (2nd ed.). Thousand Oaks, CA: Sage.

Henderson, K.A. (1998). Are volunteers worth their weight in gold? *Parks and Recreation*, *23*(11), 40–43.

Henderson, K.A. and Bialeschki, M.D. (2002). *Evaluating leisure services: Making enlightened decisions*. State College, PA: Venture.

Knowledge Development Center, (n.d.). *Volunteer value calculator*. Retrieved July 12, 2007 from http://www.kdc-cdc.ca/vvc/eng

Knowledge Development Center (n.d.). *Assigning economic value to volunteer activity: Eight tools for efficient program management*. Retrieved July 18, 2007 from http://www.nonprofitscan.ca/ page.asp?vvc_toolkit

MacKay, K. and Crompton, J.L. (1990). Measuring the quality of recreation services. *Journal of Park and Recreation Administration*, *8*(3), 47–56.

Nardi, P. (2003). *Doing survey research: A guide to quantitative methods*. Boston: Allyn and Bacon.

Parasuraman, A., Zeithaml, V. and Berry, L. (1988). SERVQUAL: A multiple item scale for measuring consumer perceptions of service quality. *Journal of Retailing, 68*(1), 12–40.

Riddick, C.C. and Russell, R.V. (1999). *Evaluative research in recreation, park, and sport settings: Searching for useful information*. Champaign, IL: Sagamore.

Rossman, J. and Schlatter, B. (2003). *Recreation programming: Designing leisure experiences* (4th ed.). Champaign, IL: Sagamore.

Salant, P. and Dillman, D.A. (1994). *How to conduct your own survey*. New York: John Wiley and Sons.

Survey Monkey, (n.d.). *The simple way to create surveys*. Retrieved June 22, 2007 from http://www.surveymonkey.com

Survey System (n.d.). *Sample size calculator*. Retrieved June 20, 2007 from http://www.surveysystem.com/sscalc.htm

Chapter 9   Event bidding

Bens, I. (2000). *Facilitating with ease!: A step-by-step guidebook*. San Francisco. CA: Jossey-Bass Inc.

Crockett, S. (1994). Tourism sport – Bidding for international events. *Journal of Tourism Sport, 1*(4), 11–21.

Emery, P. (2002). Bidding to host a major sports event: The local organizing committee perspective. *The International Journal of Public Sector Management, 15*, 316–335.

Fédération Internationale de Football Association (FIFA). (2006). *Green goal: The environmental concept for the 2006 FIFA World Cup*. Frankfort, Germany, Report published by the Organizing Committee, 2006 FIFA World Cup.

Gore, A. (2006). *An inconvenient truth*. New York: Rodale.

Greenberg, J. (2002). *Managing behaviour in organizations*. New Jersey, NY: Prentice Hall.

Hart, S. (1997). Beyond greening: Strategies for a sustainable world. *Harvard Business Review, 75*(1), 67–76.

Horte, S. and Persson, C. (2000). How Salt Lake City and its rival bidders campaigned for the 2002 Olympic Winter Games. *Event Management, 6*, 65–83.

Ingerson, L. and Westerbeek, H. (2000). Determining key success criteria for attracting hallmark sporting events. *Pacific Tourism Review, 3*, 239–253.

International Federation of Motorcycling (IFM). (2006). *Environmental code.* Switzerland.

International Olympic Committee (2006). *IOC guide on sport, environment and sustainable development.* Switzerland: Lausanne.

International Olympic Committee. (2007). Retrieved February 6, 2007 from: http://www.olympic.org/uk/organisation/missions/environment/full_story_uk.asp?id=1544

Kerzner, H. (1995). *Project management: A systems approach to planning, scheduling, and controlling* (5th ed.). Princeton, NJ: Van Nostrand Reinhold.

Persson, C. (2000). The International Olympic Committee and site decisions: The case of the 2002 Winter Olympics. *Event Management, 6*, 135–153.

Vidal, R. (2004). The vision conference: Facilitating creative processes. *Systemic Practice and Action Research, 17*(5), 385–405.

Westerbeek, H., Turner, P. and Ingerson, L. (2002). Key success factors in bidding for hallmark sporting events. *International Marketing Review, 19*, 303–322.

Chapter 10 Facilitating quality in event management

Crosby, P.B. (1979). *Quality is free: The art of making quality certain.* New York: McGraw Hill.

Garvin, D.A. (1988). *Managing quality: The strategic and competitive edge.* New York: The Free Press.

Ford, H. and Crowther, S. (1922). *My life and work.* New York: Doubleday Page.

Reeves, C.A. and Bednar, D.A. (1994). Defining quality: Alternatives and implications. *Academy of Management Review, 19*(3), 419–445.

Saad, G.H. and Siha, S. (2000). Managing quality: Critical links and a contingency model. *International Journal of Operations & Production Management, 20*(10), 1146–1163.

Watkins, D. (2006). Reflections on the future of quality. *Quality Progress, 39*(1), 23–28.

Zeithaml, V.A., Parasuraman, A. and Berry, L.L. (1990). *Delivering quality service: Balancing customer perceptions and expectations.* New York: The Free Press.

Chapter 11 An Integral approach to experiential learning: A foundation for event management and personal development

Andresen, L., Boud, D. and Cohen, R. (2000). Experience-based learning. In G. Foley (Ed.), *Understanding adult education and training* (2nd ed.) (pp. 225–239). St. Leonards, NSW, Australia: Allen and Unwin.

Argyris, C. (May 1991). Teaching smart people how to learn. *Harvard Business Review*, 1–15.

Agryris, C. and Schön, D.A. (1996). *Organizational learning II: Theory, method, and practice*. Reading, MA: Addison-Wesley.

Boud, D. (1993). Experience as the base for learning. *Higher Education Research and Development, 12*(1), 33–44.

Boud, D. (2001). Using journal writing to enhance reflective practice. In L.M. English and M.A. Gillen (Eds), *Promoting journal writing in adult education*(No. 90), (pp. 9–18). San Francisco: Jossey-Bass.

Boud, D. and Knights, S. (1996). Course design for reflective practice. In N. Gould and I. Taylor (Eds), *Reflective learning for social work: Research, theory and practice* (pp. 23–34). Aldershot, Hants: Arena.

Boud, D. and Walker, D. (1990). Making the most of experience. *Studies in Continuing Education, 12*(2), 61–80.

Boud, D. and Walker, D. (1991). *Experience and learning: Reflection at work*. Geelong, Victoria: Deakin University Press.

Boud, D., Keogh, R. and Walker, D. (1985). *Reflection: Turning experience into learning*. London: Kogan Page.

Brookfield, S. (1990). Using critical incidents to explore learners' assumptions. In J. Mezirow and Associates (Eds), *Fostering critical reflection in adulthood: A guide to transformative and emancipatory learning* (pp. 177–193). San Francisco: Jossey-Bass.

Cameron, B.L. and Mitchell, A.M. (1993). Reflective peer journals: Developing authentic nurses. *Journal of Advanced Nursing, 18*, 290–297.

Cuneen, J. and Sidwell, J.M. (1994). *Sport management field experiences*. Morgantown, WV: Fitness Information Technology.

Davies, E. (1995). Reflective practice: A focus for caring. *Journal of Nursing Education, 34*(4), 167–174.

References

Dewey, J. (1938). *Experience and education*. New York: Collier Books.

Fenwick, T.J. (2000). Expanding conceptions of experiential learning: A review of five contemporary perspectives on cognition. *Adult Education Quarterly, 50*(4), 243–272.

Fenwick, T.J. (2001). *Experiential learning: A theoretical critique from five perspectives*. Information Series No. 385, Columbus: The Ohio State University, ERIC Clearinghouse on Adult, Career and Vocational Education.

Heinrich, K.T. (1992). The intimate dialogue: Journal writing by students. *Nurse Educator, 17*(6), 17–21.

Holman, D., Pavlica, K. and Thorpe, R. (1997). Rethinking Kolb's theory of experiential learning in management education. *Management Learning, 28*(2), 135–148.

Ingersoll, E. (2005). An introduction to integral psychology. *AQAL: Journal of Integral Theory and Practice, 1*(3), 1–16.

Kayes, C.D. (2002). Experiential learning and its critics: Preserving the role of experience in management learning and education. *Academy of Management Learning and Education, 1*(2), 137–149.

Kolb, D.A. (1984). *Experiential learning*. Englewood Cliffs, NJ: Prentice Hall.

Langer, E.J. (1989). *Mindfulness*. Reading, MA: Addison-Wesley.

Lederman, L.C. (1992). Debriefing: Toward a systematic assessment of theory and practice. *Simulation and Gaming, 23*(2), 145–159.

Lewin, K. (1951). *Field theory in social sciences*. New York: Harper and Row.

Loughran, J.J. (1996). *Developing reflective practice: Learning about teaching and learning through modeling*. Washington, DC: Falmer Press.

Mezirow, J. (1991). *Transformation dimensions of adult learning*. San Francisco: Jossey-Bass.

Moon, J. (1999a). *Learning journals: A handbook for academics, students and professional development*. London: Kogan Page.

Moon, J. (1999b). Learning through reflection: The use of learning journals. In:*Reflection in learning and professional development*. (pp. 186–202). London: Kogan Page.

Neck, C. and Manz, C. (2006). *Mastering self-leadership: Empowering yourself for personal excellence* (4th ed.). Upper Saddle River, NJ: Pearson/Prentice Hall.

Patterson, B. (1995). Developing and maintaining reflection in clinical journals. *Nurse Education Today, 15*, 211–220.

Piaget, J. (1951). *Play, dreams and imitation in childhood.* New York: W.W. Norton.

Pierson, W. (1998). Reflection and nursing education. *Journal of Advanced Nursing, 27*, 165–170.

Ray, D. (1994). Reflection, dialogue, and writing: turning the apple inside out. *The Writing Notebook, 11*(3), 4–6.

Rittman, M. (1995). Storytelling: An innovative approach to staff development. *Journal of Nursing Staff Development, 11*(1), 15–19.

Robinson, J., Saberston, S. and Griffin, V. (1985). *Learning partnerships: Interdependent learning in adult education.* Toronto, Canada: Department of Adult Education, Ontario Institute for Studies in Education.

Rogers, R.R. (2001). Reflection in higher education: A concept analysis. *Innovative Higher Education, 26*(1), 37–57.

Schön, D.A. (1983). *The reflective practioner: How professionals think in action.* New York: Basic Books.

Schön, D.A. (1987). *Educating the reflective practioner.* San Francisco: Jossey-Bass.

Seibert, K.W. and Daudelin, M.W. (1999). *The role of reflection in managerial learning: Theory, research and practice.* Westport, CT: Quorum.

Sweitzer, H.F. and King, M.A. (1999). *The successful internship: transformation and empowerment.* Pacific Grove, CA: Brooks/Cole.

Taylor, E.W. (1998). *The theory and practice of transformative learning: A critical review.* Information Series No. 37 IV. Columbus: The Ohio State University.

Vince, R. (1998). Behind and beyond Kolb's learning cycle. *Journal of Management Education, 22*(3), 304–319.

Wilber, K. (1995). An informal overview of transpersonal studies. *Journal of Transpersonal Psychology, 27*(2), 107–129.

Wilber, K. (2000a). *A theory of everything: An integral vision for business, politics, science, and spirituality.* Boston: Shambala.

Wilber, K. (2000b). *Sex, ecology and spirituality: The spirit of evolution.* Boston: Shambala.

Wilber, K. (2006). *Integral spirituality: A startling new role for religion in the modern and postmodern world.* Boston: Shambala.

Yorks, L. and Kasl, E. (2002). Toward a theory and practice for whole-person learning: Reconceptualizing experience and the role of affect. *Adult Education Quarterly, 52*(3), 176–192.

Chapter 12   Conclusions

Schön, D. (1983). *The reflective practitioner: How professionals think in action.* New York: Basic Books.

Index